Learning JavaScript Data Structures and Algorithms

Second Edition

Hone your skills by learning classic data structures and algorithms in JavaScript

Loiane Groner

BIRMINGHAM - MUMBAI

Learning JavaScript Data Structures and Algorithms

Second Edition

First published: October 2014

Second edition: June 2016

Production reference: 1160616

Published by Packt Publishing Ltd.
Livery Place
35 Livery Street
Birmingham
B3 2PB, UK.
ISBN 978-1-78528-549-3

www.packtpub.com

Credits

Author

Loiane Groner

Reviewer

Tessa B. Silver

Commissioning Editor

Wilson Dsouza

Acquisition Editor

Smeet Thakkar

Content Development Editor

Prashanth G Rao

Technical Editor

Sunith Shetty

Copy Editors

Shruti Iyer

Sonia Mathur

Project Coordinator

Bijal Patel

Proofreader

Safis Editing

Indexer

Hemangini Bari

Graphics

Jason Monteiro

Production Coordinator

Melwyn Dsa

About the Author

Loiane Groner has over 10 years of experience in developing enterprise applications. She has worked at multinational companies, such as IBM, and nowadays she works as Software Development Manager at a financial institution, where she manages overseas solutions. Her areas of expertise include Java, Sencha technologies (Ext JS), and hybrid mobile development with PhoneGap and Ionic.

She is passionate about technology, and she has dedicated herself to spreading knowledge in the software development community through her blog http://loiane.com, as guest speaker in IT conferences, and also as guest professor in university extension courses.

While at university, she worked as teacher's assistant for 2 years for the Algorithms, Data Structures, and Computing Theory classes. She represented her university at the ACM International Collegiate Programming Contest – Brazilian Finals (South America Regionals) and also worked as Student Delegate of SBC (Brazilian Computing Society). She won a merit award in her Senior year for being one of top three students with better GPAs in the Computer Science department and has also graduated with honors.

Loiane is also the author of the books *Ext JS 4 First Look*, *Mastering Ext JS*, *Mastering Ext JS - Second Edition*, *Sencha Architect App Development*, *Learning JavaScript Data Structures and Algorithms*, and *JavaScript Regular Expression*, all of them published by Packt Publishing.

If you want to keep in touch, you can find Loiane on Facebook (https://www.facebook.com/loianegroner), Twitter (@loiane), and also on Github (https://github.com/loiane).

I would like to thank my parents for giving me education, guidance, and advice through all these years, and helping me to be a better human being and professional. A very special thanks to my husband for being patient and supportive and giving me encouragement to keep doing what I love. I would like to thank Packt for the amazing opportunity to write books about topics I really love! Thanks to all the people involved in the process of creating, reviewing, and publishing the books!

I also would like to thank the readers of this book and other books I have written for the support and feedback. Your feedback is very valuable to me to improve as an author and as a professional. Thank you very much!

About the Reviewer

Tessa B. Silver has a background in print design and traditional illustration. She has evolved, over the years, into web and interactive development, in which she focuses on usability and interface design as well as visualizing data primarily with JavaScript, HTML5, and CSS.

In addition to freelance consulting and technical writing via hyper^{3}media LLC (pronounced hyper-cube-media), Tessa is currently a frontend mobile app and web developer for Capella University. She can be found and contacted via Twitter at `@tessaract` and on her personal site, `http://tessaract.info`.

Tessa has authored five other Packt Publishing titles, including *WordPress Theme Design* and *WordPress 3.0 jQuery*. She's currently working on *Mastering Reactive JavaScript Programming with Bacon.js and RxJS* for Packt.

I send a huge thank you to the Packt team who have made this title possible. Special thanks to Loiane Groner for authoring such a wonderful book, revealing the logic and secrets of data structures and algorithms for the rest of us to (finally!) fully comprehend. I'd also like to thank Smeet Thakkar for being the title's Aquisition Editor, and last, I'd like to send out an additional big-time thank you to Bijal Patel for the truly thankless, backbreaking work and diligence that it takes to keep to a schedule.

www.PacktPub.com

eBooks, discount offers, and more

Did you know that Packt offers eBook versions of every book published, with PDF and ePub files available? You can upgrade to the eBook version at www.PacktPub.com and as a print book customer, you are entitled to a discount on the eBook copy. Get in touch with us at customercare@packtpub.com for more details.

At www.PacktPub.com, you can also read a collection of free technical articles, sign up for a range of free newsletters and receive exclusive discounts and offers on Packt books and eBooks.

https://www2.packtpub.com/books/subscription/packtlib

Do you need instant solutions to your IT questions? PacktLib is Packt's online digital book library. Here, you can search, access, and read Packt's entire library of books.

Why subscribe?

- Fully searchable across every book published by Packt
- Copy and paste, print, and bookmark content
- On demand and accessible via a web browser

Table of Contents

Preface

JavaScript is one of the most popular programming language nowadays. It is known as the Internet language due the fact that browsers understand JavaScript natively without installing any plugins in them. JavaScript has grown so much that is no longer just a frontend language; it is also present now on the server (NodeJS) and database as well (MongoDB).

Learning data structures is very important for any technology professional. Working as a developer means that you are able to solve problems with the help of programming languages, and data structures are an indispensible piece of the solutions that we need to create to solve these problems. Choosing the wrong data structure can also impact on performance of the program we write. That is why is important to get to know different data structures and how to apply them properly.

Algorithms are the state of art of Computer Science. There are so many ways of solving the same problem, and some approaches are better than others. This is why it is also very important to know the most famous algorithms.

This book was written for beginners who want to learn data structures and algorithms, and also for those that are already familiar with data structures and algorithms but want to learn it using JavaScript.

Happy coding!

What this book covers

Chapter 1, *JavaScript—A Quick Overview*, covers the basics of JavaScript needed prior to learning data structures and algorithms. It also covers the setup of the development environment that we need for this book.

Chapter 2, *Arrays*, explains how to use the most basic and most used data structure, which are arrays. This chapter demonstrates how to declare, initialize, add, and remove elements from an array. It also covers how to use native JavaScript Array methods.

Chapter 3, *Stacks*, introduces the stack data structure, demonstrating how to create a stack and add and remove elements. It also demonstrates how to use stack to solve some computer science problems.

Chapter 4, *Queues*, covers the queue data structure, demonstrating how to create a queue and add and remove elements. It also demonstrates how to use queues to solve some computer science problems, and explains the major differences between queues and stacks.

Chapter 5, *Linked Lists*, explains how to create the linked list data structure from scratch using objects and the pointer concept. Besides covering how to declare, create, add, and remove elements, it also covers the various types of linked lists, such as doubly-linked lists and circular-linked lists.

Chapter 6, *Sets*, introduces the set data structure and how you can use it to store nonrepeated elements. It also explains the different types of set operations and how to implement and use them.

Chapter 7, *Dictionaries and Hashes*, explains the dictionary and hash data structures and the differences between them. This chapter covers how to declare, create, and use both data structures. It also explains how to handle collisions in hash, and the techniques to create better hash functions.

Chapter 8, *Trees*, covers the tree data structure and its terminology, focusing on Binary Search Tree data its methods to search, traverse, add, and remove nodes. It also introduces the next steps to dive into the world of trees, mentioning the tree algorithms that we should learn next.

Chapter 9, *Graphs*, introduces the amazing world of graphs and their application in real-world problems. This chapter covers the most common graph terminology, different ways of representing a graph, and how to traverse graphs using the Breadth-First-Search and Depth-First-Search algorithms and their applications.

Chapter 10, *Sorting and Searching Algorithms*, explores the most used sorting algorithms, such as the Bubble sort (and its improved version), Selection sort, Insertion sort, Merge sort, and Quick sort. It also covers searching algorithms, such as the sequential and binary search.

Chapter 11, *Patterns of Algorithm*, introduces some algorithm techniques and some of the most famous algorithms. It covers the recursion concept and some advanced algorithm techniques, such as dynamic programming and greedy algorithms.

Chapter 12, *Algorithm Complexity*, introduces the Big-O notation and its concepts along with a cheat sheet of the complexity of the algorithms implemented in this book. It covers an introduction to NP-Completeness problems and heuristic solutions. Finally it explains how to take your algorithm knowledge to the next level.

What you need for this book

You can set up three different development environments for this book. You do not need to have all the three environments; you can select one or give all of them a try!

For the first option, you need a browser. We recommended one of the following:

- Chrome (`https://www.google.com/chrome/browser/`)
- Firefox (`https://www.mozilla.org/en-US/firefox/new/`)

The second option is setting up a local webserver:

- A browser listed in the first option
- A webserver. If you do not have any installed in your computer, you can install XAMMP from `https://www.apachefriends.org`

The third option is a 100% JavaScript environment!

- A browser listed in the first option
- NodeJS (`http://nodejs.org/`)
- After installing NodeJS, install the `http-server` package:

```
npm install http-server -g
```

You can find more detailed instructions in the first chapter as well.

Who this book is for

If you are a student of Computer Science or are at the start of your technology career and want to explore JavaScript's optimum ability, this book is for you. You need a basic knowledge of JavaScript and programming logic to start having fun with algorithms.

Conventions

In this book, you will find a number of text styles that distinguish between different kinds of information. Here are some examples of these styles and an explanation of their meaning.

Code words in text, database table names, folder names, filenames, file extensions, pathnames, dummy URLs, user input, and Twitter handles are shown as follows: "Using the `isEmpty` method, we can simply verify whether the length of the internal array is 0."

A block of code is set as follows:

```
function Stack() {
  //properties and methods go here
}
```

When we wish to draw your attention to a particular part of a code block, the relevant lines or items are set in bold:

```
class Stack {
  constructor () {    this.items = []; //{1}  }
  push(element){
    this.items.push(element);
  }
  //other methods
}
```

Any command-line input or output is written as follows:

```
stack.push(5);
stack.push(8);
```

New terms and **important words** are shown in bold. Words that you see on the screen, for example, in menus or dialog boxes, appear in the text like this: "When you open Firebug (simply click on its icon), you will see the **Console** tab, and you will be able to write all your JavaScript code in its command-line area."

 Warnings or important notes appear in a box like this.

 Tips and tricks appear like this.

Reader feedback

Feedback from our readers is always welcome. Let us know what you think about this book—what you liked or disliked. Reader feedback is important for us as it helps us develop titles that you will really get the most out of.

To send us general feedback, simply e-mail feedback@packtpub.com, and mention the book's title in the subject of your message.

If there is a topic that you have expertise in and you are interested in either writing or contributing to a book, see our author guide at www.packtpub.com/authors.

Customer support

Now that you are the proud owner of a Packt book, we have a number of things to help you to get the most from your purchase.

Downloading the example code

You can download the example code files for this book from your account at http://www.packtpub.com. If you purchased this book elsewhere, you can visit http://www.packtpub.com/support and register to have the files e-mailed directly to you.

You can download the code files by following these steps:

1. Log in or register to our website using your e-mail address and password.
2. Hover the mouse pointer on the **SUPPORT** tab at the top.
3. Click on **Code Downloads & Errata**.
4. Enter the name of the book in the **Search** box.
5. Select the book for which you're looking to download the code files.
6. Choose from the drop-down menu where you purchased this book from.
7. Click on **Code Download**.

You can also download the code files by clicking on the **Code Files** button on the book's webpage at the Packt Publishing website. This page can be accessed by entering the book's name in the **Search** box. Please note that you need to be logged in to your Packt account.

Once the file is downloaded, please make sure that you unzip or extract the folder using the latest version of:

- WinRAR / 7-Zip for Windows
- Zipeg / iZip / UnRarX for Mac
- 7-Zip / PeaZip for Linux

The code bundle for the book is also hosted on GitHub at https://github.com/loiane/javascript-datastructures-algorithms. We also have other code bundles from our rich catalog of books and videos available at https://github.com/PacktPublishing/. Check them out!

Downloading the color images of this book

We also provide you with a PDF file that has color images of the screenshots/diagrams used in this book. The color images will help you better understand the changes in the output. You can download this file from `https://www.packtpub.com/sites/default/files/downloads/LearningJavaScriptDataStructuresandAlgorithmsSecondEdition_ColorImages.pdf`.

Errata

Although we have taken every care to ensure the accuracy of our content, mistakes do happen. If you find a mistake in one of our books—maybe a mistake in the text or the code—we would be grateful if you could report this to us. By doing so, you can save other readers from frustration and help us improve subsequent versions of this book. If you find any errata, please report them by visiting `http://www.packtpub.com/submit-errata`, selecting your book, clicking on the **Errata Submission Form** link, and entering the details of your errata. Once your errata are verified, your submission will be accepted and the errata will be uploaded to our website or added to any list of existing errata under the Errata section of that title.

To view the previously submitted errata, go to `https://www.packtpub.com/books/content/support` and enter the name of the book in the search field. The required information will appear under the **Errata** section.

Piracy

Piracy of copyrighted material on the Internet is an ongoing problem across all media. At Packt, we take the protection of our copyright and licenses very seriously. If you come across any illegal copies of our works in any form on the Internet, please provide us with the location address or website name immediately so that we can pursue a remedy.

Please contact us at `copyright@packtpub.com` with a link to the suspected pirated material.

We appreciate your help in protecting our authors and our ability to bring you valuable content.

Questions

If you have a problem with any aspect of this book, you can contact us at `questions@packtpub.com`, and we will do our best to address the problem.

1
JavaScript—A Quick Overview

JavaScript is a very powerful language. It is the most popular language in the world and is one of the most prominent languages on the Internet. For example, GitHub (the world's largest code host, available at `https://github.com`) hosts over 400,000 JavaScript repositories (the largest number of projects is in JavaScript; refer to `http://goo.gl/ZFx6m g`). The number of projects in JavaScript in GitHub grows every year.

JavaScript is not a language that can only be used on the frontend. It can also be used in the backend, and Node.js is the technology responsible for this. The number of **Node Package modules** (`https://www.npmjs.org/`) also grows exponentially.

JavaScript is a must-have on your résumé if you are or will become a web developer.

In this chapter, you will learn the syntax and some necessary basic functionalities of Javascript, so we can start developing our own data structure and algorithms. We will cover:

- Setting up the environment
- Javascript basics
- Control structures
- Functions
- Object-oriented programming in Javascript
- Debugging and tools
- Introduction to ECMAScript 6 and ECMAScript 7

JavaScript data structure and algorithms

In this book, you will learn about the most-used data structures and algorithms. However, why use JavaScript to learn about data structures and algorithms? We have already answered this question. JavaScript is very popular and is appropriate to learn about data structures because it is a functional language. Also, this can be a very fun way of learning something new as it is very different from (and easier than) learning about data structures with a standard language such as **C** or **Java**. And who said data structures and algorithms were only made for languages such as C and Java? You might need to implement some of these languages while developing for the frontend as well.

Learning about data structures and algorithms is very important. The first reason is that data structures and algorithms can solve the most common problems efficiently. This will make a difference to the quality of the source code you write in the future (including performance; if you choose the incorrect data structure or algorithm, depending on the scenario, you may have some performance issues). Secondly, algorithms are studied in college together with the introductory concepts of computer science. And thirdly, if you are planning to get a job in the greatest **IT** (**Information Technology**) companies (such as Google, Amazon, Ebay, and so on), data structures and algorithms are the subjects of interview questions.

Let's get the fun started!

Setting up the environment

One of the pros of the JavaScript language compared to other languages is that you do not need to install or configure a complicated environment to get started with it. Every computer has the required environment already, even though the user may never write a single line of source code. All we need is a browser!

To execute the examples in this book, it is recommended that you have Google Chrome or Firefox installed (you can use the one you like the most), an editor of your preference (such as Sublime Text), and a web server (XAMPP or any other of your preference, but this step is optional). Chrome, Firefox, Sublime Text, and XAMPP are available for Windows, Linux, and Mac OS.

If you use Firefox, it is also recommended to install the **Firebug** add-on (`https://getfire bug.com/`). We will present you with three options to set up your environment.

The minimum setup to work with JavaScript

The simplest environment that you can use is a browser.

You can use Firefox along with Firebug. When you have Firebug installed, you will see the following icon in the upper-right corner:

When you open Firebug (simply click on its icon), you will see the **Console** tab, and you will be able to write all your JavaScript code in its command-line area, as demonstrated in the following screenshot (to execute the source code, you need to click on the **Run** button):

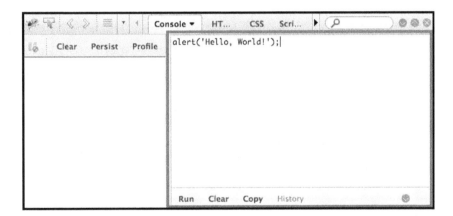

You can also expand the command line to fit the entire available area of the Firebug add-on.

You can also use Google Chrome. Chrome already comes with **Google Developer Tools**. To open it, locate the setting and control icon and navigate to **Tools | Developer Tools**, as shown in the following screenshot:

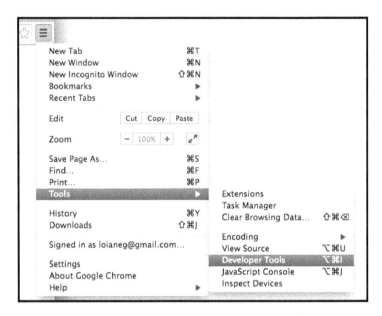

Then, in the **Console** tab, you can write your own JavaScript code for testing, as follows:

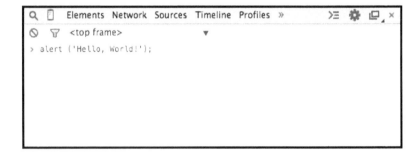

Using web servers (XAMPP)

The second environment you might want to install on your computer is also simple, but it's a little bit more complex than just using a browser.

You will need to install XAMPP (`https://www.apachefriends.org`) or any web server of your preference. Then, inside the XAMPP installation folder, you will find the `htdocs` directory. You can create a new folder in which you can execute the source code we will implement in this book, or you can download the source code from this book and extract it to the `htdocs` directory, as follows:

Then, you can access the source code from your browser using your localhost URL (after starting the XAMPP server), as shown in the following screenshot (do not forget to enable Firebug or Google Developer Tools to see the output):

When executing the examples, always remember to have Google Developer Tools or Firebug open to see the output.

It's all about JavaScript (Node.js)

The third option is having an environment that is 100 percent JavaScript! Instead of using XAMPP, which is an Apache server, we can use a JavaScript server.

To do so, we need to have Node.js installed. Go to `http://nodejs.org/` and download and install Node.js. After this, open the terminal application (if you are using Windows, open the command prompt with Node.js, which was installed with Node.js) and run the following command:

```
npm install http-server -g
```

Make sure you type the command and don't copy and paste it. Copying the command might give you some errors.

You can also execute the command as an administrator. For Linux and Mac systems, use the following command:

```
sudo npm install http-server -g
```

This command will install `http-server`, which is a JavaScript server. To start a server and run the examples from this book in the terminal application, change the directory to the folder that contains the book's source code and type `http-server`, as displayed in the following screenshot:

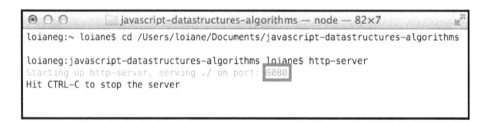

To execute the examples, open the browser and access the localhost on the port specified by the `http-server` command, as follows:

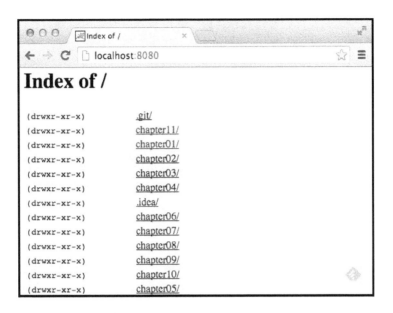

Detailed steps to download the code bundle are mentioned in the Preface of this book. Please have a look. The code bundle for the book is also hosted on GitHub at `https://github.com/loiane/javascript-data structures-algorithms`. We also have other code bundles from our rich catalog of books and videos available at `https://github.com/Pack tPublishing/`. Check them out!

JavaScript basics

Before we start diving into the various data structures and algorithms, let's have a quick overview of the JavaScript language. This section will present the JavaScript basics required to implement the algorithms we will create in the subsequent chapters.

To start, let's take a look at the two different ways we can use JavaScript code on an HTML page:

```
<!DOCTYPE html>
<html>
  <head>
```

```
      <meta charset="UTF-8">
  </head>
  <body>
    <script>
      alert('Hello, World!');
    </script>
  </body>
</html>
```

The first way is demonstrated by the previous code. We need to create an HTML file and write this code on it. In this example, we are declaring the `script` tag inside the HTML file and, inside the `script` tag, we have the JavaScript code.

For the second example, we need to create a JavaScript file (we can save it as `01-HelloWorld.js`) and, inside this file, we will insert the following code:

```
alert('Hello, World!');
```

Then, our HTML file will look similar to this:

```
<!DOCTYPE html>
<html>
  <head>
    <meta charset="UTF-8">
  </head>
  <body>
    <script src="01-HelloWorld.js">
    </script>
  </body>
</html>
```

The second example demonstrates how to include a JavaScript file inside an HTML file.

By executing any of these two examples, the output will be the same. However, the second example is best practice.

 You may find JavaScript `include` statements or JavaScript code inside the `head` tag in some examples on the Internet. As best practice, we will include any JavaScript code at the end of the `body` tag. This way, the HTML will be parsed by the browser and displayed before the scripts are loaded. This boosts the performance of the page.

Variables

Variables store data that can be set, updated, and retrieved whenever needed. Values that are assigned to a variable belong to a type. In JavaScript, the available types are numbers, strings, Booleans, functions, and objects. We also have undefined and null, along with arrays, dates, and regular expressions.

 Although JavaScript has different available variable types, it is not a **strongly typed** language such as C/C++, C#, Java. In strongly typed languages, we need to declare the type of the variable along with its declaration (in Java, for example, to declare an integer variable, we use `int num = 1;`). In JavaScript, we only need to use the keyword `var`, and we do not need to declare the variable type. For this reason, JavaScript is not a strongly typed language.

The following is an example of how to use variables in JavaScript:

```
var num = 1; //{1}
num = 3; //{2}
var price = 1.5; //{3}
var name = 'Packt'; //{4}
var trueValue = true; //{5}
var nullVar = null; //{6}
var und;  //{7}
```

- On line {1}, we have an example of how to declare a variable in JavaScript (we are declaring a number). Although it is not necessary to use the `var` keyword declaration, it is good practice to always specify when we declare a new variable.
- On line {2}, we updated an existing variable. JavaScript is not a strongly typed language. This means you can declare a variable, initialize it with a number, and then update it with a string or any other datatype. Assigning a value to a variable that is different from its original type is also not good practice.
- On line {3}, we also declared a number, but this time it is a decimal floating point. On line {4}, we declared a string; on line {5}, we declared a Boolean. On line {6}, we declared a `null` value, and on line {7}, we declared an undefined variable. A `null` value means no value, and `undefined` means a variable that has been declared but not yet assigned a value. Take a look at the following:

```
console.log("num: "+ num);
console.log("name: "+ name);
console.log("trueValue: "+ trueValue);
console.log("price: "+ price);
console.log("nullVar: "+ nullVar);
```

```
console.log("und: "+ und);
```

If we want to see the value of each variable we declared, we can use `console.log` to do so, as listed in the previous code snippet.

 We have three ways of outputting values in JavaScript that we can use with the examples of this book. The first one is `alert('My text here')`, which outputs an alert window on the browser, and the second one is `console.log('My text here')`, which outputs text on the **Console** tab of the debug tool (Google Developer Tools or Firebug, depending on the browser you are using). The third way is outputting the value directly on the HTML page that is rendered by the browser using `document.write('My text here')`. You can use the option that you feel most comfortable with.

The `console.log` method also accepts more than just arguments. Instead of `console.log("num: "+ num)`, we can also use `console.log("num: ", num)`.

We will discuss functions and objects later in this chapter.

Variable scope

Scope refers to where in the algorithm we can access the variable (it can also be a function when we work with function scopes). There are local and global variables.

Let's look at an example:

```
var myVariable = 'global';
myOtherVariable = 'global';

function myFunction(){
  var myVariable = 'local';
  return myVariable;
}

function myOtherFunction(){
  myOtherVariable = 'local';
  return myOtherVariable;
}

console.log(myVariable);      //{1}
console.log(myFunction());   //{2}

console.log(myOtherVariable);     //{3}
console.log(myOtherFunction()); //{4}
```

```
console.log(myOtherVariable);    //{5}
```

- Line {1} will output global because we are referring to a global variable.
- Line {2} will output local because we declared the myVariable variable inside the myFunction function as a local variable, so the scope will only be inside myFunction.
- Line {3} will output global because we are referencing the global variable named myOtherVariable that was initialized on the second line of the example.
- Line {4} will output local. Inside the myOtherFunction function, we referencing the myOtherVariable global variable and assigning the value local to it because we are not declaring the variable using the var keyword.
- For this reason, line {5} will output local (because we changed the value of the variable inside myOtherFunction).

You may hear that global variables in JavaScript are evil and this is true. Usually, the quality of JavaScript source code is measured by the number of global variables and functions (a large number is bad). So, whenever possible, try avoiding global variables.

Operators

We need operators when performing any operation in a programming language. JavaScript also has arithmetic, assignment, comparison, logical, bitwise, and unary operators, among others. Let's take a look at these:

```
var num = 0; // {1}
num = num + 2;
num = num * 3;
num = num / 2;
num++;
num--;

num += 1; // {2}
num -= 2;
num *= 3;
num /= 2;
num %= 3;

console.log('num == 1 : ' + (num == 1)); // {3}
console.log('num === 1 : ' + (num === 1));
console.log('num != 1 : ' + (num != 1));
console.log('num > 1 : ' + (num > 1));
console.log('num < 1 : ' + (num < 1));
```

```
console.log('num >= 1 : ' + (num >= 1));
console.log('num <= 1 : ' + (num <= 1));

console.log('true && false : ' + (true && false)); // {4}
console.log('true || false : ' + (true || false));
console.log('!true : ' + (!true));
```

On line {1}, we have the arithmetic operators. In the following table, we have the operators and their descriptions:

Arithmetic operator	Description
+	Addition
−	Subtraction
*	Multiplication
/	Division
%	Modulus (remainder of a division operation)
++	Increment
−−	Decrement

On line {2}, we have the assignment operators. In the following table, we have the operators and their descriptions:

Assignment operator	Description
=	Assignment
+=	Addition assignment $(x \mathrel{+}= y) == (x = x + y)$
−=	Subtraction assignment $(x \mathrel{-}= y) == (x = x - y)$
*=	Multiplication assignment $(x \mathrel{*}= y) == (x = x * y)$
/=	Division assignment $(x \mathrel{/}= y) == (x = x / y)$
%=	Remainder assignment $(x \mathrel{\%}= y) == (x = x \% y)$

On line {3}, we have the comparison operators. In the following table, we have the operators and their descriptions:

Comparison operator	Description
==	Equal to
===	Equal to (value and object type both)
!=	Not equal to
>	Greater than
>=	Greater than or equal to
<	Less than
<=	Less than or equal to

Finally, on line {4}, we have the logical operators. In the following table, we have the operators and their descriptions:

Logical operator	Description
&&	And
||	Or
!	Not

JavaScript also supports bitwise operators, which are shown as follows:

```
console.log('5 & 1:', (5 & 1));
console.log('5 | 1:', (5 | 1));
console.log('~ 5:', (~5));
console.log('5 ^ 1:', (5 ^ 1));
console.log('5 << 1:', (5 << 1));
console.log('5 >> 1:', (5 >> 1));
```

The following table contains a more detailed description of the bitwise operators:

Bitwise operator	Description
&	And
|	Or

~	Not
^	Xor
<<	Left shift
>>	Right shift

The `typeof` operator returns the type of the variable or expression. For example, have a look at the following code:

```
console.log('typeof num:', typeof num);
console.log('typeof Packt:', typeof 'Packt');
console.log('typeof true:', typeof true);
console.log('typeof [1,2,3]:', typeof [1,2,3]);
console.log('typeof {name:John}:', typeof {name:'John'});
```

The output will be as follows:

```
typeof num: number
typeof Packt: string
typeof true: boolean
typeof [1,2,3]: object
typeof {name:John}: object
```

JavaScript also supports the `delete` operator, which deletes a property from an object. Take a look at the following code:

```
var myObj = {name: 'John', age: 21};
delete myObj.age;
console.log(myObj); //outputs Object {name: "John"}
```

In this book's algorithms, we will use some of these operators.

Truthy and falsy

In JavaScript, true and false are a little bit tricky. In most languages, the Boolean values `true` and `false` represent the true/false results. In JavaScript, a string such as "Packt" has the value true, for example.

The following table can help us better understand how true and false work in JavaScript:

Value type	Result
undefined	`false`
null	`false`
Boolean	true is `true` and false is `false`
Number	The result is `false` for +0, −0, or NaN; otherwise, the result is `true`
String	The result is `false` if the string is empty (length is 0); otherwise, the result is `true` (length > 1)
Object	`true`

Let's consider some examples and verify their output:

```
function testTruthy(val){
    return val ? console.log('truthy') : console.log('falsy');
}

testTruthy(true); //true
testTruthy(false); //false
testTruthy(new Boolean(false)); //true (object is always true)

testTruthy(''); //false
testTruthy('Packt'); //true
testTruthy(new String('')); //true (object is always true)

testTruthy(1); //true
testTruthy(-1); //true
testTruthy(NaN); //false
testTruthy(new Number(NaN)); //true (object is always true)

testTruthy({}); //true (object is always true)

var obj = {name:'John'};
testTruthy(obj); //true
testTruthy(obj.name); //true
testTruthy(obj.age); //false (age does not exist)
```

Functions of the equals operators (== and ===)

The two equal operators supported by JavaScript can cause a little bit of confusion when working with them.

When using ==, values can be considered equal even when they are of different types. This can be confusing even for a senior JavaScript developer. Let's analyze how == works using the following table:

Type(x)	Type(y)	Result
null	undefined	`true`
undefined	null	`true`
Number	String	`x == toNumber(y)`
String	Number	`toNumber(x) == y`
Boolean	Any	`toNumber(x) == y`
Any	Boolean	`x == toNumber(y)`
String or Number	Object	`x == toPrimitive(y)`
Object	String or Number	`toPrimitive(x) == y`

If *x* and *y* are of the same type, then JavaScript will use the `equals` method to compare the two values or objects. Any other combination that is not listed in the table gives a false result.

The `toNumber` and `toPrimitive` methods are internal and evaluate the values according to the tables that follow.

The `toNumber` method is presented here:

Value type	Result
undefined	This is `NaN`.
null	This is `+0`.
Boolean	If the value is `true`, the result is `1`; if the value is `false`, the result is `+0`.
Number	This is the value of the number.

String	This parses the string into a number. If the string consists of alphabetical characters, the result is NaN; if the string consists of numbers, it is transformed into a number.
Object	This is `toNumber(toPrimitive(value))`.

Finally, `toPrimitive` is presented here:

Value type	Result
Object	If `valueOf` returns a primitive value, this returns the primitive value; otherwise, if `toString` returns a primitive value, this returns the primitive value and otherwise returns an error.

Let's verify the results of some examples. First, we know that the output of the following code is `true` (string length > 1):

```
console.log('packt' ? true : false);
```

Now, what about the following code? Let's take a look:

```
console.log('packt' == true);
```

The output is `false`, so let's understand why:

- First, it converts the Boolean value using `toNumber`, so we have `packt == 1`.
- Then, it converts the string value using `toNumber`. As the string consists of alphabetical characters, it returns `NaN`, so we have `NaN == 1`, which is false.

What about the following code? Let's take a look:

```
console.log('packt' == false);
```

The output is also `false`, and the following are the steps:

- First, it converts the Boolean value using `toNumber`, so we have `packt == 0`.
- Then, it converts the string value using `toNumber`. As the string consists of alphabetical characters, it returns `NaN`, so we have `NaN == 0`, which is false.

What about the `===` operator? It is much easier. If we are comparing two values of different types, the result is always false. If they have the same type, they are compared according to the following table:

Type(x)	Values	Result
Number	x has the same value as y (but not `NaN`)	`true`
String	x and y are identical characters	`true`
Boolean	x and y are both `true` or both `false`	`true`
Object	x and y reference the same object	`true`

If x and y are different types, then the result is false.

Let's consider some examples:

```
console.log('packt' === true); //false

console.log('packt' === 'packt'); //true

var person1 = {name:'John'};
var person2 = {name:'John'};
console.log(person1 === person2); //false, different objects
```

Control structures

JavaScript has a similar set of control structures as the C and Java languages. Conditional statements are supported by `if...else` and `switch`. Loops are supported by the `while`, `do...while`, and `for` constructs.

Conditional statements

The first conditional statement we will take a look at is the `if...else` construct. There are a few ways we can use the `if...else` construct.

We can use the `if` statement if we want to execute a script only if the condition is `true`, as follows:

```
var num = 1;
if (num === 1) {
```

```
    console.log("num is equal to 1");
}
```

We can use the if...else statement if we want to execute a script and the condition is true or another script just in case the condition is false (else), as follows:

```
var num = 0;
if (num === 1) {
    console.log("num is equal to 1");
} else {
    console.log("num is not equal to 1, the value of num is " + num);
}
```

The if...else statement can also be represented by a ternary operator. For example, take a look at the following if...else statement:

```
if (num === 1){
    num--;
} else {
    num++;
}
```

It can also be represented as follows:

```
(num === 1) ? num-- : num++;
```

Also, if we have several scripts, we can use if...else several times to execute different scripts based on different conditions, as follows:

```
var month = 5;
if (month === 1) {
    console.log("January");
} else if (month === 2){
    console.log("February");
} else if (month === 3){
    console.log("March");
} else {
    console.log("Month is not January, February or March");
}
```

Finally, we have the switch statement. If the condition we are evaluating is the same as the previous one (however, it is being compared to different values), we can use the switch statement:

```
var month = 5;
switch(month) {
    case 1:
    console.log("January");
```

```
    break;
    case 2:
    console.log("February");
    break;
    case 3:
    console.log("March");
    break;
    default:
    console.log("Month is not January, February or March");
}
```

One thing that is very important in a `switch` statement is the usage of the `case` and `break` keywords. The `case` clause determines whether the value of `switch` is equal to the value of the `case` clause. The `break` statement stops the `switch` statement from executing the rest of the statement (otherwise, it will execute all the scripts from all `case` clauses below the matched case until a `break` statement is found in one of the `case` clauses). Finally, we have the `default` statement, which is executed by default if none of the case statements are `true` (or if the executed `case` statement does not have the `break` statement).

Loops

Loops are very often used when we work with arrays (which are the subject of the next chapter). Specifically, we will use the `for` loop in our algorithms.

The `for` loop is exactly the same as in C and Java. It consists of a loop counter that is usually assigned a numeric value, then the variable is compared against another value (the script inside the `for` loop is executed while this condition is true), and finally the numeric value is increased or decreased.

- In the following example, we have a `for` loop. It outputs the value of `i` on the console, while `i` is less than `10`; `i` is initiated with , so the following code will output the values 0 to 9:

  ```
  for (var i=0; i<10; i++) {
    console.log(i);
  }
  ```

- The next loop construct we will look at is the `while` loop. The script inside the `while` loop is executed while the condition is true. In the following code, we have a variable, `i`, initiated with the value , and we want the value of `i` to be output while `i` is less than 10 (or less than or equal to 9). The output will be the values from 0 to 9:

```
var i = 0;
while(i<10)
{
  console.log(i);
  i++;
}
```

- The do...while loop is very similar to the while loop. The only difference is that in the while loop, the condition is evaluated before executing the script, and in the do...while loop, the condition is evaluated after the script is executed. The do...while loop ensures that the script is executed at least once. The following code also outputs the values from 0 to 9:

```
var i = 0;
do {
  console.log(i);
  i++;
} while (i<10)
```

Functions

Functions are very important when working with JavaScript. We will also use functions a lot in our examples.

The following code demonstrates the basic syntax of a function. It does not have arguments or the return statement:

```
function sayHello() {
  console.log('Hello!');
}
```

To call this code, we simply use the following call:

```
sayHello();
```

We can also pass arguments to a function. Arguments are variables with which a function is supposed to do something. The following code demonstrates how to use arguments with functions:

```
function output(text) {
  console.log(text);
}
```

To use this function, we can use the following code:

```
output('Hello!');
```

You can use as many arguments as you like, as follows:

```
output('Hello!', 'Other text');
```

In this case, only the first argument is used by the function and the second one is ignored.

A function can also return a value, as follows:

```
function sum(num1, num2) {
  return num1 + num2;
}
```

This function calculates the sum of two given numbers and returns its result. We can use it as follows:

```
var result = sum(1,2);
output(result);
```

Object-oriented programming in Javascript

JavaScript objects are very simple collections of name-value pairs. There are two ways of creating a simple object in JavaScript. The first way is as follows:

```
var obj = new Object();
```

And the second way is as follows:

```
var obj = {};
```

We can also create an object entirely, as follows:

```
obj = {
  name: {
    first: 'Gandalf',
    last: 'the Grey'
  },
  address: 'Middle Earth'
};
```

As we can see, to declare a JavaScript object, *[key, value]* pairs are used, where the key can be considered an attribute of the object and the value is the attribute value. All classes that we will create in this book are JavaScript objects, such as `Stack`, `Set`, `LinkedList`, `Dictionary`, `Tree`, `Graph`, and so on.

In **object-oriented programming** (**OOP**), an object is an instance of a class. A class defines the characteristics of the object. For our algorithms and data structures, we will create some classes that will represent them. This is how we can declare a class that represents a book:

```
function Book(title, pages, isbn){
  this.title = title;
  this.pages = pages;
  this.isbn = isbn;
}
```

To instantiate this class, we can use the following code:

```
var book = new Book('title', 'pag', 'isbn');
```

Then, we can access its attributes and update them as follows:

```
console.log(book.title); //outputs the book title
book.title = 'new title'; //updates the value of the book title
console.log(book.title); //outputs the updated value
```

A class can also contain functions. We can declare and use a function as the following code demonstrates:

```
Book.prototype.printTitle = function(){
  console.log(this.title);
};
book.printTitle();
```

We can declare functions directly inside the class definition as well:

```
function Book(title, pages, isbn){
  this.title = title;
  this.pages = pages;
  this.isbn = isbn;
  this.printIsbn = function(){
  console.log(this.isbn);
  }
}
book.printIsbn();
```

In the prototype example, the `printTitle` function will be shared between all the instances and only one copy will be created. When we use a class-based definition, as in the previous example, each instance will have its own copy of the functions. Using the prototype method saves memory and processing cost with regard to assigning the functions to the instance. However, you can only declare public functions and properties using the prototype method. With a class-based definition, you can declare private functions and properties and the other methods inside the class can also access them. ECMAScript 6 introduces a simplified syntax very similar to the class-based example and it is prototype based. We will discuss more on this later in this chapter.

Debugging and tools

Knowing how to program with JavaScript is important, but so is knowing how to debug your code. Debugging is very useful in helping you find bugs in your code, but it can also help you execute your code at a lower speed so that you can see everything that is happening (the stack of methods called, variable assignment, and so on). It is highly recommended that you spend some time debugging the source code of this book to see every step of the algorithm (it might help you understand it better as well).

Both Firefox and Chrome support debugging. A great tutorial from Google that shows you how to use Google Developer Tools to debug JavaScript can be found at `https://developer.chrome.com/devtools/docs/javascript-debugging`.

You can use any text editor of your preference. However, there are other great tools that can help you be more productive when working with JavaScript as well, which are as follows:

- **Aptana**: This is a free and open source IDE that supports JavaScript, CSS3, and HTML5, among other languages (`http://www.aptana.com/`).
- **WebStorm**: This is a very powerful JavaScript IDE with support for the latest web technologies and frameworks. It is a paid IDE, but you can download a 30-day trial version (`http://www.jetbrains.com/webstorm/`).
- **Sublime Text**: This is a lightweight text editor and you can customize it by installing plugins. You can buy the license to support the development team, but you can also use it for free (the trial version does not expire) at `http://www.sublimetext.com/`.
- **Atom:** This is also a free lightweight text editor created by GitHub. It has great support for JavaScript and it can also be customized by installing plugins (`https://atom.io/`).

Introducing ECMAScript

If you follow the news and latest trends about JavaScript, you might have heard the hype about **ECMAScript** 6 and **ECMAScript** 7. What does ECMAScript have to do with JavaScript and is there a difference?

ECMAScript is a scripting language specification. JavaScript is an implementation of this specification, as are **Jscript** and **ActionScript**.

ECMAScript 6 and ECMAScript 7

As we know, JavaScript is a language that runs mostly on browsers (also in servers using NodeJS), and each browser can implement its own version of the available functionalities of JavaScript (as you will learn later on in this book). This specific implementation is based on ECMAScript. Thus, the browsers offer mostly the same functionalities (our JavaScript code will run in all browsers); however, each functionality's behavior may be a little bit different from browser to browser.

All the code presented in this chapter so far is based on ECMAScript 5, which became a standard in December 2009. The most recent release of ECMAScript, at the time this book is being written, is ECMAScript 6, which was standardized in July 2015, almost 6 years after its previous version. The committee responsible for drafting the ECMAScript specifications made the decision to move to a yearly model to define new standards, where new features would be added as they were approved. For this reason, ECMAScript sixth edition was renamed to ECMAScript 2015 (**ES6**). There is a new version that is also being prepared to be released in the summer of 2016, which is called ECMAScript 2016 or ECMAScript 7 (**ES7**).

In this topic, we will cover some of the new functionalities introduced in ES6 and ES7.

The compatibility table

It is important to know that, even though ES6 has already been released, its features might not be supported by all browsers. For a better experience, it is best to use the latest version available for the browser you choose to use (Firefox or Chrome).

At the following links, you can verify which features are available in each browser:

- **ES6**: http://kangax.github.io/compat-table/es6/
- **ES7**: http://kangax.github.io/compat-table/es7/

Even if the features are not yet available, we can start using new syntax and new functionalities today.

By default, Firefox adds support to ES6 and ES7 as their team ships the implementation of the functionalities.

In Google Chrome, you can enable the functionalities by enabling the experimental JavaScript flag by opening the URL `chrome://flags`, as demonstrated in the following image:

Even with the **Enable Experimental JavaScript** flag enabled, some of the ES6 features might not be supported in Chrome. The same can be applied to Firefox. To know exactly which features are already supported in each browser, take a look at the compatibility table.

Using Babel.js

Babel (`https://babeljs.io`) is a JavaScript transpiler, also known as a source-to-source compiler. It converts JavaScript code with ES6 and ES7 language features to equivalent code that uses only language features from the widely supported ES5 specification.

There are many different ways of using Babel.js. One of them is installing it according to its setup (`https://babeljs.io/docs/setup/`). Another one is using it directly in the browser through its **Try it out** option (`https://babeljs.io/repl/`), as demonstrated in the following screenshot:

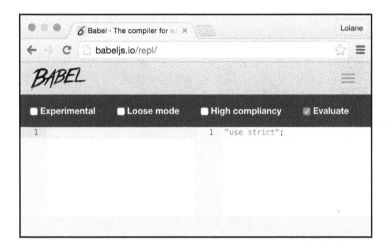

Along with each example of ES6 and ES7 that will be presented in the following topics, we will also provide a link so that you can run and test the examples in Babel.

ECMAScript 6 functionalities

In this topic, we will demonstrate how to use some of the new functionalities of ES6, which may be useful in the everyday JavaScript coding and which will also be useful to simplify the examples presented in the next chapters of this book. Among the functionalities, we will cover the following ones:

- `let` and `const`
- Template literals
- Destructuring
- Spread operator
- Arrow functions using =>
- Classes

Declaring variables with let instead of var

Until ES5, we could declare variables in any place of our code, even if we overwrote the variables declaration, as in the following code:

```
var framework = 'Angular';
var framework = 'React';
console.log(framework);
```

The output of the preceding code is `React` as the last variable declared, named framework, was assigned this value. In the previous code, we had two variables with the same name; this is very dangerous and might drive the code to an incorrect output.

Other languages, such as C, Java, and C#, do no allow this behavior. With ES6, a new keyword was introduced, called `let`. Let is the new `var` keyword, meaning we can simply substitute the keyword `var` for `let`. In the following code, we have an example:

```
let language = 'JavaScript!'; //{1}
let language = 'Ruby!'; // {2} - throws error
console.log(language);
```

Line {2} will throw an error because a variable named language is already declared in the same scope (line {1}). We will discuss the `let` and variables scope in the next topic.

 The preceding code can be tested and executed at the URL https://goo.gl/he0udZ.

Variables scope with let

To understand how variables declared with `let` keyword work, let's use the following example (you can run the example using the URL https://goo.gl/NbsVvg):

```
let movie = 'Lord of the Rings'; //{1}
//var movie = 'Batman v Superman'; //throws error, variable movie already
declared

function starWarsFan(){
  let movie = 'Star Wars'; //{2}
  return movie;
}

function marvelFan(){
  movie = 'The Avengers'; //{3}
```

```
    return movie;
}

function blizzardFan(){
  let isFan = true;
  let phrase = 'Warcraft'; //{4}
  console.log('Before if: ' + phrase);
  if (isFan){
    let phrase = 'initial text'; //{5}
    phrase = 'For the Horde!';    //{6}
    console.log('Inside if: ' + phrase);
  }
  phrase = 'For the Alliance!';    //{7}
  console.log('After if: ' + phrase);
}

console.log(movie); //{8}
console.log(starWarsFan()); //{9}
console.log(marvelFan()); //{10}
console.log(movie);        //{11}
blizzardFan(); //{12}
```

This will be the output from the previous code:

```
Lord of the Rings
Star Wars
The Avengers
The Avengers
Before if: Warcraft
Inside if: For the Horde!
After if: For the Alliance!
```

Now, we will discuss the reason we got this output.

- On line {1}, we declared a variable `movie` with the value `Lord of the Rings`, and we output its value on line {8}. This variable has global scope, as you learned in the *Variable scope* section of this chapter.
- On line {9}, we executed the `starWarsFan` function. Inside this function, we also declared a variable named `movie` on line {2}. The output from this function is `Star Wars` because the variable from line {2} has local scope, meaning it is only valid inside this function.

- On line {10}, we executed the `marvelFan` function. Inside this function, we changed the value of the `movie` variable (line {3}). This variable made a reference to the global variable declared on line {1}. This is why we got the output `The Avengers` on line {10} and also on line {11}, where we output the global variable.
- Finally, we executed the `blizzardFan` function on line {12}. Inside this function, we declared a variable named `phrase` (line {4}) with the scope of the function. Then, on line {5}, again, we will declare a variable named `phrase`, but this time, this variable will have only a scope inside the `if` statement.
- On line {6}, we changed the value of `phrase`. As we are still inside the `if` statement, only the variable declared on line {5} would have its value changed.
- Then, on line {7}, we again changed the value of `phrase`, but as we are not inside the block of the `if` statement, the value of the variable declared on line {4} is changed.

Again, this scope behavior is the same as in other programming languages, such as Java or C. However, this was only introduced in JavaScript through ES6.

Constants

ES6 also introduced the keyword `const`. Its behavior is the same thing as the keyword `let`; the only difference is that a variable defined as `const` has a read-only value, meaning a constant value.

For example, consider the following code:

```
const PI = 3.141593;
PI = 3.0; //throws error
console.log(PI);
```

When we try to assign a new value to `PI` or even try to redeclare it as `var PI` or `let PI`, the code will throw an error saying that `PI` is read only.

 The preceding code can be executed at `https://goo.gl/4xuWrC`.

Template literals

Template literals are really nice because we can create strings without the need to concatenate the values.

For example, consider the following examples written with ES5:

```
var book = {
   name: 'Learning JavaScript DataStructures and Algorithms'
};
console.log('You are reading ' + book.name + '.,\n     and this is a new
line\n    and so is this.');
```

We can improve the syntax of the previous `console.log` output with the following code:

```
console.log(`You are reading ${book.name}.,
and this is a new line
and so is this.`);
```

Template literals are enclosed by backticks (` `` `). To interpolate a variable value, we will simply set the variable value inside a dollar sign and curly braces (`${ }`), as we did with `book.name`.

Template literals can also be used for multiline strings. There is no need to use \n anymore. Simply hit *Enter* on the keyboard to take the string to a new line, as was done with `and this is a new line` in the previous example.

This functionality will be very useful in our examples to simplify the output!

 The preceding examples can be executed at `https://goo.gl/PTqnw0`.

Arrow functions

Arrow functions are a great way of simplifying the syntax of functions in ES6. Consider the following example:

```
var circleArea = function circleArea(r) {
   var PI = 3.14;
   var area = PI * r * r;
   return area;
};
```

```
console.log(circleArea(2));
```

We can simplify the syntax of the preceding code to the following code:

```
let circleArea = (r) => { //{1}
  const PI = 3.14;
  let area = PI * r * r;
  return area;
}
console.log(circleArea(2));
```

The main difference is on line {1} of the example, on which we can omit the keyword function using =>.

If the function has a single statement, we can use a simpler version as well, by omitting the keyword `return`. Take a look at the following:

```
let circleArea2 = (r) => 3.14 * r * r;
console.log(circleArea2(2));
```

 The preceding examples can be executed at `https://goo.gl/CigniJ`.

Default parameter values for functions

With ES6, it is also possible to define default parameter values for functions. The following is an example:

```
function sum (x = 1, y = 2, z = 3) {
  return x + y + z
};
console.log(sum(4,2)); //outputs 9
```

As we are not passing `z` as a parameter, it will have value 3 by default. So, `4 + 2 + 3 == 9`.

Before ES6, we would have to write the preceding function as the following code:

```
function sum (x, y, z) {
  if (x === undefined)
  x = 1;
  if (y === undefined)
  y = 2;
  if (z === undefined)
```

```
  z = 3;
  return x + y + z;
};
```

With ES6, we can save a few lines of code using the default parameter values functionality.

 The preceding example can be executed at `https://goo.gl/2MiJ59`.

Declaring the spread and rest operators

In ES5, we can turn arrays into parameters using the `apply()` function. ES6 has the spread operator (...) for this purpose. For example, consider the function sum we declared in the previous topic. We can execute the following code to pass the x, y, and z parameters:

```
var params = [3, 4, 5];
console.log(sum(...params));
```

The preceding code is the same as the code written in ES5, as follows:

```
var params = [3, 4, 5];
console.log(sum.apply(undefined, params));
```

The spread operator (...) can also be used as a rest parameter in functions to replace `arguments`. Consider the following example:

```
function restParamaterFunction (x, y, ...a) {
  return (x + y) * a.length;
}
console.log(restParamaterFunction(1, 2, "hello", true, 7)); //outputs 9;
```

The preceding code is the same as the following:

```
function restParamaterFunction (x, y) {
  var a = Array.prototype.slice.call(arguments, 2);
  return (x + y) * a.length;
};
```

 The spread operator example can be executed at `https://goo.gl/8equk5`, and the rest parameter example can be executed at `https://goo.gl/LaJZqU`.

Enhanced object properties

ES6 introduces a concept called **array destructuring**, which is a way of initializing variables at once. For example, consider the following:

```
var [x, y] = ['a', 'b'];
```

Executing the preceding code is the same as doing the following:

```
var x = 'a';
var y = 'b';
```

Array destructuring can also be performed to swap values at once without the need to create temp variables, as follows:

```
[x, y] = [y, x];
```

The preceding code is the same as the following one:

```
var temp = x;
x = y;
y = temp;
```

This will be very useful when you learn sorting algorithms as this swap values is very common.

There is also another functionality, called property shorthand, which is another way of performing the destructuring of objects. For example, consider the following example:

```
var [x, y] = ['a', 'b'];
var obj = { x, y };
console.log(obj); // { x: "a", y: "b" }
```

The preceding code is the same as doing the following:

```
var x = 'a';
var y = 'b';
var obj2 = { x: x, y: y };
console.log(obj2); // { x: "a", y: "b" }
```

The last functionality we will discuss in this topic is called the method property. This allows developers to declare functions inside objects as if they were properties. The following is an example:

```
var hello = {
  name : 'abcdef',
  printHello(){
  console.log('Hello');
```

```
  }
}
console.log(hello.printHello());
```

The preceding code can also be written as follows:

```
var hello = {
  name: 'abcdef',
  printHello: function printHello() {
  console.log('Hello');
  }
};
```

The three examples presented can be executed at:

- **Array destructuring**: https://goo.gl/VsLecp
- **Variable swap**: https://goo.gl/EyFAII
- **Property shorthand**: https://goo.gl/DKU2PN

Object-oriented programming with classes

ES6 also introduced a cleaner way of declaring classes. You learned that we can declare a class named Book in the *Object oriented programming* section this way:

```
function Book(title, pages, isbn){ //{1}
  this.title = title;
  this.pages = pages;
  this.isbn = isbn;
}
Book.prototype.printTitle = function(){
  console.log(this.title);
};
```

With ES6, we can simplify the syntax and use the following code:

```
class Book { //{2}
  constructor (title, pages, isbn) {
  this.title = title;
  this.pages = pages;
  this.isbn = isbn;
  }
  printIsbn(){
    console.log(this.isbn);
  }
}
```

We can simply use the keyword `class` and declare a class with a `constructor` function and other functions as well—for example, the `printIsbn` function. The code for the class `Book` declared on line {1} has the same effect and output as the code declared on line {2}:

```
let book = new Book('title', 'pag', 'isbn');
console.log(book.title); //outputs the book title
book.title = 'new title'; //update the value of the book title
console.log(book.title); //outputs the book title
```

 The preceding example can be executed at `https://goo.gl/UhK1n4`.

Inheritance

As we have a new way of declaring classes, there is also a simplified syntax to use inheritance between classes. Let's take a look at an example:

```
class ITBook extends Book { //{1}
  constructor (title, pages, isbn, technology) {
    super(title, pages, isbn); //{2}
    this.technology = technology;
  }
  printTechnology(){
    console.log(this.technology);
  }
}

let jsBook = new ITBook('Learning JS Algorithms', '200', '1234567890',
'JavaScript');
console.log(jsBook.title);
console.log(jsBook.printTechnology());
```

We can extend another class and inherit its behavior using the keyword `extends` (line {1}). Inside the constructor, we can also refer to the `constructor` superclass using the keyword `super` (line {2}).

Although the syntax of this new way of declaring classes in JavaScript is very similar to other programming languages such as Java and C/C++, it is good to remember that JavaScript object-oriented programming is done through a prototype.

The preceding example can be executed at `https://goo.gl/hgQvo9`.

Working with getters and setters

With the new class syntax, it is also possible to create getter and setter functions for the class attributes. Although class attributes are not private as in other object-oriented languages (the encapsulation concept), it is good to follow a naming pattern.

The following is an example of a class declaring a `get` and `set` function along with its use:

```
class Person {
  constructor (name) {
    this._name = name; //{1}
  }
  get name() { //{2}
    return this._name;
  }
  set name(value) { //{3}
    this._name = value;
  }
}

let lotrChar = new Person('Frodo');
console.log(lotrChar.name); //{4}
lotrChar.name = 'Gandalf';    //{5}
console.log(lotrChar.name);
lotrChar._name = 'Sam'; //{6}
console.log(lotrChar.name);
```

To declare a `get` and `set` function, we simply need to use the keyword `get` or `set` in front of the function name (lines {2} and {3}), which is the name we want to expose and to be used. We can declare the class attributes with the same name, or we can use underscore in front of the attribute name (line {1}) to make it seem as though the attribute is private.

Then, to take a look at the `get` or `set` functions, we can simply refer to their names as it was a simple attribute (lines {4} and {5}).

It is also good to remember that the _name attribute is not really private, and we can still make a reference to it. However, we will talk about this later on in this book.
This example can be executed at `https://goo.gl/SMRYsv`.

Other functionalities

ES6 also has some other functionalities; among them, we can list iterators, typed arrays, Set, Map, WeakSet, WeakMap, modules, tail calls, and Symbol. We will cover some of these other functionalities in other chapters of this book.

 For more information about all the functionalities of ES6 and its specification, refer to `http://www.ecma-international.org/ecma-26 2/6.0/`.

ECMAScript 7 functionalities

Until the date that this book is being written, only one functionality is confirmed to be shipped with ES7 (or ECMAScript 2016), which is called `Array.prototype.includes`.

There are other functionalities that are almost ready and may be included in ES7 but still not confirmed, which are:

- The exponentiation operator
- SIMD.JS – SIMD APIs + polyfill
- Async functions
- `Object.values/Object.entries`
- String padding
- Trailing commas in function parameter lists and calls

The exponentiation operator may come in handy when working with math, and it simplifies the `Math.pow(2, 3)` code to `2 ** 3`, where `**` is designed to be the new exponentiation operator.

You will learn more about the `Array.prototype.includes` functionality in the next `Chapter 2`, *Arrays*.

 For more information about ES7, visit `https://tc39.github.io/ecma2 62/`.

ES6 and ES7 backward compatibility

Do I need to update my current JavaScript code to ES6 or Es7? Of course not! ES6 and ES7 are subsets of the JavaScript language. Everything that was standardized as ES5 will continue working as is today. However, you can start using ES6 and ES7 to leverage the new syntax and make your code simpler and easier to read.

In the following chapters of this book, we will try to use ES6 and ES7 as much as we can. In case you want to write the example code using ES5, you can always use Babel to transpiler the code of this book into ES5 code.

 Some of the examples we will create are also available in ES5 syntax by accessing the branch master of the Github repository at `https://github.com/loiane/javascript-datastructures-algo rithms`.

Now, we have covered all the basic JavaScript concepts that are needed for us to start having some fun with data structures and algorithms!

Summary

In this chapter, you learned how to set up the development environment to be able to create or execute the examples in this book.

We also covered the basics of the JavaScript language that are needed prior to getting started with constructing the algorithms and data structures covered in this book.

You also learned some of the ECMAScript 6 and ECMAScript 7 functionalities that will help us simplify the syntax of our upcoming examples.

In the next chapter, we will look at our first data structure, which is the array, the most basic data structure that many languages support natively, including JavaScript.

2
Arrays

An **array** is the simplest memory data structure. For this reason, all programming languages have a built-in array datatype. JavaScript also supports arrays natively, even though its first version was released without array support. In this chapter, we will dive into the array data structure and its capabilities.

An array stores values sequentially that are all of the same datatype. Although JavaScript allows us to create arrays with values from different datatypes, we will follow best practices and assume that we cannot do this (most languages do not have this capability).

Why should we use arrays?

Let's consider that we need to store the average temperature of each month of the year of the city that we live in. We could use something similar to the following to store this information:

```
var averageTempJan = 31.9;
var averageTempFeb = 35.3;
var averageTempMar = 42.4;
var averageTempApr = 52;
var averageTempMay = 60.8;
```

However, this is not the best approach. If we store the temperature for only one year, we could manage 12 variables. However, what if we need to store the average temperature for more than one year? Fortunately, this is why arrays were created, and we can easily represent the same information mentioned earlier as follows:

```
var averageTemp = [];
averageTemp[0] = 31.9;
averageTemp[1] = 35.3;
averageTemp[2] = 42.4;
```

```
averageTemp[3] = 52;
averageTemp[4] = 60.8;
```

We can also represent the `averageTemp` array graphically:

Creating and initializing arrays

Declaring, creating, and initializing an array in JavaScript is as simple, as shown by the following:

```
var daysOfWeek = new Array(); //{1}
var daysOfWeek = new Array(7); //{2}
var daysOfWeek = new Array('Sunday', 'Monday', 'Tuesday', 'Wednes day',
'Thursday', 'Friday', 'Saturday'); //{3}
```

We can simply declare and instantiate a new array using the keyword `new` (line {1}). Also, using the keyword `new`, we can create a new array specifying the length of the array (line {2}). A third option would be passing the array elements directly to its constructor (line {3}).

However, using the `new` keyword is not best practice. If you want to create an array in JavaScript, we can assign empty brackets (`[]`), as in the following example:

```
var daysOfWeek = [];
```

We can also initialize the array with some elements, as follows:

```
var daysOfWeek = ['Sunday', 'Monday', 'Tuesday', 'Wednesday', 'Thursday',
'Friday', 'Saturday'];
```

If we want to know how many elements are in the array (its size), we can use the `length` property. The following code will give an output of 7:

```
console.log(daysOfWeek.length);
```

Accessing elements and iterating an array

To access a particular position of the array, we can also use brackets, passing the index of the position we would like to access. For example, let's say we want to output all the elements from the `daysOfWeek` array. To do so, we need to loop the array and print the elements, as follows:

```
for (var i=0; i<daysOfWeek.length; i++){
    console.log(daysOfWeek[i]);
}
```

Let's take a look at another example. Let's say that we want to find out the first 20 numbers of the Fibonacci sequence. The first two numbers of the Fibonacci sequence are 1 and 2, and each subsequent number is the sum of the previous two numbers:

```
var fibonacci = []; //{1}
fibonacci[1] = 1; //{2}
fibonacci[2] = 1; //{3}

for(var i = 3; i < 20; i++){
    fibonacci[i] = fibonacci[i-1] + fibonacci[i-2]; ////{4}
}

for(var i = 1; i<fibonacci.length; i++){ //{5}
    console.log(fibonacci[i]);           //{6}
}
```

- So, in line {1}, we declared and created an array.
- In lines {2} and {3}, we assigned the first two numbers of the Fibonacci sequence to the second and third positions of the array (in JavaScript, the first position of the array is always referenced by 0, and as there is no 0 in the Fibonacci sequence, we will skip it).
- Then, all we have to do is create the third to the twentieth number of the sequence (as we know the first two numbers already). To do so, we can use a loop and assign the sum of the previous two positions of the array to the current position (line {4}, starting from index 3 of the array to the 19th index).
- Then, to take a look at the output (line {6}), we just need to loop the array from its first position to its length (line {5}).

We can use `console.log` to output each index of the array (lines {5} and {6}), or we can also use `console.log(fibonacci)` to output the array itself. Most browsers have a nice array representation in `console.log`.

If you would like to generate more than 20 numbers of the Fibonacci sequence, just change the number 20 to whatever number you like.

Adding elements

Adding and removing elements from an array is not that difficult; however, it can be tricky. For the examples we will use in this section, let's consider that we have the following numbers array initialized with numbers from 0 to 9:

```
var numbers = [0,1,2,3,4,5,6,7,8,9];
```

If we want to add a new element to this array (for example, the number 10), all we have to do is reference the latest free position of the array and assign a value to it:

```
numbers[numbers.length] = 10;
```

 In JavaScript, an array is a mutable object. We can easily add new elements to it. The object will grow dynamically as we add new elements to it. In many other languages, such as C and Java, we need to determine the size of the array, and if we need to add more elements to the array, we need to create a completely new array; we cannot simply add new elements to it as we need them.

Using the push method

However, there is also a method called push that allows us to add new elements to the end of the array. We can add as many elements as we want as arguments to the push method:

```
numbers.push(11);
numbers.push(12, 13);
```

The output of the numbers array will be the numbers from 0 to 13.

Inserting an element in the first position

Now, let's say we need to add a new element to the array and would like to insert it in the first position, not the last one. To do so, first, we need to free the first position by shifting all the elements to the right. We can loop all the elements of the array, starting from the last position + 1 (length) and shifting the previous element to the new position to finally assign the new value we want to the first position (-1). Run the following code for this:

```
for (var i=numbers.length; i>=0; i--){
  numbers[i] = numbers[i-1];
}
numbers[0] = -1;
```

We can represent this action with the following diagram:

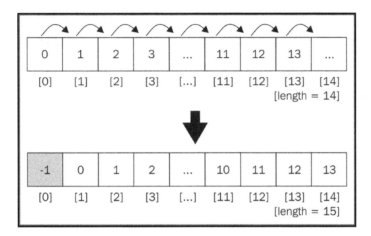

Using the unshift method

The JavaScript array class also has a method called unshift, which inserts the values passed in the method's arguments at the start of the array:

```
numbers.unshift(-2);
numbers.unshift(-4, -3);
```

So, using the unshift method, we can add the value -2 and then -3 and -4 to the beginning of the numbers array. The output of this array will be the numbers from -4 to 13.

Removing elements

So far, you have learned how to add values to the end and at the beginning of an array. Let's take a look at how we can remove a value from an array.

To remove a value from the end of an array, we can use the pop method:

```
numbers.pop();
```

The `push` and `pop` methods allow an array to emulate a basic `stack` data structure, which is the subject of the next chapter.

The output of our array will be the numbers from -4 to 12. The length of our array is 17.

Removing an element from first position

To remove a value from the beginning of the array, we can use the following code:

```
for (var i=0; i<numbers.length; i++){
  numbers[i] = numbers[i+1];
}
```

We can represent the previous code using the following diagram:

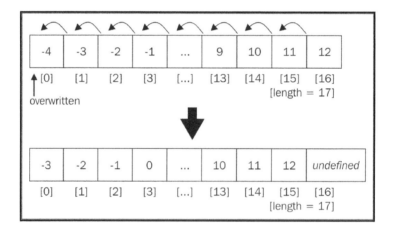

We shifted all the elements one position to the left. However, the **length** of the array is still the same (**17**), meaning we still have an extra element in our array (with an undefined value). The last time the code inside the loop was executed, `i+1` was a reference to a position that does not exist. In some languages such as Java, C/C++, or C#, the code would throw an exception, and we would have to end our loop at `numbers.length -1`.

As you can note, we have only overwritten the array's original values, and we did not really remove the value (as the length of the array is still the same and we have this extra undefined element).

Using the shift method

To actually remove an element from the beginning of the array, we can use the `shift` method, as follows:

```
numbers.shift();
```

So, if we consider that our array has the value -4 to 12 and a length of 17, after we execute the previous code, the array will contain the values -3 to 12 and have a length of 16.

> The `shift` and `unshift` methods allow an array to emulate a basic `queue` data structure, which is the subject of `Chapter 4`, *Queues*.

Adding and removing elements from a specific position

So far, you have learned how to add elements at the end and at the beginning of an array, and you have also learned how to remove elements from the beginning and end of an array. What if we also want to add or remove elements from any particular position of our array? How can we do this?

We can use the `splice` method to remove an element from an array by simply specifying the position/index that we would like to delete from and how many elements we would like to remove, as follows:

```
numbers.splice(5,3);
```

This code will remove three elements, starting from index 5 of our array. This means the numbers [5],numbers [6], and numbers [7] will be removed from the numbers array. The content of our array will be -3, -2, -1, 0, 1, 5, 6, 7, 8, 9, 10, 11, and 12 (as the numbers 2, 3, and 4 have been removed).

> As with JavaScript arrays and objects, we can also use the `delete` operator to remove an element from the array, for example, `remove numbers[0]`. However, the position 0 of the array will have the value `undefined`, meaning that it would be the same as doing `numbers[0] = undefined`. For this reason, we should always use the `splice`, `pop`, or `shift` (which you will learn next) methods to remove elements.

Now, let's say we want to insert numbers 2 to 4 back into the array, starting from the position 5. We can again use the `splice` method to do this:

```
numbers.splice(5,0,2,3,4);
```

The first argument of the method is the index we want to remove elements from or insert elements into. The second argument is the number of elements we want to remove (in this case, we do not want to remove any, so we will pass the value 0 (zero)). And the third argument (onwards) are the values we would like to insert into the array (the elements 2, 3, and 4). The output will be values from -3 to 12 again.

Finally, let's execute the following code:

```
numbers.splice(5,3,2,3,4);
```

The output will be values from -3 to 12. This is because we are removing three elements, starting from the index 5, and we are also adding the elements 2, 3, and 4, starting at index 5.

Two-dimensional and multidimensional arrays

At the beginning of this chapter, we used the *temperature measurement* example. We will now use this example one more time. Let's consider that we need to measure the temperature hourly for a few days. Now that we already know we can use an array to store the temperatures, we can easily write the following code to store the temperatures over two days:

```
var averageTempDay1 = [72,75,79,79,81,81];
var averageTempDay2 = [81,79,75,75,73,72];
```

However, this is not the best approach; we can write better code! We can use a matrix (two-dimensional array) to store this information, in which each row will represent the day, and each column will represent an hourly measurement of temperature, as follows:

```
var averageTemp = [];
averageTemp[0] = [72,75,79,79,81,81];
averageTemp[1] = [81,79,75,75,73,72];
```

JavaScript only supports one-dimensional arrays; it does not support matrices. However, we can implement matrices or any multidimensional array using an array of arrays, as in the previous code. The same code can also be written as follows:

```
//day 1
averageTemp[0] = [];
averageTemp[0][0] = 72;
averageTemp[0][1] = 75;
averageTemp[0][2] = 79;
averageTemp[0][3] = 79;
averageTemp[0][4] = 81;
averageTemp[0][5] = 81;
//day 2
averageTemp[1] = [];
averageTemp[1][0] = 81;
averageTemp[1][1] = 79;
averageTemp[1][2] = 75;
averageTemp[1][3] = 75;
averageTemp[1][4] = 73;
averageTemp[1][5] = 72;
```

In the previous code, we specified the value of each day and hour separately. We can also represent this example in a diagram similar to the following:

	[0]	[1]	[2]	[3]	[4]	[5]
[0]	72	75	79	79	81	81
[1]	81	79	75	75	73	73

Each row represents a day, and each column represents an hour of the day (temperature).

Iterating the elements of two-dimensional arrays

If we want to take a look at the output of the matrix, we can create a generic function to log its output:

```
function printMatrix(myMatrix) {
  for (var i=0; i<myMatrix.length; i++){
    for (var j=0; j<myMatrix[i].length; j++){
      console.log(myMatrix[i][j]);
    }
  }
}
```

We need to loop through all the rows and columns. To do this, we need to use a nested `for` loop in which the variable `i` represents rows, and `j` represents the columns.

We can call the following code to take a look at the output of the averageTemp matrix:

```
printMatrix(averageTemp);
```

Multi-dimensional arrays

We can also work with multidimensional arrays in JavaScript. For example, let's create a 3 x 3 matrix. Each cell contains the sum i (row) + j (column) + z (depth) of the matrix, as follows:

```
var matrix3x3x3 = [];
for (var i=0; i<3; i++){
  matrix3x3x3[i] = [];
  for (var j=0; j<3; j++){
    matrix3x3x3[i][j] = [];
    for (var z=0; z<3; z++){
      matrix3x3x3[i][j][z] = i+j+z;
    }
  }
}
```

It does not matter how many dimensions we have in the data structure; we need to loop each dimension to access the cell. We can represent a 3 x 3 x 3 matrix with a cube diagram, as follows:

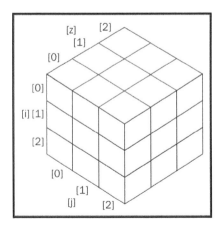

To output the content of this matrix, we can use the following code:

```
for (var i=0; i<matrix3x3x3.length; i++){
  for (var j=0; j<matrix3x3x3[i].length; j++){
    for (var z=0; z<matrix3x3x3[i][j].length; z++){
      console.log(matrix3x3x3[i][j][z]);
    }
  }
}
```

If we had a 3 x 3 x 3 x 3 matrix, we would have four nested `for` statements in our code and so on.

References for JavaScript array methods

Arrays in JavaScript are modified objects, meaning that every array we create has a few methods available to be used. JavaScript arrays are very interesting because they are very powerful and have more capabilities available than primitive arrays in other languages. This means that we do not need to write basic capabilities ourselves, such as adding and removing elements in/from the middle of the data structure.

The following is a list of the core available methods in an array object. We have covered some methods already:

Method	Description
concat	This joins multiple arrays and returns a copy of the joined arrays
every	This iterates every element of the array, verifying a desired condition (function) until `false` is returned
filter	This creates an array with each element that evaluates to `true` in the function provided
forEach	This executes a specific function on each element of the array
join	This joins all the array elements into a string
indexOf	This searches the array for specific elements and returns its position
lastIndexOf	This returns the position of last item in the array that matches the search criteria
map	This creates a new array from a function that contains the criteria/condition and returns the elements of the array that match the criteria

reverse	This reverses the array so that the last items become the first and vice versa
slice	This returns a new array from the specified index
some	This iterates every element of the array, verifying a desired condition (function) until `true` is returned
sort	This sorts the array alphabetically or by the supplied function
toString	This returns the array as a string
valueOf	Similar to the `toString` method, this returns the array as a string

We have already covered the `push`, `pop`, `shift`, `unshift`, and `splice` methods. Let's take a look at these new ones. These methods will be very useful in the subsequent chapters of this book, where we will code our own data structure and algorithms.

Joining multiple arrays

Consider a scenario where you have different arrays and you need to join all of them into a single array. We could iterate each array and add each element to the final array. Fortunately, JavaScript already has a method that can do this for us named the `concat` method, which looks as follows:

```
var zero = 0;
var positiveNumbers = [1,2,3];
var negativeNumbers = [-3,-2,-1];
var numbers = negativeNumbers.concat(zero, positiveNumbers);
```

We can pass as many arrays and objects/elements to this array as we desire. The arrays will be concatenated to the specified array in the order that the arguments are passed to the method. In this example, `zero` will be concatenated to `negativeNumbers`, and then `positiveNumbers` will be concatenated to the resulting array. The output of the `numbers` array will be the values -3, -2, -1, 0, 1, 2, and 3.

Iterator functions

Sometimes, we need to iterate the elements of an array. You learned that we can use a loop construct to do this, such as the `for` statement, as we saw in some previous examples.

JavaScript also has some built-in iterator methods that we can use with arrays. For the examples of this section, we will need an array and also a function. We will use an array with values from 1 to 15 and also a function that returns `true` if the number is a multiple of 2 (even) and `false` otherwise. Run the following code:

```
var isEven = function (x) {
  // returns true if x is a multiple of 2.
  console.log(x);
  return (x % 2 == 0) ? true : false;
};
var numbers = [1,2,3,4,5,6,7,8,9,10,11,12,13,14,15];
```

> `return (x % 2 == 0) ? true : false` can also be represented as `return (x % 2 == 0)`.

Iterating using the every method

The first method we will take a look at is the `every` method. The `every` method iterates each element of the array until the return of the function is `false`, as follows:

```
numbers.every(isEven);
```

In this case, our first element of the `numbers` array is the number 1. 1 is not a multiple of 2 (it is an odd number), so the `isEven` function will return `false`, and this will be the only time the function will be executed.

Iterating using the some method

Next, we have the `some` method. It has the same behavior as the `every` method; however, the `some` method iterates each element of the array until the return of the function is `true`:

```
numbers.some(isEven);
```

In our case, the first even number of our `numbers` array is 2 (the second element). The first element that will be iterated is the number 1; it will return `false`. Then, the second element that will be iterated is the number 2, which will return `true`, and the iteration will stop.

Iterating using forEach

If we need the array to be completely iterated no matter what, we can use the `forEach` function. It has the same result as using a `for` loop with the function's code inside it, as follows:

```
numbers.forEach(function(x){
    console.log((x % 2 == 0));
});
```

Using map and filter

JavaScript also has two other iterator methods that return a new array with a result. The first one is the `map` method, which is as follows:

```
var myMap = numbers.map(isEven);
```

The `myMap` array will have the following values: `[false, true, false, true, false, true, false, true, false, true, false, true, false, true, false]`. It stores the result of the `isEven` function that was passed to the `map` method. This way, we can easily know whether a number is even or not. For example, `myMap[0]` returns `false` because 1 is not even, and `myMap[1]` returns `true` because 2 is even.

We also have the `filter` method. It returns a new array with the elements that the function returned `true`, as follows:

```
var evenNumbers = numbers.filter(isEven);
```

In our case, the `evenNumbers` array will contain the elements that are multiples of 2: `[2, 4, 6, 8, 10, 12, 14]`.

Using the reduce method

Finally, we have the `reduce` method. The `reduce` method also receives a function with the following parameters: `previousValue`, `currentValue`, `index`, and `array`. We can use this function to return a value that will be added to an accumulator, which will be returned after the `reduce` method stops being executed. It can be very useful if we want to sum up all the values in an array. Here's an example:

```
numbers.reduce(function(previous, current, index){
    return previous + current;
});
```

The output will be 120.

 The JavaScript Array class also has two other important methods: map and reduce. The method names are self-explanatory, meaning that the map method will map values when given a function, and the reduce method will reduce the array containing the values that match a function as well. These three methods (map, filter, and reduce) are the base of the functional programming of JavaScript, which we will explore in Chapter 11, *Patterns of Algorithms*.

ECMAScript 6 and new Array functionalities

As you learned in Chapter 1, *JavaScript—A Quick Overview*, the JavaScript language has new functionalities according to the **ECMAScript 6** (**ES6** or **ES2015**) and **ECMAScript 7** (**ES7** or **ES2016**) specifications.

The following is a list of the new methods added in ES6 and ES7:

Method	Description
@@iterator	This returns an iterator object that contains the key/value pairs of the array that can be synchronously called to retrieve key/value of the array elements.
copyWithin	This copies a sequence of values of the array into the position of a start index.
entries	This returns @@iterator, which contains key/value pairs.
includes	This returns true in case an element is found in the array, and false otherwise. This was added in ES 7.
find	This searches for an element in the array given a desired condition (callback function) and returns the element in case it is found.
findIndex	This searches for an element in the array given a desired condition (callback function) and returns the element index in case it is found.
fill	This fills the array with a static value.
from	This creates a new array from an existing one.
keys	This returns @@iterator, which contains the keys of the array.
of	This creates a new array from the arguments passed to the method.
values	This returns @@iterator, which contains the values of the array.

Along with these new methods, we also have a new way of iterating the array, which uses the new `for..of` loop and also the Iterator object that can be retrieved from the array instance.

We will demonstrate all these new functionalities in the following topics.

Iterating using forEach with arrow functions

We can use arrow functions to simplify the way we iterate all the elements of an array using the `forEach` method. Consider the following example:

```
numbers.forEach(function (x) {
  console.log(x % 2 == 0);
});
```

We can simplify the preceding code with the following one:

```
numbers.forEach(x => {
  console.log((x % 2 == 0));
});
```

Iterating using the for...of loop

You have learned that we can iterate an array using the `for` loop and the `forEach` method. ES6 also introduces the `for..of` loop, which iterates through the values of an array. We can take a look at an example of how to use the `for..of` loop here:

```
for (let n of numbers) {
  console.log((n % 2 == 0) ? 'even' : 'odd');
}
```

This example can be executed at `https://goo.gl/qHYAN1`.

Using the new ES6 iterator (@@iterator)

The `Array` class also has a property named `@@iterator` that was introduced in ES6. To use this, we need to access the `Symbol.iterator` property of the array as follows:

```
let iterator = numbers[Symbol.iterator]();
console.log(iterator.next().value); //1
console.log(iterator.next().value); //2
console.log(iterator.next().value); //3
console.log(iterator.next().value); //4
console.log(iterator.next().value); //5
```

Then, we can individually call the `next` method of the iterator to retrieve the next value of the array. For the numbers array, we need to call the `iterator.next().value` 15 times because we have 15 values in the array.

When the array is iterated and there are no more values to be iterated, the `iterator.next()` code will return `undefined`.

The preceding code has the same output as executing `numbers.value()`, which you will learn in the next topic.

 This example can be executed at `https://goo.gl/L81UQW`.

Array entries, keys, and values

ES6 also introduced three ways of retrieving iterators from an array. The first one you will learn is the `entries` method.

The `entries` method returns `@@iterator`, which contains key/value pairs. The following is an example of how we can use this method:

```
let aEntries = numbers.entries(); //retrieve iterator of key/value
console.log(aEntries.next().value); //[0, 1] - position 0, value 1
console.log(aEntries.next().value); //[1, 2] - position 1, value 2
console.log(aEntries.next().value); //[2, 3] - position 2, value 3
```

As the `number` array only contains numbers, `key` will be the position of the array, and `value` will be value stored in the array index.

To be able to retrieve key/value pairs is very useful when we are working with sets, dictionaries, and hash maps. This functionality will be very useful to us in the later chapters of this book.

The `keys` method returns `@@iterator`, which contains the keys of the array. The following is an example of how we can use this method:

```
let aKeys = numbers.keys(); //retrieve iterator of keys
console.log(aKeys.next()); // {value: 0, done: false }
console.log(aKeys.next()); // {value: 1, done: false }
console.log(aKeys.next()); // {value: 2, done: false }
```

For the `numbers` array, the `keys` will be the indexes of the array. Once there are no values to be iterated, the code `aKeys.next()` will return `undefined` as `value` and `done` as `true`. When `done` has the value `false`, it means that there are still more keys of the array to be iterated.

The `values` method returns `@@iterator`, which contains the values of the array. The following is an example of how we can use this method:

```
let aValues = numbers.values();
console.log(aValues.next()); // {value: 1, done: false }
console.log(aValues.next()); // {value: 2, done: false }
console.log(aValues.next()); // {value: 3, done: false }
```

 It is valid to remember that not all functionalities from ES6 work on the browsers yet. Because of this, the best way to test this code is using **Babel**. Examples can be executed at `https://goo.gl/eojEGk`.

Using the from method

The `Array.from` method creates a new array from an existing one. For example, if we want to copy the array numbers into a new one, we can use the following code:

```
let numbers2 = Array.from(numbers);
```

It is also possible to pass a function so that we can determine which values we want to filter. Consider the following code:

```
let evens = Array.from(numbers, x => (x % 2 == 0));
```

The preceding code created a new array named `evens` and only retrieves the even values from the numbers array.

This example can be executed at `https://goo.gl/n4rOY4`.

Using Array.of

The `Array.of` method creates a new array from the arguments passed to the method. For example, let's consider the following example:

```
let numbers3 = Array.of(1);
let numbers4 = Array.of(1,2,3,4,5,6);
```

The preceding code would be the same as performing the following:

```
let numbers3 = [1];
let numbers4 = [1,2,3,4,5,6];
```

We can also use this method to make a copy of an existing array. Here, we have an example:

```
let numbersCopy = Array.of(...numbers4);
```

The preceding code is the same as using `Array.from(numbers4)`. The difference here is that we are using the `spread` operator that you learned in Chapter 1, *JavaScript—A Quick Overview*. The spread operator (`...`) will spread each of the values of the `numbers4` array into arguments.

The examples can be executed at `https://goo.gl/FoJYNf`.

Using the fill method

The `fill` method fills the array with a value. For example, consider the following array:

```
let numbersCopy = Array.of(1,2,3,4,5,6);
```

The `numbersCopy` array has the length 6, meaning we have 6 positions. Let's use the following code:

```
numbersCopy.fill(0);
```

Here, the `numbersCopy` array will have all its positions with value (`[0,0,0,0,0,0]`).

We can also pass the start index that we want to fill the array with, as follows:

```
numbersCopy.fill(2, 1);
```

In the preceding example, all the positions of the array will have the value 2, starting from position 1 (`[0,2,2,2,2,2]`).

It is also possible to pass the end index that we want to fill the array with:

```
numbersCopy.fill(1, 3, 5);
```

In the preceding example, we will fill the array with value 1 from index 3 to 5 (not inclusive), resulting in the following array: `[0,2,2,1,1,2]`.

The `fill` method is great when we want to create an array and initialize its values, as demonstrated here:

```
let ones = Array(6).fill(1);
```

The preceding code will create an array of length 6 and all its values as 1 (`[1,1,1,1,1,1]`).

 The preceding examples can be executed at `https://goo.gl/sqiHSK`.

Using the copyWithin method

The `copyWithin` method copies a sequence of values of the array into the position of a start index. For example, let's consider the following array for our examples:

```
let copyArray = [1, 2, 3, 4, 5, 6];
```

Now, let's say we want to copy the values 4,5, and 6 to the first three positions of the array, resulting in the `[4,5,6,4,5,6]` array. We can use the following code to achieve this result:

```
copyArray.copyWithin(0, 3);
```

Now, consider that we want to copy the values 4 and 5 (the positions 3 and 4) to the positions 1 and 2. We can use the following code to do this:

```
copyArray = [1, 2, 3, 4, 5, 6];
copyArray.copyWithin(1, 3, 5);
```

In this case, we will copy the elements starting in position 3 and ending in position 5 (not inclusive) to the position 1 of the array, resulting in the [1,4,5,4,5,6] array.

 This example can be executed at https://goo.gl/hZhBE1.

Sorting elements

Throughout this book, you will learn how to write the most-used searching and sorting algorithms. However, JavaScript also has a sorting method and a couple of searching methods available. Let's take a look at them.

First, let's take our `numbers` array and put the elements out of order (1, 2, 3, ... 15 are already sorted). To do this, we can apply the `reverse` method, in which the last item will be the first and vice versa, as follows:

```
numbers.reverse();
```

So now, the output for the `numbers` array will be [15, 14, 13, 12, 11, 10, 9, 8, 7, 6, 5, 4, 3, 2, 1]. Then, we can apply the `sort` method as follows:

```
numbers.sort();
```

However, if we output the array, the result will be [1, 10, 11, 12, 13, 14, 15, 2, 3, 4, 5, 6, 7, 8, 9]. This is not ordered correctly. This is because the `sort` method sorts the elements lexicographically, and it assumes all the elements are strings.

We can also write our own comparison function. As our array has numeric elements, we can write the following code:

```
numbers.sort(function(a,b){
   return a-b;
});
```

This code will return a negative number if b is bigger than a, a positive number if a is bigger than b, and (Zero) if they are equal. This means that if a negative value is returned, it implies that a is smaller than b, which is further used by the sort function to arrange the elements.

The previous code can be represented by the following code as well:

```
function compare(a, b) {
  if (a < b) {
    return -1;
  }
  if (a > b) {
    return 1;
  }
  // a must be equal to b
  return 0;
}

numbers.sort(compare);
```

This is because the sort function from the JavaScript Array class can receive a parameter called compareFunction, which is responsible for sorting the array. In our example, we declared a function that will be responsible for comparing the elements of the array, resulting in an array sorted in ascending order.

Custom sorting

We can sort an array with any type of object in it, and we can also create compareFunction to compare the elements as we need to. For example, suppose we have an object, Person, with name and age, and we want to sort the array based on the age of the person. We can use the following code:

```
var friends = [
  {name: 'John', age: 30},
  {name: 'Ana', age: 20},
  {name: 'Chris', age: 25}
];

function comparePerson(a, b){
  if (a.age < b.age){
  return -1
  }
  if (a.age > b.age){
  return 1
  }
}
```

```
    return 0;
  }

  console.log(friends.sort(comparePerson));
```

In this case, the output from the previous code will be Ana (20), Chris (25), and John (30).

Sorting strings

Suppose we have the following array:

```
var names =['Ana', 'ana', 'john', 'John'];
console.log(names.sort());
```

What do you think would be the output? The answer is as follows:

["Ana", "John", "ana", "john"]

Why does ana come after John when "a" comes first in the alphabet? The answer is because JavaScript compares each character according to its ASCII value. For example, A, J, a, and j have the decimal ASCII values of **A: 65**, **J: 74**, **a: 97**, and **j: 106**.

Therefore, J has a lower value than a, and because of this, it comes first in the alphabet.

For more information about the ASCII table, visit http://www.asciitab le.com/.

Now, if we pass compareFunction, which contains the code to ignore the case of the letter, we will have the output ["Ana", "ana", "John", "john"], as follows:

```
names.sort(function(a, b){
  if (a.toLowerCase() < b.toLowerCase()){
    return -1
  }
  if (a.toLowerCase() > b.toLowerCase()){
    return 1
  }
  return 0;
});
```

For accented characters, we can use the `localeCompare` method as well:

```
var names2 = ['Maève', 'Maeve'];
console.log(names2.sort(function(a, b){
  return a.localeCompare(b);
}));
```

The output will be `["Maeve", "Maève"]`.

Searching

We have two options to search: the `indexOf` method, which returns the index of the first element that matches the argument passed, and `lastIndexOf`, which returns the index of the last element found that matches the argument passed. Let's go back to the `numbers` array that we were using before:

```
console.log(numbers.indexOf(10));
console.log(numbers.indexOf(100));
```

In the previous example, the output in the console would be 9 for the first line and −1 (because it does not exist in our array) for the second line.

We can get the same result with the following code:

```
numbers.push(10);
console.log(numbers.lastIndexOf(10));
console.log(numbers.lastIndexOf(100));
```

We added a new element with the value 10, so the second line will output 15 (our array now has values from 1 to 15 + 10), and the third line will output −1 (because the element 100 does not exist in our array).

ECMAScript 6 – the find and findIndex methods

Consider the followingexample:

```
let numbers = [1,2,3,4,5,6,7,8,9,10,11,12,13,14,15];
function multipleOf13(element, index, array) {
  return (element % 13 == 0) ? true : false;
}
console.log(numbers.find(multipleOf13));
console.log(numbers.findIndex(multipleOf13));
```

The `find` and `findIndex` methods receive a callback function that will search for a value that satisfies the condition presented in the testing function (callback). For this example, we are looking whether the array numbers contain any multiple of 13.

The difference between `find` and `findIndex` is that the `find` method returns the first value of the array that satisfies the proposed condition. The `findIndex` method, on the other hand, returns the index of the first value of the array that satisfies the condition. In case the value is not found, it returns `undefined`.

This example can be executed at `https://goo.gl/2vAaCh`.

ECMAScript 7 – using the includes method

The `includes` method returns `true` in case an element is found in the array, and `false` otherwise. The following is an example of how to use this method:

```
console.log(numbers.includes(15));
console.log(numbers.includes(20));
```

In this example the `includes(15)` will return `true` and `includes(20)` will return `false` because the element `20` does not exist in the `numbers` array.

It is also possible to pass a starting index where we want the array to start searching for the value:

```
let numbers2 = [7,6,5,4,3,2,1];
console.log(numbers2.includes(4,5));
```

The output from the example above will be `false` because the element `4` does not exist after position `5`.

This example can be executed at `https://goo.gl/tTY9bc`.

Outputting the array into a string

Finally, we come to the final two methods: `toString` and `join`.

If we want to output all the elements of the array into a single string, we can use the `toString` method as follows:

```
console.log(numbers.toString());
```

This will output the values 1, 2, 3, 4, 5, 6, 7, 8, 9, 10, 11, 12, 13, 14, 15, and 10 to the console.

If we want to separate the elements by a different separator, such as –, we can use the `join` method to do just this, as follows:

```
var numbersString = numbers.join('-');
console.log(numbersString);
```

The output will be as follows:

```
1-2-3-4-5-6-7-8-9-10-11-12-13-14-15-10
```

This can be useful if we need to send the array's content to a server or to be decoded (and then, knowing the separator, it is easy to decode).

> There are some great resources that you can use to boost your knowledge about arrays and their methods.
> The first one is the arrays page from w3schools at `http://www.w3school s.com/js/js_arrays.asp`.
> The second one is the array methods page from w3schools at `http://www .w3schools.com/js/js_array_methods.asp`.
> Mozilla also has a great page about arrays and their methods with great examples at `https://developer.mozilla.org/en-US/docs/Web/Jav aScript/Reference/Global_Objects/Array` (`http://goo.gl/vu1d iT`).
> There are also great libraries that are very useful when working with arrays in JavaScript projects, which are as follows:
> **The Underscore library**: `http://underscorejs.org/`
> **The Lo-Dash library**: `http://lodash.com/`

The TypedArray class

We can store any data type in JavaScript arrays. This is because JavaScript arrays are not strongly typed as in other languages such as C and Java.

`TypeArray` was created so that we could work with arrays with a single datatype. Its syntax is `let myArray = new TypedArray(length)`, where `TypedArray` needs to be replaced with one `TypedArray` class, as specified in the following table:

TypedArray	Description
Int8Array	8-bit twos complement signed integer
Uint8Array	8-bit unsigned integer
Uint8ClampedArray	8-bit unsigned integer
Int16Array	16-bit twos complement signed integer
Uint16Array	16-bit unsigned integer
Int32Array	32-bit twos complement signed integer
Uint32Array	32-bit unsigned integer
Float32Array	32-bit IEEE floating point number
Float64Array	64-bit IEEE floating point number

The following is an example:

```
let length = 5;
let int16 = new Int16Array(length);

let array16 = [];
array16.length = length;

for (let i=0; i<length; i++){
  int16[i] = i+1;
}
console.log(int16);
```

Typed arrays are great to work with WebGL APIs, manipulate bits, and manipulate files and images. Typed arrays work exactly like simple arrays, and we can also use the same methods and functionalities that you learned in this chapter.

At the following link, you can find a good tutorial on how to use typed arrays to manipulate binary data and its applications in real-world projects:

`http://goo.gl/kZBsGx.`

Summary

In this chapter, we covered the most-used data structure: arrays. You learned how to declare, initialize, and assign values as well as add and remove elements. You also learned about two-dimensional and multidimensional arrays as well as the main methods of an array, which will be very useful when we start creating our own algorithms in later chapters.

You also learned the new methods and functionalities that were added to the `Array` class in the ECMAScript 2015 and 2016 specifications.

In the next chapter, you will learn about stacks, which are arrays with a special behavior.

3
Stacks

You learned in the previous chapter how to create and use arrays, which are the most common type of data structure in Computer Science. As you learned, we can add and remove elements from an array at any index desired. However, sometimes we need some form of data structure where we have more control over adding and removing items. There are two data structures that have some similarities to arrays, but which give us more control over the addition and removal of elements. These data structures are stacks and queues.

In this chapter, we will cover the following topics:

- The stack data structure
- Adding elements to a stack
- Popping elements from a stack
- How to use the Stack class
- The decimal to binary problem

The stack data structure

A stack is an ordered collection of items that follows the **LIFO (Last In First Out)** principle. The addition of new items or the removal of existing items takes place at the same end. The end of the stack is known as the top, and the opposite side is known as the base. The newest elements are near the top, and the oldest elements are near the base.

We have several examples of stacks in real life, for example, a pile of books, as we can see in the following image, or a stack of trays in a cafeteria or food court:

A stack is also used by compilers in programming languages, and by computer memory to store variables and method calls.

Creating a stack

We are going to create our own class to represent a stack. Let's start from the basics, and declare our class:

```
function Stack() {
  //properties and methods go here
}
```

First, we need a data structure that will store the elements of the stack. We can use an array to do this:

```
let items = [];
```

Next, we need to declare the methods available for our stack:

- push(element(s)): This adds a new item (or several items) to the top of the stack.
- pop(): This removes the top item from the stack. It also returns the removed element.

- peek(): This returns the top element from the stack. The stack is not modified (it does not remove the element; it only returns the element for information purposes).
- isEmpty(): This returns true if the stack does not contain any elements, and false if the size of the stack is bigger than 0.
- clear(): This removes all the elements of the stack.
- size(): This returns the number of elements that the stack contains. It is similar to the length property of an array.

Pushing elements to the stack

The first method that we will implement is the push method. This method is responsible for adding new elements to the stack with one very important detail: we can only add new items to the top of the stack, meaning at the end of the stack. The push method is represented as follows:

```
this.push = function(element){
  items.push(element);
};
```

As we are using an array to store the elements of the stack, we can use the push method from the JavaScript array class that we covered in the previous chapter.

Popping elements from the stack

Next, we are going to implement the pop method. This method is responsible for removing the items from the stack. As the stack uses the LIFO principle, the last item that we added is the one that is removed. For this reason, we can use the pop method from the JavaScript array class that we also covered in the previous chapter. The pop method is represented as follows:

```
this.pop = function(){
  return items.pop();
};
```

With the push and pop methods being the only methods available for adding and removing items from the stack, the LIFO principle will apply to our own Stack class.

Peeking the element from the top of the stack

Now, let's implement some additional `helper` methods for our class. If we would like to know what the last item added to our stack was, we can use the `peek` method. This method will return the item from the top of the stack:

```
this.peek = function(){
    return items[items.length-1];
};
```

As we are using an array to store the items internally, we can obtain the last item from an array using `length - 1` as follows:

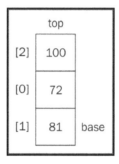

For example, in the previous diagram, we have a stack with three items; therefore, the length of the internal array is 3. The last position used in the internal array is 2. As a result, the `length - 1` (3 − 1) is 2!

Verifying if the stack is empty

The next method is the `isEmpty` method, which returns `true` if the stack is empty (no item has been added), and `false` otherwise:

```
this.isEmpty = function(){
    return items.length == 0;
};
```

Using the `isEmpty` method, we can simply verify whether the length of the internal array is 0.

Similar to the `length` property from the `array` class, we can also implement `length` for our `Stack` class. For collections, we usually use the term `size` instead of `length`. And again, as we are using an array to store the items internally, we can simply return its `length`:

```
this.size = function(){
   return items.length;
};
```

Clearing and printing the elements of the stack

Finally, we are going to implement the `clear` method. The `clear` method simply empties the stack, removing all its elements. The simplest way of implementing this method is as follows:

```
this.clear = function(){
   items = [];
};
```

An alternative implementation would be calling the `pop` method until the stack is empty.

And we are done! Our `Stack` class is implemented. Just to make our lives easier while studying the examples, to help us inspect the contents of our stack, let's implement a `helper` method called `print` that is going to output the content of the stack on the console:

```
this.print = function(){
   console.log(items.toString());
};
```

And now we are really done!

Using the Stack class

Before we dive into some examples, we need to learn how to use the `Stack` class.

The first thing we need to do is instantiate the `Stack` class we just created. Next, we can verify whether it is empty (the output is `true`, because we have not added any elements to our stack yet):

```
let stack = new Stack();
console.log(stack.isEmpty()); //outputs true
```

Next, let's add some elements to it (let's push the numbers 5 and 8; you can add any element type to the stack):

```
stack.push(5);
stack.push(8);
```

If we call the `peek` method, the output will be the number 8, because it was the last element that was added to the stack:

```
console.log(stack.peek()); // outputs 8
```

Let's also add another element:

```
stack.push(11);
console.log(stack.size()); // outputs 3
console.log(stack.isEmpty()); //outputs false
```

We added the element 11. If we call the `size` method, it will give the output as 3, because we have three elements in our stack (5, 8, and 11). Also, if we call the `isEmpty` method, the output will be `false` (we have three elements in our stack). Finally, let's add another element:

```
stack.push(15);
```

The following diagram shows all the `push` operations we have executed so far, and the current status of our stack:

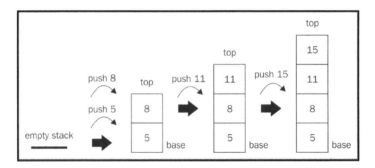

Next, let's remove two elements from the stack by calling the `pop` method twice:

```
stack.pop();
stack.pop();
console.log(stack.size()); // outputs 2
stack.print(); // outputs [5, 8]
```

Before we called the pop method twice, our stack had four elements in it. After the execution of the pop method two times, the stack now has only two elements: 5 and 8. The following diagram exemplifies the execution of the pop method:

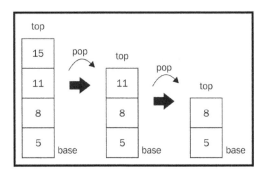

EcmaScript 6 and the Stack class

Let's take a moment to analyze our code and see if we can improve it using some of the new **EcmaScript 6** (**ES6**) functionalities.

We created a Stack function that can be used as a sort of class; since JavaScript functions have constructors, we can simulate the class behavior. We declared a variable named items that is private and only accessible to the Stack function/class. However, this approach creates a copy of the variable items for each class instance created. Therefore, it does not escalate well in case we need to use several instances of the Stack class at the same time.

Let's see how we can declare the same Stack class using the new ES6 syntax and compare its pros and cons against the approach we used in this chapter.

Declaring the Stack class using ES6 syntax

The first code we will analyze is the following:

```
class Stack {
  constructor () {    this.items = []; //{1}  }
  push(element){
    this.items.push(element);
  }
  //other methods
}
```

We simply transformed the `Stack` function into a `Stack` class using the ES6 simplified syntax. Using this approach, we cannot declare variables in the body of the class as other languages (Java, C++, C#), so we need to declare them inside the class `constructor` (line {1}), and we can make a reference to the variable using `this.nameofVariable` in other functions of the class.

Although the code looks cleaner and it is more beautiful, the variable `items` are `public`. The ES6 classes are prototype based. Although a prototype-based class saves memory and escalates better than function-based classes, this approach does not allow us to declare `private` properties (variables) or methods. And, in this case, we want the user of the `Stack` class to have access only to the methods we are exposing in the class. Otherwise, it is possible to remove elements from the middle of the stack (since we are using an array to store its values), and we do not want to allow this action.

Let's take a look at other approaches that can allow us to have private properties using ES6 syntax.

ES6 classes with scoped Symbols

ES6 introduced a new primitive type called `Symbol` that is immutable, and it can be used as an object property. Let's see how we can use it to declare the `items` property in the `Stack` class:

```
let _items = Symbol(); //{1}

class Stack {
  constructor () {
    this[_items] = []; //{2}
  }
  //Stack methods
}
```

In the preceding code, we declare the variable _items as a `Symbol` (line {1}), and initiate its value inside the class `constructor` (line {2}). To access the variable _items, we simply need to replace all `this.items` occurrences with `this[_items]`.

This approach provides a false class private property, because the method `Object.getOwnPropertySymbols` was also introduced in ES6, and it can be used to retrieve all the property `Symbols` declared in the class. An example of how we can explore and hack the `Stack` class is given as follows:

```
let stack = new Stack();
stack.push(5);
```

```
stack.push(8);
let objectSymbols = Object.getOwnPropertySymbols(stack);
console.log(objectSymbols.length); // 1
console.log(objectSymbols); // [Symbol()]
console.log(objectSymbols[0]); // Symbol()
stack[objectSymbols[0]].push(1);
stack.print(); //outputs 5, 8, 1
```

As we can see from the preceding code, it is possible to retrieve the _items Symbol by accessing stack[objectSymbols[0]]. And, as the _items property is an array, we can do any array operation such as removing or adding an element to the middle of the array. But this is not what we want as we are working with a stack.

So let's see a third option.

ES6 classes with WeakMap

There is one data type we can use to ensure that the property will be private in a class, and it is called WeakMap. We will explore the *Map data structure* in detail in Chapter 7, *Dictionaries and Hashes*, but for now, we need to know that a WeakMap can store a key/value pair, where the key is an object and the value can be any data type.

Let's see what the Stack class would look like if we use WeakMap to store the items variable:

```
const items = new WeakMap(); //{1}

class Stack {
  constructor () {
    items.set(this, []); //{2}
  }
  push(element){
    let s = items.get(this); //{3}
    s.push(element);
  }
  pop(){
    let s = items.get(this);
    let r = s.pop();
    return r;
  }
  //other methods
}
```

- In line {1}, we declare the items variable as a WeakMap

- In line {2}, we set the `items` value inside the constructor by setting this (reference to the `Stack` class) as the key of the `WeakMap` and the array that represents the stack as its value
- In line {3}, we retrieve the value of the `items` by retrieving the value from the `WeakMap`, that is, by passing this as the key (that we set in line {2})

Now we know that the `items` property is truly private in the `Stack` class. But there is one more step we need to do. Right now, the `items` variable is still declared outside the `Stack` class, so anyone can change it. We will wrap the `Stack` class with a `closure` (an outer function), so the `WeakMap` has scope only inside the function:

```
let Stack = (function () {
  const items = new WeakMap();
  class Stack {
    constructor () {
      items.set(this, []);
    }
    //other methods
  }
  return Stack; //{5}
})();
```

When the constructor of the `Stack` function is called, it will return an instance of the `Stack` class (line {5}).

 To learn more about JavaScript closures please read `http://www.w3scho ols.com/js/js_function_closures.asp`

Now the `Stack` class has a private property named `items`. It is still an ugly solution, but it works regarding the privacy of the properties. However, with this approach, it is not possible to inherit the private properties if we extend this class; we cannot have it all!

If we compare the preceding code with the code that we initially used in this chapter to declare the `Stack` class, we will notice some similarities:

```
function Stack() {
  let items = [];
  //other methods
}
```

The truth is that although, ES 6 introduced the class syntax, we still cannot declare private properties or methods as it is possible in other programming languages. There are different approaches with which we can achieve the same result, but each one has its pros and cons regarding a simpler syntax or performance.

Which approach is better? It depends on how you use the algorithms presented in this book in real-life projects. It depends on the volume of data you will be dealing with, on the number of instances that you need of the classes we create, among other constraints. Ultimately, the decision is yours.

 For every data structure class we create in this book, you will find the simple function class and also the ES6 `WeakMap` with closure approach when downloading the source code of this book.

Solving problems using stacks

Stacks have a variety of applications in real-world problems. They can be used for backtracking problems to remember tasks or paths visited, and to undo actions (we will learn how to apply this example when we discuss graphs and backtracking problems later on this book). The Java and C# programming languages use stacks to store variables and method calls and there is a stack overflow exception that can be thrown specially when working with recursive algorithms (which we will cover later on this book as well).

Now that we know how to use the `Stack` class, let's use it to solve some Computer Science problems. In this section, we will learn the three most famous algorithm examples of using a stack. We will cover the decimal to binary problem, where we will also transform the algorithm to a base converter algorithm, the balanced parenthesis problem, and, finally, we will learn how to solve the tower of Hanoi problem using stacks.

Decimal to binary

You are probably already aware of the decimal base. However, binary representation is very important in Computer Science, as everything in a computer is represented by binary digits (0 and 1). Without the ability to convert back and forth between decimal and binary numbers, it would be a little bit difficult to communicate with a computer.

To convert a decimal number to a binary representation, we can divide the number by 2 (binary is a base 2 number system) until the division result is 0. As an example, we will convert the number 10 into binary digits:

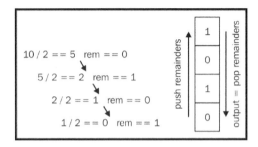

This conversion is one of the first things you learn in college (Computer Science classes). The following is our algorithm:

```
function divideBy2(decNumber){

    var remStack = new Stack(),
    rem,
    binaryString = '';

    while (decNumber > 0){ //{1}
        rem = Math.floor(decNumber % 2); //{2}
        remStack.push(rem); //{3}
        decNumber = Math.floor(decNumber / 2); //{4}
    }

    while (!remStack.isEmpty()){ //{5}
        binaryString += remStack.pop().toString();
    }

    return binaryString;
}
```

In this preceding code, while the division result is not zero (line {1}), we get the remainder of the division (mod), and push it to the stack (lines {2} and {3}), and finally, we update the number that will be divided by 2 (line {4}). An important observation: JavaScript has a numeric data type, but it does not distinguish integers from floating points. For this reason, we need to use the Math.floor function to obtain only the integer value from the division operations. Finally, we pop the elements from the stack until it is empty, concatenating the elements that were removed from the stack into a string (line {5}).

We can try the previous algorithm, and output its result on the console using the following code:

```
console.log(divideBy2(233));
console.log(divideBy2(10));
console.log(divideBy2(1000));
```

The base converter algorithm

We can easily modify the previous algorithm to make it work as a converter from decimal to any base. Instead of dividing the decimal number by 2, we can pass the desired base as an argument to the method and use it in the divisions, as shown in the following algorithm:

```
function baseConverter(decNumber, base){

  var remStack = new Stack(),
  rem,
  baseString = '',
  digits = '0123456789ABCDEF'; //{6}

  while (decNumber > 0){
    rem = Math.floor(decNumber % base);
    remStack.push(rem);
    decNumber = Math.floor(decNumber / base);
  }

  while (!remStack.isEmpty()){
    baseString += digits[remStack.pop()]; //{7}
  }

  return baseString;
}
```

There is one more thing we need to change. In the conversion from decimal to binary, the remainders will be 0 or 1; in the conversion from decimal to octagonal, the remainders will be from 0 to 8, but in the conversion from decimal to hexadecimal, the remainders can be 0 to 8 plus the letters A to F (values 10 to 15). For this reason, we need to convert these values as well (lines {6} and {7}).

We can use the previous algorithm, and output its result on the console as follows:

```
console.log(baseConverter(100345, 2));
console.log(baseConverter(100345, 8));
console.log(baseConverter(100345, 16));
```

You will also find the balanced parentheses and the **Hanoi Tower** examples when you download the source code of this book.

Summary

In this chapter, you learned about the stack data structure. We implemented our own algorithm that represents a stack, and you learned how to add and remove elements from it using the `push` and `pop` methods.

We compared different syntaxes that can be used to create the Stack class, and presented the pros and cons of each one. We also covered how to solve one of the most famous problems in Computer Science using stacks.

In the next chapter, you will learn about queues, which are very similar to stacks, but use a principle different than LIFO.

4

Queues

You have already learned how stacks work. Queues are very similar, but instead of LIFO, they use a different principle that you will learn about in this chapter.

The queue data structure

A **queue** is an ordered collection of items that follows the **FIFO (First In First Out)**, also known as the *first-come first-served* principle. The addition of new elements in a queue is at the tail, and the removal is from the front. The newest element added to the queue must wait at the end of the queue.

The most popular example of a queue in real life is the typical line that we form from time to time:

We have lines for movies, the cafeteria, and a checkout line at a grocery store among other examples. The first person that is in the line is the first one that will be attended to.

A very popular example in Computer Science is the printing line. Let's say we need to print five documents. We open each document and click on the print button. Each document will be sent to the print line. The first document that we asked to be printed is going to be printed first and so on, until all the documents are printed.

Creating a queue

We are now going to create our own class to represent a queue. Let's start from the basics and declare our class:

```
function Queue() {
  //properties and methods go here
}
```

First, we need a data structure that will store the elements of the queue. We can use an array to do it, just like we used it for the `Stack` class in the previous chapter (you will notice the `Queue` and `Stack` class are very similar, just the principles for adding and removing the elements are different):

```
let items = [];
```

Next, we need to declare the methods available for a queue:

- `enqueue(element(s))`: This adds a new item (or several items) at the back of the queue.
- `dequeue()`: This removes the first item from the queue (the item that is in the front of the queue). It also returns the removed element.
- `front()`: This returns the first element from the queue, the first one added, and the first one that will be removed from the queue. The queue is not modified (it does not remove the element; it only returns the element for information purposes-very similar to the `peek` method from the `Stack` class).
- `isEmpty()`: This returns `true` if the queue does not contain any elements, and `false` if the queue is bigger than 0.
- `size()`: This returns the number of elements the queue contains. It is similar to the `length` property of the array.

Enqueue elements to the queue

The first method that we will implement is the `enqueue` method. This method will be responsible for adding new elements to the queue with one very important detail-we can only add new items to the end of the queue:

```
this.enqueue = function(element){
    items.push(element);
};
```

As we are using an array to store the elements for the stack, we can use the `push` method from the JavaScript `array` class that we covered in `Chapter 2`, *Arrays*, and also in `Chapter 3`, *Stacks*.

Dequeue elements from the queue

Next, we are going to implement the `dequeue` method. This method is responsible for removing the items from the queue. As the queue uses the FIFO principle, the first item that we added is the one that is removed. For this reason, we can use the `shift` method from the JavaScript `array` class that we also covered in `Chapter 2`, *Arrays*. If you remember, the `shift` method removes the element that is stored at the index 0 (first position) of the array:

```
this.dequeue = function(){
    return items.shift();
};
```

With the `enqueue` and `dequeue` methods being the only methods available for adding and removing items from the queue, we assured the FIFO principle for our own `Queue` class.

Peeking the element from the front of the queue

Now, let's implement some additional `helper` methods for our class. If we want to know what the front item of our queue is, we can use the `front` method. This method will return the item from the front of the queue (index 0 of the array):

```
this.front = function(){
    return items[0];
};
```

Verifying if the queue is empty

The next method is the `isEmpty` method, which returns `true` if the queue is empty, and `false` otherwise (note that this method is the same as the one in the `Stack` class):

```
this.isEmpty = function(){
    return items.length == 0;
};
```

For the `isEmpty` method, we can simply verify that the length of the internal array is 0.

Like the `length` property of the `array` class, we can also implement the same for our `Queue` class. The `size` method is also the same for the `Stack` class:

```
this.size = function(){
    return items.length;
};
```

Printing the elements of the queue

And we are done! Our `Queue` class is implemented. Just like we did for the `Stack` class, we can also add the `print` method:

```
this.print = function(){
    console.log(items.toString());
};
```

And now we are really done!

 The `Queue` and `Stack` class are very similar. The only difference is the `dequeue` and `front` methods, which is because of the difference between the FIFO and LIFO principles.

Using the Queue class

The first thing we need to do is instantiate the `Queue` class that we just created. Next, we can verify that it is empty (the output is `true`, because we have not added any elements to our queue yet):

```
let queue = new Queue();
console.log(queue.isEmpty()); //outputs true
```

Next, let's add some elements to it (let's `enqueue` the elements `"John"` and `"Jack"`—you can add any element type to the queue):

```
queue.enqueue("John");
queue.enqueue("Jack");
```

Let's add another element:

```
queue.enqueue("Camila");
```

Let's also execute some other commands:

```
queue.print();
console.log(queue.size()); //outputs 3
console.log(queue.isEmpty()); //outputs false
queue.dequeue();
queue.dequeue();
queue.print();
```

If we ask to print the contents of the queue, we will get John, Jack, and Camila. The size of the queue will be 3, because we have three elements queued in it (and it is also not going to be empty).

The following diagram exemplifies all the `enqueue` operations we executed so far, and the current status of our queue:

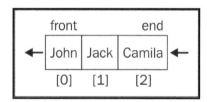

Next, we asked to `dequeue` two elements (the `dequeue` method is executed twice). The following diagram exemplifies the `dequeue` method execution:

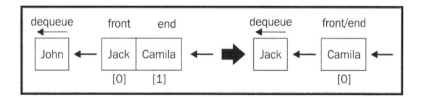

And when we finally ask to print the content of the queue again, we only have the element `Camila`. The first two queued elements were dequeued; the final element queued to the data structure is the last one that will be dequeued from it. That is, we follow the FIFO principle.

The Queue class using ECMAScript 6 syntax

As we learned in Chapter 3, *Stacks*, we can also write the same `Queue` class using the ECMAScript 6 syntax. In this approach, we will use a `WeakMap` to keep the property `items` private, and we will also use an outer function (`closure`) to encapsulate the `Queue` class.

The code is presented as follows:

```
let Queue2 = (function () {

  const items = new WeakMap();

  class Queue2 {
    constructor () {
      items.set(this, []);
    }
    enqueue(element) {
      let q = items.get(this);
      q.push(element);
    }
    dequeue() {
      let q = items.get(this);
      let r = q.shift();
      return r;
    }
    //other methods
  }
  return Queue2;
})();
```

You can use either of the `Queue` class that we created; the output of our tests will be the same.

The priority queue

As queues are largely applied in Computer Science and also in our lives, there are some modified versions of the default queue that we implemented in the previous topic.

One modified version is the priority queue. Elements are added and removed based on a priority. An example from real life is the boarding line at the airport. The first class and business class passengers get priority over the coach class passengers. In some countries, elderly people and pregnant women (or women with newborn children) also get priority over other passengers for boarding

Another example from real life is the waiting room for patients in a hospital (emergency department). Patients that are in a severe condition are seen by a doctor prior to patients in a less severe condition. Usually, a nurse will do the triage and assign a code to the patient depending on the severity of the condition.

There are two options when implementing a priority queue: you can set the priority and add the element at the correct position, or you can queue the elements as they are added to the queue, and remove them according to priority. For this example, we will add the elements at their correct position, so we can `dequeue` them by default:

```
function PriorityQueue() {
  let items = [];
  function QueueElement (element, priority){ // {1}
    this.element = element;
    this.priority = priority;
  }

  this.enqueue = function(element, priority){
    let queueElement = new QueueElement(element, priority);

    let added = false;
    for (let i=0; i<items.length; i++){
      if (queueElement.priority < items[i].priority){ // {2}
        items.splice(i,0,queueElement);                // {3}
        added = true;
        break; // {4}
      }
    }
    if (!added){
      items.push(queueElement); //{5}
    }
  };

  this.print = function(){
    for (let i=0; i<items.length; i++){
```

```
        console.log(`${items[i].element}  -
        ${items[i].priority}`);
      }
   };
   //other methods - same as default Queue implementation
 }
```

The difference between the implementation of the default Queue and PriorityQueue classes is that we need to create a special element (line {1}) to be added to PriorityQueue. This element contains the element that we want to add to the queue (it can be any type), plus the priority on the queue.

First we need to compare its priority to the rest of the elements (line {2}). When we find an item that has a higher priority than the element we are trying to add, then we insert the new element one position before (with this logic, we also respect the other elements with the same priority, but which were added to the queue first). To do this, we can use the splice method from the JavaScript array class that you learned about in Chapter 2, *Arrays*. Once we find an element with a higher priority, we insert the new element (line{3}), and we stop looping the queue (line {4}). This way, our queue will also be sorted and organized by priority.

Also, if the priority we are adding is greater than any priority already added, or if the queue is empty, we simply add to the end of the queue (line {5}):

```
let priorityQueue = new PriorityQueue();
priorityQueue.enqueue("John", 2);
priorityQueue.enqueue("Jack", 1);
priorityQueue.enqueue("Camila", 1);
priorityQueue.print();
```

In the previous code, we can see an example of how to use the PriorityQueue class. We can see each command result in the following diagram (a result of the previous code):

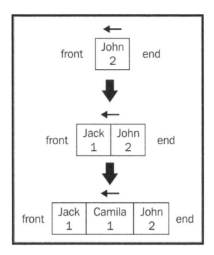

The first element that was added was `John` with priority 2. Because the queue was empty, this is the only element in it. Then, we added `Jack` with priority 1. As `Jack` has higher priority than `John`, it is the first element in the queue. Then, we added `Camila`, also with priority 1. As `Camila` has the same priority as `Jack`, it will be inserted after `Jack` (as it was inserted first); and as `Camila` has a higher priority than `John`, it will be inserted before this element.

The priority queue we implemented is called a min priority queue, because we are adding the element with the lower value (1 has higher priority) to the front of the queue. There is also the max priority queue, which, instead of adding the element with the lower value to front of the queue, adds the element with the greater value to the front of the queue.

The circular queue – Hot Potato

We also have another modified version of the queue implementation, which is the circular queue. An example of a circular queue is the *Hot Potato* game. In this game, children are organized in a circle, and they pass the hot potato to their neighbor as fast as they can. At a certain point of the game, the hot potato stops being passed around the circle of children, and the child that has the hot potato is removed from the circle. This action is repeated until there is only one child left (the winner).

For this example, we will implement a simulation of the Hot Potato game:

```
function hotPotato (nameList, num){

  let queue = new Queue(); // {1}

  for (let i=0; i<nameList.length; i++){
    queue.enqueue(nameList[i]); // {2}
  }

  let eliminated = '';
  while (queue.size() > 1){
    for (let i=0; i<num; i++){
      queue.enqueue(queue.dequeue()); // {3}
    }
    eliminated = queue.dequeue();// {4}
    console.log(eliminated + ' was eliminated from the Hot Potato  game.');
  }

  return queue.dequeue();// {5}
}

let names = ['John','Jack','Camila','Ingrid','Carl'];let winner =
hotPotato(names, 7);console.log('The winner is: ' + winner);
```

To implement a simulation of this game, we will use the Queue class we implemented at the beginning of this chapter (line {1}). We will get a list of names, and queue all of them (line {2}). Given a number, we need to iterate the queue. We will remove an item from the beginning of the queue, and add it to the end of (line {3}) to simulate the hot potato (if you passed the hot potato to your neighbor, you are not threatened to be eliminated right away). Once we reach the number, the person that has the hot potato is eliminated (removed from the queue-line {4}). When there is only one person left, this person is declared the winner (line {5}).

The output from the previous algorithm is:

```
Camila was eliminated from the Hot Potato game.
Jack was eliminated from the Hot Potato game.
Carl was eliminated from the Hot Potato game.
Ingrid was eliminated from the Hot Potato game.
The winner is: John
```

This output is simulated in the following diagram:

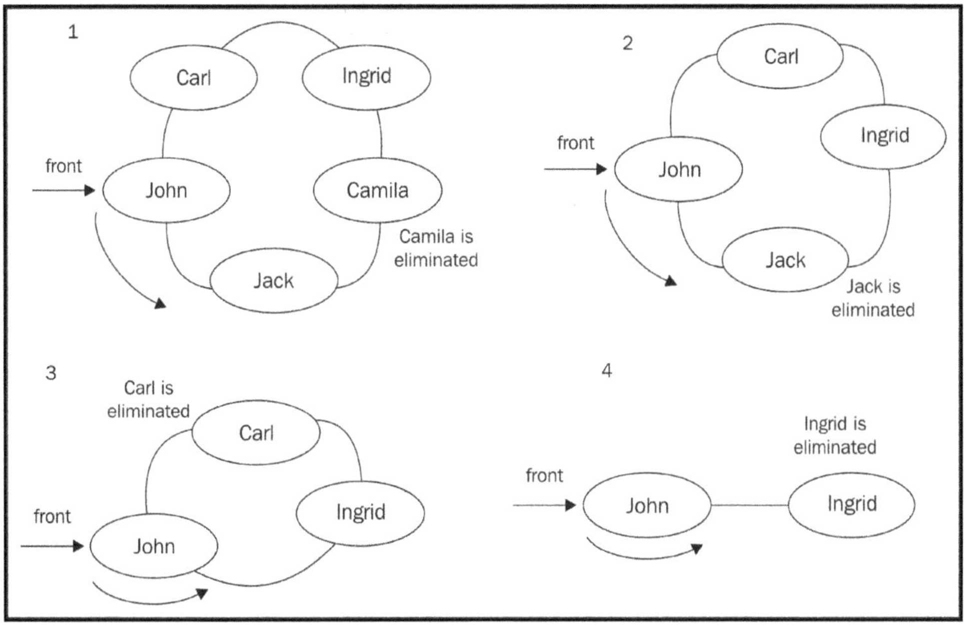

You can change the number passed to the `hotPotato` function to simulate different scenarios.

JavaScript task queues

Since we are using JavaScript in this book, why not explore a little bit more how the language works?

When we open a new tab in the browser, a task queue is created. This is because only a single thread handles all the tasks for a single tab, and it is called an **event loop**. The browser is responsible for several tasks, such as rendering the HTML, executing JavaScript code commands, handling user interaction (user input, mouse clicks, and so on), executing and processing asynchronous requests. You can learn more about the event loop at the following link: `https://goo.gl/ayF840`.

It is really nice to know that a popular and powerful language such as JavaScript uses such a basic data structure to handle internal control.

Summary

In this chapter, you learned about the `queue` data structure. We implemented our own algorithm that represents a queue; you learned how to add and remove elements from it using the `enqueue` and `dequeue` methods. We also covered two very famous special implementations of the queue: the priority queue and the circular queue (using the Hot Potato game implementation).

In the next chapter, you will learn about linked lists, a more complex data structure than the array.

5
Linked Lists

In Chapter 2, *Arrays*, we learned about the data structure, array. An array (we can also call it a list) is a very simple data structure that stores a sequence of data. In this chapter, you will learn how to implement and use a linked list, which is a dynamic data structure, meaning that we can add or remove items from it at will and it will grow as needed.

In this chapter, we will cover the following topics:

- The linked list data structure
- Adding elements to a linked list
- Removing elements from a linked list
- How to use the LinkedList class
- Doubly linked lists
- Circular linked lists

The linked list data structure

Arrays (or lists) are probably the most common data structure used to store a collection of elements. As we mentioned before in this book, each language has its own implementation of arrays. This data structure is very convenient and provides a handy [] syntax to access its elements. However, this data structure has a disadvantage: the size of the array is fixed (in most languages) and inserting or removing items from the beginning or from the middle of the array is expensive, because the elements need to be shifted over (even though we learned that JavaScript has methods from the array class that will do that for us, this is what happens behind the scenes as well).

Linked lists store a sequential collection of elements; but unlike arrays, in linked lists, the elements are not placed contiguously in memory. Each element consists of a node that stores the element itself and also a reference (also known as a pointer or link) that points to the next element. The following diagram exemplifies the structure of a linked list:

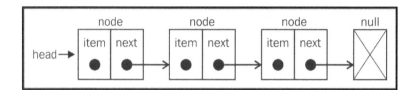

One of the benefits of a linked list over a conventional array is that we do not need to shift elements over when adding or removing them. However, we need to use pointers when working with a linked list and, because of it, we need to pay some extra attention when implementing a linked list. Another detail in the array is that we can directly access any element at any position; with the linked list, if we want to access an element from the middle, we need to start from the beginning (**head**) and iterate the list until we find the desired element.

We have some real-world examples that can be exemplified as a linked list. The first example is a conga line. Each person is an element, and the hands would be the pointer that links to the next person in the conga line. You can add people to the line—you just need to find the spot where you want to add this person, decouple the connection, then insert the new person and make the connection again.

Another example would be a scavenger hunt. You have a clue, and this clue is the pointer to the place where you can find the next clue. With this link, you go to the next place and get another clue that will lead to the next one. The only way to get a clue from the middle of the list is to follow the list from the beginning (from the first clue).

We have another example—which might be the most popular one used to exemplify linked lists—that of a train. A train consists of a series of vehicles (also known as wagons). Each vehicle or wagon is linked to each other. You can easily decouple a wagon, change its place, or add or remove it. The following figure demonstrates a train. Each wagon is an element of the list and the link between the wagons is the pointer:

In this chapter, we will cover the linked list and also the doubly linked list. But let's start with the easiest data structure first.

Creating a linked list

Now that you understand what a linked list is, let's start implementing our data structure. This is the skeleton of our `LinkedList` class:

```
function LinkedList() {

  let Node = function(element){ // {1}
    this.element = element;
    this.next = null;
  };

  let length = 0; // {2}
  let head = null; // {3}

  this.append = function(element){};
  this.insert = function(position, element){};
  this.removeAt = function(position){};
  this.remove = function(element){};
  this.indexOf = function(element){};
  this.isEmpty = function() {};
  this.size = function() {};
  this.toString = function(){};
  this.print = function(){};
}
```

For the `LinkedList` data structure, we need a `helper` class called `Node` (line {1}). The `Node` class represents the item that we want to add to the list. It contains an `element` attribute, which is the value that we want to add to the list, and a `next` attribute, which is the pointer that contains the link to the next node item of the list.

There is also the `length` property (line {2}) in the `LinkedList` class (internal/private variable) that stores the number of items we have on the list.

Another important note is that we need to store a reference for the first node as well. To do this, we can store this reference inside a variable that we will call head (line {3}).

Then we have the methods of the LinkedList class. Let's see what each method will be responsible for before we implement each one:

- append(element): This adds a new item to the end of the list.
- insert(position, element): This inserts a new item at a specified position in the list.
- remove(element): This removes an item from the list.
- indexOf(element): This returns the index of the element in the list. If the element is not in the list, it returns -1.
- removeAt(position): This removes an item from a specified position in the list.
- isEmpty(): This returns true if the linked list does not contain any elements and false if the size of the linked list is bigger than 0.
- size(): This returns the number of elements the linked list contains. It is similar to the length property of the array.
- toString(): As the list uses a Node class as an item, we need to overwrite the default toString method inherited from the JavaScript object to output only the element values.

Appending elements to the end of the linked list

When adding an element to the end of a LinkedList object, there can be two scenarios: one where the list is empty and we are adding its first element, or one where the list is not empty and we are appending elements to it.

The following is the implementation of the append method:

```
this.append = function(element){

  let node = new Node(element), //{1}
  current; //{2}

  if (head === null){ //first node on list //{3}
  head = node;

  } else {

    current = head; //{4}
```

```
        //loop the list until find last item
        while(current.next){
          current = current.next;
        }

        //get last item and assign next to node to make the link
        current.next = node; //{5}
      }

      length++; //update size of list //{6}
    };
```

The first thing we need to do is to create the `Node` item passing `element` as its value (line {1}).

Let's implement the first scenario first: adding an element when the list is empty. When we create a `LinkedList` object, the head will point to `null`:

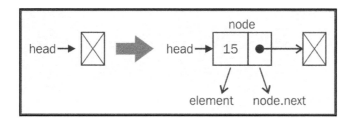

If the `head` element is `null` (the list is empty-line {3}), it means we are adding the first element to the list. So, all we have to do is point the `head` element to the `node` element. The next `node` element will be `null` automatically (check the source code from the previous topic).

 The last node from the list always has `null` as the next element.

So, we have covered the first scenario. Let's go to the second one, which is adding an element to the end of the list when it is not empty.

To add an element to the end of the list, we first need to find the last element. Remember that we only have a reference to the first element (line {4}), so we need to iterate through the list until we find the last item. To do so, we need a variable that points to the `current` item of the list (line {2}).

When looping through the list, we know we'll reached its end when the `current.next` element is `null`. Then, all we have to do is link the current element's (which is the last one) next pointer to the node we want to add to the list (line {5}). The following diagram exemplifies this action:

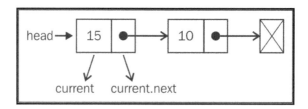

And as with when we create a `Node` element, its next pointer will always be `null`. We are OK with this, because we know that it is going to be the last item of the list.

And of course, we cannot forget to increment the size of the list so that we can control it and easily get the list size (line {6}).

We can use and test the data structure we've created so far with the following code:

```
let list = new LinkedList();
list.append(15);
list.append(10);
```

Removing elements from the linked list

Now, let's see how we can remove elements from the `LinkedList` object. Again there are two scenarios when removing elements: the first one is removing the first element, and the second one is removing any element but the first one. We are going to implement two `remove` methods: the first one is removing an element from a specified position, and the second one is based on the element value (we will present the second `remove` method later).

```
this.removeAt = function(position){

  //check for out-of-bounds values
  if (position > -1 && position < length){ // {1}

    let current = head, // {2}
    previous, // {3}
    index = 0; // {4}

    //removing first item
```

```
    if (position === 0){ // {5}
      head = current.next;
    } else {

      while (index++ < position){ // {6}

        previous = current;     // {7}
        current = current.next; // {8}
      }

      //link previous with current's next: skip it to remove
      previous.next = current.next; // {9}
    }

    length--; // {10}

    return current.element;

  } else {
    return null; // {11}
  }
};
```

We will dive into this code step by step. As the method is going to receive the position of the element that needs to be removed, we need to verify that the position value is a valid one (line {1}). A valid position would be from 0 (included) to the size of the list (size – 1, as the index starts from zero). If it is not a valid position, we return null (meaning no element was removed from the list).

Let's write the code for the first scenario—we want to remove the first element from the list (position === 0, line {5}). The following diagram exemplifies this:

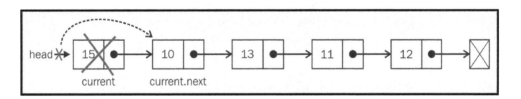

So, if we want to remove the first element, all we have to do is point head to the second element of the list. We will make a reference to the first element of the list using the current variable (line {2}; we will also use this to iterate the list, but we will get there in a minute). So, the current variable is a reference to the first element of the list. If we assign head to current.next, we will be removing the first element.

Now, let's say we want to remove the last item of the list, or an item from the middle of the list. To do so, we need to iterate the list until the desired position (line {6}—we will use an index variable for internal control and increment) with one detail: the current variable will always make a reference to the current element of the list that we are looping through (line {8}). And we also need to make a reference to the element that comes before the current element (line {7}); we will name it previous (line {3}).

So, to remove the current element from the list, all we have to do is link `previous.next` with `current.next` (line {9}). This way, the current element will be lost in the computer memory and will be available to be cleaned by the garbage collector.

 To understand better how the JavaScript garbage collector works, please read https://developer.mozilla.org/en-US/docs/Web/JavaScript/Memory_Management.

Let's try to understand this better with some diagrams. First, let's consider that we want to remove the last element:

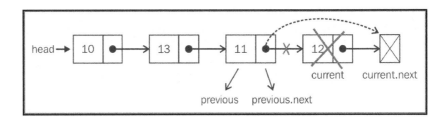

In the case of the last element, when we get off the loop in line {6}, the current variable will be a reference to the last element of the list (the one we want to remove). The `current.next` value will be `null` (because it is the last element). As we also keep a reference of the `previous` element (one element before the current one), `previous.next` will point to `current`. So to remove `current`, all we have to do is change the value of `previous.next` to `current.next`.

Now let's see whether the same logic applies to an element from the middle of the list:

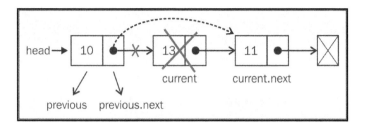

The `current` variable is a reference to the element that we want to remove. The `previous` variable is a reference to the element that comes before the element we want to remove. So to remove the `current` element, all we need to do is link `previous.next` to `current.next`. So, our logic works for both cases.

Inserting an element at any position

Next, we are going to implement the `insert` method. This method provides you with the capability to insert an element at any position. Let's take a look at its implementation:

```
this.insert = function(position, element){

  //check for out-of-bounds values
  if (position >= 0 && position <= length){ //{1}

    let node = new Node(element),
    current = head,
    previous,
    index = 0;

    if (position === 0){ //add on first position

      node.next = current; //{2}
      head = node;

    } else {
      while (index++ < position){ //{3}
        previous = current;
        current = current.next;
      }
      node.next = current; //{4}
      previous.next = node; //{5}
    }

    length++; //update size of list
```

```
        return true;

    } else {
       return false; //{6}
    }
};
```

As we are handling positions, we need to check the out-of-bound values (line {1}, just like we did in the `remove` method). If it is out of bounds, we return the value `false` to indicate that no item was added to the list (line {6}).

Now we are going to handle the different scenarios. The first scenario is the case where we need to add an element at the beginning of the list, meaning the *first position*. The following diagram exemplifies this scenario:

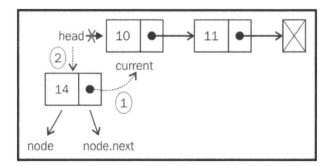

In the preceding diagram, we have the `current` variable making a reference to the first element of the list. What we need to do is set the value `node.next` to `current` (the first element of the list). Now we have `head` and also `node.next` pointing to `current`. Next, all we have to do is change the `head` reference to `node` (line {2}), and we have a new element in the list.

Now let's handle the second scenario: adding an element in the middle or at the end of the list. First, we need to loop through the list until we reach the desired position (line {3}). When we get out of the loop, the `current` variable will be a reference to an element present after the position where we would like to insert the new item, and `previous` will be a reference to an element present before the position where we would like to insert the new item. In this case, we want to add the new item between `previous` and `current`. So, first we need to make a link between the new item (`node`) and current item (line {4}), and then we need to change the link between `previous` and `current`. We need `previous.next` to point to `node` (line {5}).

Let's see the code in action using a diagram:

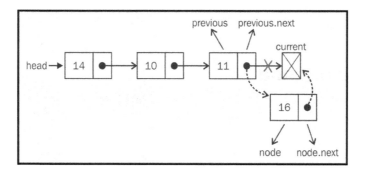

If we try to add a new element to the last position, `previous` will be a reference to the last item of the list and `current` will be null. In this case, `node.next` will point to `current`, `previous.next` will point to `node`, and we have a new item in the list.

Now, let's see how to add a new element in the middle of the list with the help of the following diagram:

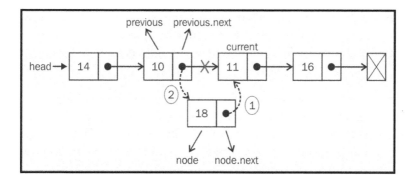

In this case, we are trying to insert the new item (`node`) between the `previous` and `current` elements. First, we need to set the value of the `node.next` pointer to `current`. Then, set the value of `previous.next` to `node`. And then we have a new item in the list!

It is very important to have variables referencing the nodes we need to control so that we do not lose the link between the nodes. We could work with only one variable (`previous`), but it would be harder to control the links between the nodes. For this reason, it is better to declare an extra variable to help us with these references.

Implementing other methods

In this section, we will learn how to implement the other methods from the `LinkedList` class, such as `toString`, `indexOf`, `isEmpty`, and `size`.

The toString method

The `toString` method converts the `LinkedList` object into a string. The following is the implementation of the `toString` method:

```
this.toString = function(){

  let current = head, //{1}
      string = '';    //{2}

  while (current) {    //{3}
     string +=current.element +(current.next ? 'n' : '');//{4}
     current = current.next;    //{5}
  }
  return string;                //{6}
};
```

First, to iterate through all the elements of the list, we need a starting point, which is `head`. We will use the `current` variable as our index (line {1}) and navigate through the list. We also need to initialize the variable that we will be using to concatenate the elements' values (line {2}).

Next, we iterate through each element of the list (line {3}). We will use `current` to check whether there is an element (if the list is empty or we reach the second last element of the list (`null`), the code inside the `while` loop will not be executed). Then, we get the element's content, and concatenate it to our string (line {4}). And finally, we iterate the next element (line {5}). At last, we return the string with the list's content (list {6}).

The indexOf method

The next method that we will implement is the `indexOf` method. The `indexOf` method receives the value of an element, and returns the position of this element if it is found. Otherwise, it returns −1.

Let's take a look at its implementation:

```
this.indexOf = function(element){

  let current = head,  //{1}
  index = -1;

  while (current) {    //{2}
    if (element === current.element) {
      return index;        //{3}
    }
    index++;                     //{4}
    current = current.next; //{5}
  }

  return -1;
};
```

As always, we need a variable that will help us iterate through the list; this variable is current, and its first value is the head (the first element of the list—we also need a variable to increment to count the position number, index (line {1})). Then, we iterate through the elements (line {2}), and check if the element we are looking for is the current one. If positive, we return its position (line {3}). If not, we continue counting (line {4}), and go to the next node of the list (line {5}).

The loop will not be executed if the list is empty, or if we reach the end of the list (current = current.next will be null). If we do not find the value, we return −1.

With this method implemented, we can implement other methods such as the remove method:

```
this.remove = function(element){
  let index = this.indexOf(element);
  return this.removeAt(index);
};
```

We already have a method that removes an element at a given position (removeAt). Now that we have the indexOf method, if we pass the element's value, we can find its position and call the removeAt method passing the position that we found. It is very simple, and it is also easier if we need to change the code from the removeAt method—it will be changed for both methods (this is what is nice about reusing code). This way, we do not need to maintain two methods to remove an item from the list—we need only one! Also, the bounds constraints will be checked by the removeAt method.

The isEmpty, size, and getHead methods

The `isEmpty` and `size` methods are the same as the ones we implemented for the classes implemented in the previous chapter. But let's take a look at them anyway:

```
this.isEmpty = function() {
  return length === 0;
};
```

The `isEmpty` method returns `true` if there is no element in the list and `false` otherwise:

```
this.size = function() {
  return length;
};
```

The `size` method returns the `length` of the list. Unlike the classes we implemented in earlier chapters, the `length` variable of the list is controlled internally, as `LinkedList` is a class built from scratch.

And finally, we have the `getHead` method:

```
this.getHead = function(){
  return head;
};
```

The `head` variable is a private variable from the `LinkedList` class (meaning it can be accessed and changed only by the `LinkedList` instance, not outside of the instance). But, if we need to iterate the list outside the class implementation, we need to provide a way to get the first element of the class.

Doubly linked lists

There are different types of linked lists. In this section, we are going to cover the **doubly linked list**. The difference between a doubly linked list and a normal linked list is that in a linked list, we make the link from one node to the next one only, while in the doubly linked list, we have a double link: one for the next element and one for the previous element, as shown in the following diagram:

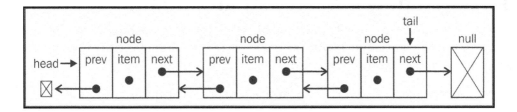

Let's get started with the changes that are needed to implement the `DoublyLinkedList` class:

```
function DoublyLinkedList() {

  let Node = function(element){

    this.element = element;
    this.next = null;
    this.prev = null; //NEW
  };

  let length = 0;
  let head = null;
  let tail = null; //NEW

  //methods here
}
```

As we can see in this code, the differences between the `LinkedList` class and the `DoublyLinkedList` class are marked by `NEW`. Inside the `Node` class, we have the `prev` attribute (a new pointer) and, inside the `DoublyLinkedList` class, we also have the `tail` attribute to keep the reference of the last item of the list.

The doubly linked list provides us with two ways to iterate the list: from the beginning to its end or vice versa. We can also go to the next element or the previous element of a particular node. In the singly linked list, when you are iterating the list and you miss the desired element, you need to go back to the beginning of the list and start iterating it again. This is one of the advantages of the doubly linked list.

Inserting a new element at any position

Inserting a new item in the doubly linked list is very similar to the linked list. The difference is that in the linked list we only control one pointer (next), and in the doubly linked list we have to control both next and prev (previous).

Here we have the algorithm to insert a new element at any position:

```
this.insert = function(position, element){

  //check for out-of-bounds values
  if (position >= 0 && position <= length){

    let node = new Node(element),
    current = head,
    previous,
    index = 0;

    if (position === 0){ //add on first position

      if (!head){                  //NEW {1}
        head = node;
        tail = node;
      } else {
        node.next = current;
        current.prev = node; //NEW {2}
        head = node;
      }
    } else  if (position === length) { //last item //NEW

      current = tail;       // {3}
      current.next = node;
      node.prev = current;
      tail = node;

    } else {
      while (index++ < position){ //{4}
        previous = current;
        current = current.next;
      }
      node.next = current; //{5}
      previous.next = node;

      current.prev = node; //NEW
      node.prev = previous; //NEW
    }
```

```
    length++; //update size of list

    return true;

} else {
    return false;
}
};
```

Let's analyze the first scenario: insert a new element at the first position of the list (the beginning of the list). If the list is empty (line {1}), we simply need to point `head` and `tail` to the new node. If not, the `current` variable will be a reference to the first element of the list. As we did for the linked list, we set `node.next` to `current` and `head` will point to the node (it will be the first element of the list). The difference now is that we also need to set a value for the previous pointer of the elements. The `current.prev` pointer will point to the new element (`node`—line {2}) instead of null. Since the node.prev pointer is already null, we do not need to update anything.

The following diagram demonstrates this process:

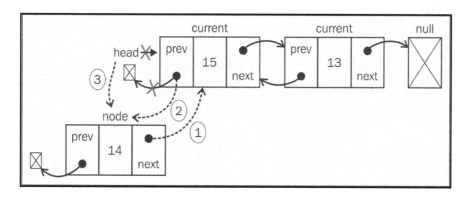

Now let's analyze this, just in case we want to add a new element as the last element of the list. As we are also controlling the pointer to the last element, this is a special case. The `current` variable will reference the last element (line {3}). Then, we start making the first link: `node.prev` will reference `current`. The `current.next` pointer (which points to null) will point to `node` (`node.next` will point to `null` already because of the constructor). Then, there is only one thing left to be done, that is updating `tail`, which will point to `node` instead of `current`.

The following diagram demonstrates all these actions:

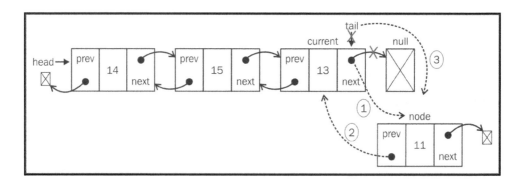

Then we have the third scenario: inserting a new element in the middle of the list. As we did for the previous methods, we will iterate the list until we get to the desired position (line {4}). We will insert the new element between the `current` and `previous` elements. First, `node.next` will point to `current` (line {5}), and `previous.next` will point to `node` so that we do not lose the link between the nodes. Then, we need to fix all the links: `current.prev` will point to `node` and `node.prev` will point to `previous`. The following diagram exemplifies this:

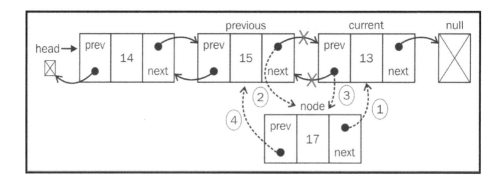

We can make some improvements in both the methods that we implemented: `insert` and `remove`. In case of a negative result, we could insert elements at the end of the list. There is also a performance improvement: for example, if `position` is greater than `length/2`, it is best to iterate from the end than start from the beginning (by doing so, we will have to iterate fewer elements from the list).

Removing elements from any position

Removing elements from a doubly linked list is also very similar to a linked list. The only difference is that we need to set the previous pointer as well. Let's take a look at the implementation:

```
this.removeAt = function(position){

  //look for out-of-bounds values
  if (position > -1 && position < length){

    let current = head,
    previous,
    index = 0;

    //removing first item
    if (position === 0){

      head = current.next; // {1}

      //if there is only one item, update tail //NEW
      if (length === 1){ // {2}
        tail = null;
      } else {
        head.prev = null; // {3}
      }

    } else if (position === length-1){ //last item //NEW

      current = tail; // {4}
      tail = current.prev;
      tail.next = null;

    } else {

      while (index++ < position){ // {5}

        previous = current;
        current = current.next;
      }

      //link previous with current's next - skip it
      previous.next = current.next; // {6}
      current.next.prev = previous; //NEW
    }

    length--;
```

```
        return current.element;

    } else {
        return null;
    }
};
```

We need to handle three scenarios: removing an element from the beginning, from the middle, and the last element.

Let's take a look how to remove the first element. The `current` variable is a reference to the first element of the list, the one we want to remove. All we need to do is change the reference from `head`; instead of `current`, it will be the next element (`current.next` —line {1}). But we also need to update the current.next previous pointer (as the first element prev pointer is a reference to null). So, we change the reference of head.prev to null (line {3} —as head also points to the new first element of the list, or we can also use current.next.prev). As we also need to control the tail reference, we can check whether the element we are trying to remove is the first one, and if positive, all we need to do is set tail to null as well (line {2}).

The following diagram illustrates the removal of the first element from a doubly linked list:

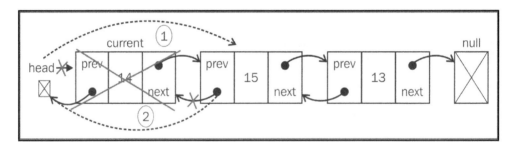

The next scenario removes an element from the last position. As we have the reference to the last element already (`tail`), we do not need to iterate the list to get to it. So, we can assign the `tail` reference to the `current` variable as well (line {4}). Next, we need to update the `tail` reference to the second-last element of the list (`current.prev` or `tail.prev` works as well). And, now that `tail` is pointing to the second-last element, all we need to do is update the `next` pointer to `null` (`tail.next = null`). The following diagram demonstrates this action:

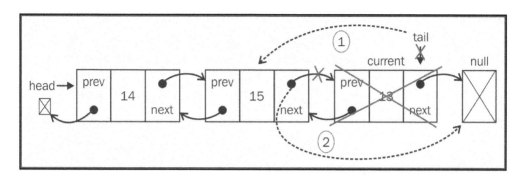

And the third and final scenario: removing an element from the middle of the list. First, we need to iterate until we get to the desired position (line {5}). The element we want to remove would be referenced by the `current` variable. So, to remove it, we can skip it in the list by updating the references of `previous.next` and `current.next.prev`. So, `previous.next` will point to `current.next`, and `current.next.prev` will point to `previous`, as demonstrated by the following diagram:

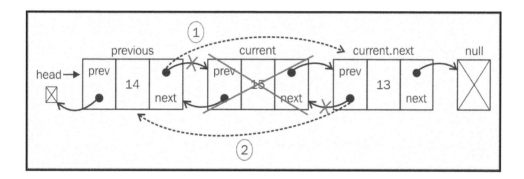

 To know the implementation of other methods of doubly linked list, refer to the source code of the book. The download link of the source code is mentioned in the *Preface* of the book.

Circular linked lists

A **circular linked list** can have only one reference direction (as with the linked list) or a double reference as with the doubly linked list. The only difference between the circular linked list and a linked list is that the last element's next (`tail.next`) pointer does not make a reference to `null`, but to the first element (`head`), as we can see in the following diagram:

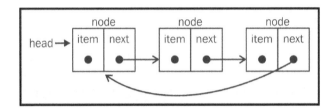

A **doubly circular linked list** has `tail.next` pointing to the `head` element, and `head.prev` pointing to the `tail` element:

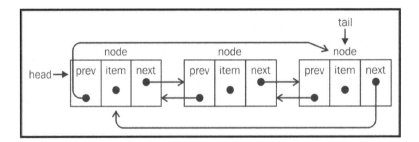

We will not cover the `CircularLinkedList` algorithm in this book (the source code is very similar to `LinkedList` and `DoublyLinkedList`). However, you can access the code by downloading this book's source code. Inside the book's source code you will also find the ECMAScript 6 version of all the three linked list classes.

Summary

In this chapter, you learned about the linked list data structure and its variants, the doubly linked list and the circular linked list. You learned how to remove and add elements at any position, and how to iterate through a linked list. You also learned that the most important advantage of a linked list over an array is that you can easily add and remove elements from a linked list without shifting over its elements. So, whenever you need to add and remove lots of elements, the best option would be a linked list instead of an array. In the next chapter, you will learn about sets, the last sequential data structure that we will cover in this book.

6
Sets

So far, you have learned about sequential data structures such as arrays (lists), stacks, queues, and linked lists (and their variants). In this chapter, we will cover a data structure called sets, which is also a sequential data structure that does not allow duplicated values.

In this chapter, you will learn how to create a set data structure, to add and remove values, and also to search whether a value already exists. You will learn how to perform mathematical operations such as union, intersection, and difference. You will also learn how to use the native ES6 (ECMAScript 6) `Set` class.

Structuring a dataset

A **set** is a collection of items that are unordered and consists of unique elements (meaning they cannot be repeated). This data structure uses the same math concept as finite sets but applied to a computer science data structure.

Let's take a look at the math concept of sets before we dive into the computer science implementation of it. In mathematics, a set is a collection of distinct objects.

For example, we have a set of natural numbers, which consists of integer numbers greater than or equal to 0—that is, $N = \{0, 1, 2, 3, 4, 5, 6, \ldots\}$. The list of the objects within the set is surrounded by $\{\}$ (curly braces).

There is also the null set concept. A set with no element is called a **null set** or an **empty set**. An example would be a set of prime numbers between 24 and 29. As there is no prime number (a natural number greater than 1 that has no positive divisors other than 1 and itself) between 24 and 29, the set will be empty. We will represent an empty set with $\{\}$.

You can also imagine a set as an array with no repeated elements and no concept or order.

In mathematics, a set also has some basic operations such as union, intersection, and difference. We will also cover these operations in this chapter.

Creating a set

The current implementation of JavaScript is based on **ECMAScript 5.1** (supported by modern browsers) published on June 2011. It contains the `Array` class implementation that we covered in earlier chapters. **ECMAScript 6** also contains an implementation of the `Set` class that you will learn how to use later on in this chapter. The class we will implement in this chapter is based on the `Set` implementation of ECMAScript 6.

This is the skeleton of our `Set` class:

```
function Set() {
   let items = {};
}
```

A very important detail here is that we are using an object to represent our set (`items`) instead of an array. However, we could also use an array to do this implementation. Let's use an object to implement things a little bit differently and discuss new ways of implementing data structures that are similar. Also, objects in JavaScript do not allow you to have two different properties on the same key, which guarantees unique elements in our set.

Next, we need to declare the methods available for a set (we will try to simulate the same `Set` class implemented in ECMAScript 6):

- `add(value)`: This adds a new item to the set.
- `delete(value)`: This removes the value from the set.
- `has(value)`: This returns `true` if the value exists in the set and `false` otherwise.
- `clear()`: This removes all the items from the set.
- `size()`: This returns how many elements the set contains. It is similar to the `length` property of the array.
- `values()`: This returns an array of all the values of the set.

The has (value) method

The first method we will implement is the `has(value)` method. We will implement this method first because it will be used in other methods, such as `add` and `remove`. We can take a look at its implementation here:

```
this.has = function(value){
  return value in items;
};
```

As we are using an object to store all the values of the set, we can use JavaScript's `in` operator to verify that the given value is a property of the `items` object.

However, there is a better way of implementing this method, which is as follows:

```
this.has = function(value){
  return items.hasOwnProperty(value);
};
```

All JavaScript objects have the `hasOwnProperty` method. This method returns a Boolean indicating whether the object has the specified property or not.

The add method

The next method we will implement is the `add` method, as follows:

```
this.add = function(value){
  if (!this.has(value)){
    items[value] = value; //{1}
    return true;
  }
  return false;
};
```

Given a value, we can check whether the `value` already exists in the set. If not, we add the `value` to the set (line `{1}`) and return `true` to indicate that the value was added. If the value already exists in the set, we simply return `false` to indicate that the value was not added.

We are adding the value as key and value because it will help us search for the value if we store it as the key as well.

The delete and clear methods

Next, we will implement the `remove` method:

```
this.delete = function(value){
  if (this.has(value)){
    delete items[value]; //{2}
    return true;
  }
  return false;
};
```

In the `remove` method, we will verify that the given `value` exists in the set. If this is positive, we will remove the `value` from the set (line {2}) and return `true` to indicate that the value was removed; otherwise, we will return `false`.

As we are using an object to store the `items` object of the set, we can simply use the `delete` operator to remove the property from the `items` object (line {2}).

To use the `Set` class, we can use the following code as an example:

```
let set = new Set();
set.add(1);
set.add(2);
```

Just out of curiosity, if we output the `items` variable on the console (`console.log`) after executing the previous code, this will be the output in Google Chrome:

Object {1: 1, 2: 2}

 As we can note, it is an object with two properties. The property name is the value we added to the set and its value, as well.

If we want to remove all the values from the set, we can use the `clear` method, as follows:

```
this.clear = function(){
  items = {}; // {3}
};
```

All we need to do to reset the `items` object is assign it to an empty object again (line {3}). We could also iterate the set and remove all the values one by one using the `remove` method, but this is too much work as we have an easier way of doing it.

The size method

The next method we will implement is the `size` method (which returns how many items are in the set). There are three ways of implementing this method.

The first method is to use a `length` variable and control it whenever we use the `add` or `remove` method, as we used in the `LinkedList` class in the previous chapter.

In the second method, we use a built-in function from the built-in `Object` class in JavaScript (ECMAScript 5+), as follows:

```
this.size = function(){
   return Object.keys(items).length;  //{4}
};
```

The `Object` class in JavaScript contains a method called `keys` that returns an array of all the properties of a given object. In this case, we can use the `length` property of this array (line {4}) to return how many properties we have in the `items` object. This code will work only in modern browsers (such as IE9+, FF4+, Chrome5+, Opera12+, Safari5+, and so on).

The third method is to extract each property of the `items` object manually, count how many properties there are, and return this number. This method will work in any browser and is the equivalent of the previous code, as follows:

```
this.sizeLegacy = function(){
   let count = 0;
   for(let key in items) {  //{5}
     if(items.hasOwnProperty(key))  //{6}
     ++count;   //{7}
   }
   return count;
};
```

So, first we will iterate through all the properties of the `items` object (line {5}) and check whether this property is really a property of our object (so that we do not count it more than once, line {6}). If positive, we will increment the `count` variable (line {7}) and at the end of the method, we will return this number.

We cannot simply use the `for-in` statement, iterate through the properties of the `items` object, and increment the `count` variable's value. We also need to use the `has` method (to verify that the `items` object has this property) because the object's prototype contains additional properties for the object, as well (properties are inherited from the base JavaScript `Object` class, but it still has properties of the object, which are not used in this data structure).

The values method

The same logic applies to the `values` method, using which we want to extract all the keys of the `items` object and return its values as an array:

```
this.values = function(){
  let values = [];
  for (let i=0, keys=Object.keys(items); i<keys.length; i++) {
    values.push(items[keys[i]]);
  }
  return values;
};
```

This code will only work in modern browsers. As we are using Google Chrome and Firefox as testing browsers in this book, the code will work.

If we want code that can be executed in any browser, we can use the following code, which is equivalent to the previous code:

```
this.valuesLegacy = function(){
  let values = [];
  for(let key in items) { //{7}
    if(items.hasOwnProperty(key)) { //{8}
      values.push(items[key]);
    }
  }
  return values;
};
```

So, first we will iterate through all the properties of the `items` object (line {7}), add them to an array (line {8}), and return this array. This method is similar to the `sizeLegacy` method we developed, but instead of counting the properties, we are adding in an array.

Using the Set class

Now that we have finished implementing our data structure, let's take a look at how we can use it. Let's give it a try and execute some commands to test our `Set` class, as follows:

```
let set = new Set();

set.add(1);
console.log(set.values()); //outputs ["1"]
console.log(set.has(1));   //outputs true
console.log(set.size());   //outputs 1

set.add(2);
console.log(set.values()); //outputs ["1", "2"]
console.log(set.has(2));   //true
console.log(set.size());   //2

set.remove(1);
console.log(set.values()); //outputs ["2"]

set.remove(2);
console.log(set.values()); //outputs []
```

So, now we have a very similar implementation of the `Set` class, as in ECMAScript 6. As mentioned before, we could also have used an array instead of an object to store the elements. As we used arrays in `Chapter 2`, *Arrays*; `Chapter 3`, *Stacks*; and `Chapter 4`, *Queues*; it is nice to know there are different ways of implementing the same thing.

Set operations

We can perform the following operations on sets:

- **Union**: Given two sets, this returns a new set with elements from both the given sets
- **Intersection**: Given two sets, this returns a new set with the elements that exist in both sets
- **Difference**: Given two sets, this returns a new set with all the elements that exist in the first set and do not exist in the second set
- **Subset**: This confirms whether a given set is a subset of another set

Set union

The mathematic concept of **union** is: the union of sets A and B, denoted by:

$$A \cup B$$

This set is defined as:

$$A \cup B = \{x \mid x \in A \vee x \in B\}$$

This means that x (the element) exists in A or x exists in B. The following diagram exemplifies the union operation:

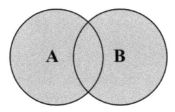

Now, let's implement the `union` method in our `Set` class via the following code:

```
this.union = function(otherSet){
    let unionSet = new Set(); //{1}

    let values = this.values(); //{2}
    for (let i=0; i<values.length; i++){
        unionSet.add(values[i]);
    }

    values = otherSet.values(); //{3}
    for (let i=0; i<values.length; i++){
        unionSet.add(values[i]);
    }

    return unionSet;
};
```

First, we need to create a new set to represent the union of two sets (line {1}). Next, we will get all the `values` from the first set (the current instance of the `Set` class), iterate through them, and add all the values to the set that represents the union (line {2}). Then, we will do the exact same thing but with the second set (line {3}). At last, we will return the result.

Let's test the previous code as follows:

```
let setA = new Set();
setA.add(1);
setA.add(2);
setA.add(3);

let setB = new Set();
setB.add(3);
setB.add(4);
setB.add(5);
setB.add(6);

let unionAB = setA.union(setB);
console.log(unionAB.values());
```

The output will be `["1", "2", "3", "4", "5", "6"]`. Note that the element 3 is present in both *A* and *B*, and it appears only once in the result set.

Set intersection

The mathematic concept of **intersection**, here the intersection of sets *A* and *B*, is denoted by:

$$A \cap B$$

This set is defined as:

$$A \cap B = \{x \mid x \in A \land x \in B\}$$

This means that *x* (the element) exists in *A*, and *x* exists in *B*. The following diagram exemplifies the intersection operation:

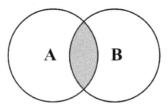

Now, let's implement the `intersection` method in our `Set` class, as follows:

```
this.intersection = function(otherSet){
  let intersectionSet = new Set(); //{1}

  let values = this.values();
  for (let i=0; i<values.length; i++){ //{2}
    if (otherSet.has(values[i])){    //{3}
      intersectionSet.add(values[i]); //{4}
    }
  }

  return intersectionSet;
}
```

For the `intersection` method, we need to find all the elements from the current instance of the `Set` class that also exist in the given `Set` instance. So, first, we will create a new `Set` instance so that we can return it with the common elements (line {1}). Next, we will iterate through all the `values` of the current instance of the `Set` class (line {2}), and we will verify that the value exists in the `otherSet` instance, as well (line {3}). We can use the `has` method, which we implemented earlier, in this chapter to verify that the element exists in the `Set` instance. Then, if the value exists in the other `Set` instance also, we will add it to the created `intersectionSet` variable (line {4}) and return it.

Let's do some testing, as follows:

```
let setA = new Set();
setA.add(1);
setA.add(2);
setA.add(3);

let setB = new Set();
setB.add(2);
setB.add(3);
```

```
setB.add(4);

let intersectionAB = setA.intersection(setB);
console.log(intersectionAB.values());
```

The output will be [`"2"`, `"3"`], as the values 2 and 3 exist in both sets.

Set difference

The mathematic concept of **difference**, here the difference between sets A and B, is denoted by $A - B$, defined as:

$$A\text{-}B = \{x \mid x \in A \land x \notin B\}$$

This means that x (the element) exists in A, but x does not exist in B. The following diagram exemplifies the difference operation between sets A and B:

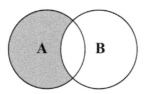

Now let's implement the `difference` method in our `Set` class by executing the following:

```
this.difference = function(otherSet){
  let differenceSet = new Set(); //{1}

  let values = this.values();
  for (let i=0; i<values.length; i++){ //{2}
    if (!otherSet.has(values[i])){     //{3}
      differenceSet.add(values[i]); //{4}
    }
  }

  return differenceSet;
};
```

The `intersection` method will get all the `values` that exist in both sets. The `difference` method will get all the values that exist in *A* but not in *B*. So, the only difference in the implementation of the method is in line {3}. Instead of getting the values that also exist in the `otherSet` instance, we will get only the values that do not exist. Lines {1}, {2}, and {4} are exactly the same.

Let's do some testing (with the same sets we used in the `intersection` section) via the following code:

```
let setA = new Set();
setA.add(1);
setA.add(2);
setA.add(3);

let setB = new Set();
setB.add(2);
setB.add(3);
setB.add(4);

let differenceAB = setA.difference(setB);
console.log(differenceAB.values());
```

The output will be `["1"]` because 1 is the only element that exists only in `setA`.

Subset

The last set operation we will cover is the subset. An example of the mathematic concept of **subset** is that *A* is a subset of (or is included in) *B*, and this is denoted by:

$$A \subseteq B$$

The set is defined as:

$$\forall x \{ x \in A \Rightarrow x \in B \}$$

This means that for every *x* (element) that exists in *A*, it also *needs to exist* in *B*. The following diagram exemplifies when *A* is a subset of *B* and when it is not:

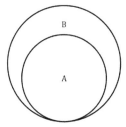

Now let's implement the `subset` method in our `Set` class through the following code:

```
this.subset = function(otherSet){

  if (this.size() > otherSet.size()){ //{1}
    return false;
  } else {
    let values = this.values();
    for (let i=0; i<values.length; i++){ //{2}
      if (!otherSet.has(values[i])){    //{3}
        return false; //{4}
      }
    }
    return true; //{5}
  }
};
```

The first verification that we need to do is to check the size of the current instance of the `Set` class. If the current instance has more elements than the `otherSet` instance, it is not a subset (line {3}). A subset needs to have a lesser or the same number of elements as the compared set.

Next, we will iterate through all the set elements (line {2}), and we will verify that the element also exists in `otherSet` (line {3}). If any element does not exist in `otherSet`, it means that it is not a subset, so we will return `false` (line {4}). If all the elements also exist in `otherSet`, line {4} will not be executed, and then we will return `true` (line {5}).

Let's try the previous code:

```
let setA = new Set();
setA.add(1);
setA.add(2);
```

```
let setB = new Set();
setB.add(1);
setB.add(2);
setB.add(3);

let setC = new Set();
setC.add(2);
setC.add(3);
setC.add(4);

console.log(setA.subset(setB));
console.log(setA.subset(setC));
```

We have three sets: `setA` is a subset of `setB` (so the output is `true`); however, `setA` is not a subset of `setC` (`setC` only contains the value 2 from `setA` and not the values 1 and 2), so the output will be `false`.

ES6 – the Set class

ECMAScript 2015 introduced a Set class as part of the JavaScript API. We developed our `Set` class based on the **ES6** `Set` class.

 You can see the details of the ECMAScript 6 `Set` class implementation at `https://developer.mozilla.org/en-US/docs/Web/JavaScript/R eference/Global_Objects/Set` (or `http://goo.gl/2li2a5`).

Now, let's take a look at how we can use the native `Set` class, as well.

Let's use the same examples we used to test our `Set` class, as follows:

```
let set = new Set();
set.add(1);
console.log(set.values()); //outputs @Iterator
console.log(set.has(1));   //outputs true
console.log(set.size);   //outputs 1
```

The difference between our `Set` class and the ES6 `Set` class is that the `values` method returns `Iterator` (which you learned in `Chapter 2`, *Arrays*) instead of the array with the values. Another difference is that we developed a `size` method to return the number of values `set` stores. The ES6 `Set` class has a property named `size`.

We can also call the `delete` method to remove an element from `set` via the following code:

```
set.delete(1);
```

The `clear` method also resets the `set` data structure. This is the same functionality we implemented.

ES6 Set class operations

We developed the mathematical operations such as union, intersection, difference, and also subset in our `Set` class. Unfortunately, the **ES6** native `Set` class does not contain these functionalities. However, we can try to simulate them in case it is needed.

We will use the following two sets in our examples:

```
let setA = new Set();
setA.add(1);
setA.add(2);
setA.add(3);

let setB = new Set();
setB.add(2);
setB.add(3);
setB.add(4);
```

Simulating the union operation

To add all the elements from two sets, we can create a third one (line {1}), iterate the other two sets (lines {2} and {3}), and add all their elements into the union set, as demonstrated by the following code:

```
let unionAb = new Set(); //{1}
for (let x of setA) unionAb.add(x); //{2}
for (let x of setB) unionAb.add(x); //{3}
```

Simulating the intersection operation

To simulate the intersection operation, we will need to create an auxiliary function to help create a new set with the common elements that both `setA` and `setB` have (line `{1}`), as demonstrated here:

```
let intersection = function(setA, setB){
  let intersectionSet = new Set();
  for (let x of setA){
    if (setB.has(x)){ //{1}
      intersectionSet.add(x);
    }
  }
  return intersectionSet;
};
let intersectionAB = intersection(setA, setB);
```

We can also use a simpler syntax to simulate the intersection, as follows:

```
intersectionAb = new Set([x for (x of setA) if (setB.has(x))]);
```

The preceding code does the same thing as the `intersection` function we developed.

 Firefox is the only browser that supports simplified syntax code. However, the `intersection` function can be executed in all modern browsers that support ES6.

Simulating the difference operation

While the intersection operation is achieved by creating a new set with the common elements that both `setA` and `setB` have, the difference operation is achieved by creating a new set with the elements that `setA` has but `setB` does not. Take a look at the following code:

```
let difference = function(setA, setB){
  let differenceSet = new Set();
  for (let x of setA){
    if (!setB.has(x)){ //{1}
      differenceSet.add(x);
    }
  }
  return differenceSet;
};
let differenceAB = difference(setA, setB);
```

The only difference between the `intersection` function and the `difference` function is line `{1}` as we only want to add the different Set elements that `setA` has and `setB` does not.

We can also write the previous function in a simpler syntax, as follows:

```
differenceAB = new Set([x for (x of setA) if (!setB.has(x))]);
```

 Firefox is the only browser that supports simplified syntax code. However, the `difference` function can be executed in all modern browsers that support ES6.

Summary

In this chapter, you learned how to implement a `Set` class from scratch, which is similar to the `Set` class defined in the definition of ECMAScript 6. We also covered some methods that are not usually present in other programming language implementations of the set data structure, such as union, intersection, difference, and subset. We implemented a very complete `Set` class compared to the current implementation of `Set` in other programming languages.

In the next chapter, we will cover hashes and dictionaries, which are nonsequential data structures.

7
Dictionaries and Hashes

In the previous chapter, you learned about sets. In this chapter, we will continue our discussion about data structures that store unique values (nonrepeated values) using dictionaries and hashes.

Sets, dictionaries, and hashes store unique values. In a set, we are interested in the value itself as the primary element. In a dictionary (or map), we store values in pairs as *[key, value]*. The same goes for hashes (they store values in pairs, such as *[key, value]*); however, the way that we implement these data structures is a little bit different, as we will see in this chapter.

Dictionaries

As you have learned, a set is a collection of distinct elements (nonrepeated elements). A **dictionary** is used to store *[key, value]* pairs, where the key is used to find a particular element. A dictionary is very similar to a set; a set stores a *[key, key]* collection of elements, and a dictionary stores a *[key, value]* collection of elements. A dictionary is also known as a **map**.

In this chapter, we will cover some examples of how to use the dictionary data structure in the real world: a dictionary itself (the words and their definitions) and an address book.

Creating a dictionary

Similarly to the Set class, ECMAScript 6 also contains an implementation of the Map class, also known as a dictionary.

The class we will implement in this chapter is based on the `Map` implementation of ECMAScript 6. You will notice that it is very similar to the `Set` class (but instead of storing a *[key, key]* pair, we will store a *[key, value]* pair).

This is the skeleton of our `Dictionary` class:

```
function Dictionary(){
    var items = {};
}
```

Similar to the `Set` class, we will also store the elements in an `Object` instance instead of an array.

Next, we need to declare the methods available for a map/dictionary, which are:

- `set(key,value)`: This adds a new item to the dictionary.
- `delete(key)`: This removes the value from the dictionary using the key.
- `has(key)`: This returns `true` if the key exists in the dictionary and `false` otherwise.
- `get(key)`: This returns a specific value searched by the key.
- `clear()`: This removes all the items from the dictionary.
- `size()`: This returns how many elements the dictionary contains. It is similar to the `length` property of the array.
- `keys()`: This returns an array of all the keys the dictionary contains.
- `values()`: This returns an array of all the values of the dictionary.

The has and set methods

The first method we will implement is the `has(key)` method. We will implement this method first because it will be used in other methods, such as `set` and `remove`. We can see its implementation in the following code:

```
this.has = function(key){
    return key in items;
};
```

The implementation is exactly the same as what we did for the `Set` class. We are using the JavaScript `in` operator to verify that `key` is a property of the `items` object.

The next method is the `set` method, as in the following code:

```
this.set = function(key, value){
  items[key] = value; //{1}
};
```

This receives a `key` and a `value` parameter. We simply set the value to the `key` property of the `items` object. This method can be used to add a new value or update an existing one.

The delete method

Next, we will implement the `delete` method. It is very similar to the `delete` method from the `Set` class; the only difference is that we will first search for `key` (instead of `value`), as follows:

```
this.delete = function(key){
  if (this.has(key)){
    delete items[key];
    return true;
  }
  return false;
};
```

Then, we will use the JavaScript `remove` operator to remove the `key` attribute from the `items` object.

The get and values methods

If we want to search for a particular item from the dictionary and retrieve its value, we can use the following method:

```
this.get = function(key) {
  return this.has(key) ? items[key] : undefined;
};
```

The `get` method will first verify that the value that we would like to retrieve exists (by searching for `key`), and if the result is positive, its value is returned. If not, an `undefined` value is returned (remember that `undefined` is different from `null`; we covered this concept in `Chapter 1`, *Javascript—A Quick Overview*).

The next method is the `values` method. This method will be used to retrieve an array of all `values` instances present in the dictionary, as follows:

```
this.values = function(){
  var values = [];
  for (var k in items) { //{1}
    if (this.has(k)) {
      values.push(items[k]); //{2}
    }
  }
  return values;
};
```

First, we will iterate through all attributes from the `items` object (line {1}). Just to make sure the value exists, we will use the `has` function to verify that `key` really exists, and then we will add its value to the `values` array (line {2}). At the end, we will simply return all the values found.

 We cannot simply use the `for-in` statement and iterate through the properties of the `items` object. We also need to use the `has` method (to verify whether the `items` object has this property) because the object's prototype contains additional properties of the object, as well. (Properties are inherited from the base JavaScript `Object` class, but it still has properties of the object that we are not interested in for this data structure.)

The clear, size, keys, and getItems methods

The `clear` and `size` methods are exactly the same as those from the `Set` class (Chapter 6, *Sets*). For this reason, we will not go through them again in this chapter.

The `keys` method returns all the keys used to identify a value in the `Dictionary` class. To retrieve all the keys from a JavaScript object, we can use the `keys` method from the `Object` class by passing our object as a parameter (all the classes we created so far in this book are also JavaScript objects, including the `Dictionary` class), as follows:

```
this.keys = function(){
  return Object.keys(items);
};
```

Finally, just so that we can verify the output of the items property, let's implement a method called getItems that will return the items variable, as follows:

```
this.getItems = function(){
  return items;
}
```

Using the Dictionary class

First, we will create an instance of the Dictionary class, and then we will add three e-mails to it. We will use this dictionary instance to exemplify an e-mail address book.

Let's execute some code using the class we created:

```
var dictionary = new Dictionary();
dictionary.set('Gandalf', 'gandalf@email.com');
dictionary.set('John', 'johnsnow@email.com');
dictionary.set('Tyrion', 'tyrion@email.com');
```

If we execute the following code, we will get the output as true:

```
console.log(dictionary.has('Gandalf'));
```

The following code will output 3 because we added three elements to our dictionary instance:

```
console.log(dictionary.size());
```

Now, let's execute the following lines of code:

```
console.log(dictionary.keys());
console.log(dictionary.values());
console.log(dictionary.get('Tyrion'));
```

The output will be as follows, in the respective order:

```
["Gandalf", "John", "Tyrion"]
["gandalf@email.com", "johnsnow@email.com", "tyrion@email.com"]
tyrion@email.com
```

Finally, let's execute some more lines of code:

```
dictionary.delete('John');
```

Let's also execute the following ones:

```
console.log(dictionary.keys());
console.log(dictionary.values());
console.log(dictionary.getItems());
```

The output will be as follows:

```
["Gandalf", "Tyrion"]
["gandalf@email.com", "tyrion@email.com"]
Object {Gandalf: "gandalf@email.com", Tyrion:
"tyrion@email.com"}
```

As we removed one element, the `dictionary` instance now contains only two elements. The highlighted line exemplifies how the `items` object is structured internally.

The hash table

In this section, you will learn about the `HashTable` class, also known as `HashMap`, a hash implementation of the `Dictionary` class.

Hashing consists of finding a value in a data structure in the shortest time possible. You learned in previous chapters that if we want to get a value from it (using a `get` method), we need to iterate through the structure until we find it. When we use a hash function, we already know which position the value is in, so we can simply retrieve it. A hash function is a function that, given a key, will return an address in the table where the value is.

For example, let's continue using the e-mail address book we used in the previous section. The hash function we will use is the most common one, called a lose lose hash function, in which we simply sum up the ASCII values of each character of the key length.

Name/Key	Hash Function	Hash Value	Hash Table	
Gandalf	71 + 97 + 110 + 100 + 97 + 108 + 102	685	[...]	
			[399]	johnsnow@email.com
John	74 + 111 + 104 + 110	399	[...]	
			[645]	tyrion@email.com
Tyrion	84 + 121 + 114 + 105 + 111 + 110	645	[...]	
			[685]	gandalf@email.com
			[...]	

Creating a hash table

We will use an array to represent our data structure to have one very similar to that which we used in the diagram in the previous topic.

As usual, let's start with the skeleton of our class via the following code:

```
function HashTable() {
  var table = [];
}
```

Next, we need to add some methods to our class. We will implement three basic methods for every class:

- `put(key, value)`: This adds a new item to the hash table (or it can also update it)
- `remove(key)`: This removes the value from the hash table using the key
- `get(key)`: This returns a specific value searched by the key

The first method that we will implement before we implement these three methods is the `hash` function. This is a private method of the `HashTable` class:

```
var loseloseHashCode = function (key) {
  var hash = 0;                              //{1}
  for (var i = 0; i < key.length; i++) {   //{2}
    hash += key.charCodeAt(i);              //{3}
  }
  return hash % 37;                         //{4}
};
```

Given a `key` parameter, we will generate a number based on the sum of each char ASCII value that composes `key`. So, first, we need a variable to store the sum (line {1}). Then, we will iterate through `key` (line {2}) and add the ASCII value of the corresponding character value from the ASCII table to the `hash` variable (to do so, we can use the `charCodeAt` method from the JavaScript `String` class line {3}). Finally, we will return this `hash` value. To work with lower numbers, we must use the rest of the division (`mod`) of the hash number using an arbitrary number (line {4}).

 For more information about ASCII, refer to
`http://www.asciitable.com/`.

Now that we have our `hash` function, we can implement the `put` method, as follows:

```
this.put = function (key, value) {
    var position = loseloseHashCode(key); //{5}
    console.log(position + ' - ' + key); //{6}
    table[position] = value; //{7}
};
```

First, for the given `key` parameter, we need to find a position in the table using the `hash` function we created (line {5}). For information purposes, we will log the position on the console (line {6}). We can remove this line from the code as it is not necessary. Then, all we have to do is add the `value` parameter to `position`, which we found using the `hash` function (line {7}).

Retrieving a value from the `HashTable` instance is also simple. We will implement the `get` method for this purpose, as follows:

```
this.get = function (key) {
    return table[loseloseHashCode(key)];
};
```

First, we will retrieve the position of the given `key` parameter using the `hash` function we created. This function will return the position of the value, and all we have to do is access this position from the `table` array and return this value.

The last method we will implement is the `remove` method, which is as follows:

```
this.remove = function(key){
    table[loseloseHashCode (key)] = undefined;
};
```

To remove an element of the `HashTable` instance, we simply need to access the desired position (which we can get using the `hash` function) and assign the `undefined` value to it.

For the `HashTable` class, we do not need to remove the position from the `table` array as we did for the `ArrayList` class. As the elements will be distributed throughout the array, some positions will not be occupied by any value, having the `undefined` value by default. We also cannot remove the position itself from the array (this will shift the other elements). Otherwise, next time we try to get or remove another existing element, the element will not be present in the position we get from the `hash` function.

Using the HashTable class

Let's test the `HashTable` class by executing some code:

```
var hash = new HashTable();
hash.put('Gandalf', 'gandalf@email.com');
hash.put('John', 'johnsnow@email.com');
hash.put('Tyrion', 'tyrion@email.com');
```

When we execute the previous code, we get the following output on the console:

```
19 - Gandalf
29 - John
16 - Tyrion
```

The following diagram represents the `HashTable` data structure with these three elements in it:

Name/Key	Hash Value	Hash Table	
		[...]	
Gandalf	19	[16]	tyrion@email.com
		[...]	
John	29	[19]	gandalf@email.com
		[...]	
Tyrion	16	[29]	johnsnow@email.com
		[...]	

Now, let's test the `get` method by executing the following code:

```
console.log(hash.get('Gandalf'));
console.log(hash.get('Loiane'));
```

We will have the following output:

```
gandalf@email.com
undefined
```

As `Gandalf` is a key that exists in `HashTable`, the `get` method will return its value. As `Loiane` is not an existing key, when we try to access its position in the array (a position generated by the `hash` function), its value will be `undefined` (nonexistent).

Next, let's try to remove `Gandalf` from `HashTable`, as follows:

```
hash.remove('Gandalf');
console.log(hash.get('Gandalf'));
```

The `hash.get('Gandalf')` method will give `undefined` as the output on the console as `Gandalf` no longer exists in the table.

Hash table versus hash set

A hash table is the same thing as a hash map. We have covered this data structure in this chapter.

In some programming languages, we also have the hash set implementation. The hash set data structure consists of a set, but to insert, remove, or get elements, we use a `hash` function. We can reuse all the code we implemented in this chapter for a hash set; the difference is that instead of adding a key-value pair, we will insert only the value, not the key. For example, we could use a hash set to store all the English words (without their definition). Similar to set, the hash set also stores only unique values, not repeated ones.

Handling collisions between hash tables

Sometimes, different keys can have the same hash value. We will call it a collision as we will try to set different values to the same position of the `HashTable` instance. For example, let's take a look at what we get in the output with the following code:

```
var hash = new HashTable();
hash.put('Gandalf', 'gandalf@email.com');
hash.put('John', 'johnsnow@email.com');
```

```
hash.put('Tyrion', 'tyrion@email.com');
hash.put('Aaron', 'aaron@email.com');
hash.put('Donnie', 'donnie@email.com');
hash.put('Ana', 'ana@email.com');
hash.put('Jonathan', 'jonathan@email.com');
hash.put('Jamie', 'jamie@email.com');
hash.put('Sue', 'sue@email.com');
hash.put('Mindy', 'mindy@email.com');
hash.put('Paul', 'paul@email.com');
hash.put('Nathan', 'nathan@email.com');
```

The following will be the output:

```
19 - Gandalf
29 - John
16 - Tyrion
16 - Aaron
13 - Donnie
13 - Ana
5 - Jonathan
5 - Jamie
5 - Sue
32 - Mindy
32 - Paul
10 - Nathan
```

 Note that `Tyrion` has the same hash value as `Aaron` (16). `Donnie` has the same hash value as `Ana` (13). `Jonathan`, `Jamie`, and `Sue` (5) have the same hash value as well, and so do `Mindy` and `Paul` (32).

What will happen to the `HashTable` instance? Which values do we have inside it after executing the previous code?

To help us find out, let's implement a `helper` method called `print`, which will log on to the console the values in the `HashTable` instance, as follows:

```
this.print = function () {
  for (var i = 0; i < table.length; ++i) {   //{1}
    if (table[i] !== undefined) {            //{2}
      console.log(i + ": " + table[i]); //{3}
    }
  }
};
```

First, we will iterate through all the elements of the array (line {1}). For the positions that have a value (line {2}), we will log the position and its value on the console (line {3}).

Now, let's use this method via the following code:

```
hash.print();
```

We will have the following output on the console:

```
5: sue@email.com
10: nathan@email.com
13: ana@email.com
16: aaron@email.com
19: gandalf@email.com
29: johnsnow@email.com
32: paul@email.com
```

Jonathan, Jamie, and Sue have the same hash value—that is, 5. As Sue was the last one to be added, Sue will be the one to occupy position 5 of HashTable. First, Jonathan will occupy it, then Jamie will overwrite it, and Sue will overwrite it again. The same will happen to the other elements that have a collision.

The idea of using a data structure to store all these values is obviously not to lose these values; it is to keep them all, somehow. For this reason, we need to handle this situation when it happens. There are a few techniques to handle collisions: separate chaining, linear probing, and double hashing. We will cover the first two in this book.

Separate chaining

The **separate chaining** technique consists of creating a linked list for each position of the table and storing the elements in it. It is the simplest technique to handle collisions; however, it requires additional memory outside the HashTable instance.

For example, if we use separate chaining in the code we used to do some testing in the previous topic, this would be the output:

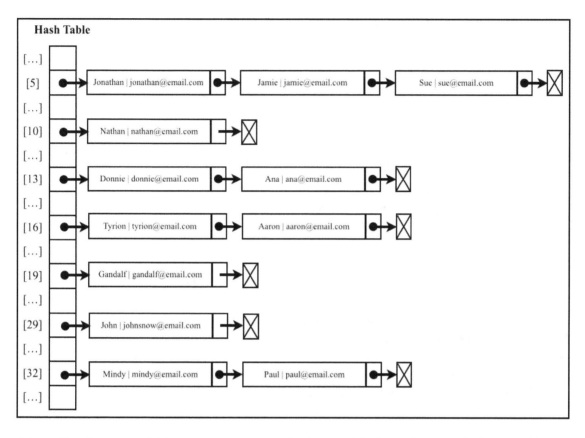

At position **5**, we would have a `LinkedList` instance with three elements in it; at positions **13**, **16**, and **32**, we would have `LinkedList` instances with two elements in it, and at positions **10**, **19**, and **29**, we would have `LinkedList` instances with a single element in it.

For separate chaining and linear probing, we only need to override three methods: `put`, `get`, and `remove`. These three methods will be different in each different technique we decide to implement.

To help us implement a `HashTable` instance using the separate chaining technique, we will need a new `helper` class to represent the element we will add to the `LinkedList` instance. We will call it the `ValuePair` class (declared inside the `HashTable` class), as follows:

```
var ValuePair = function(key, value){
  this.key = key;
  this.value = value;
```

```
    this.toString = function() {
      return '[' + this.key + ' - ' + this.value + ']';
    }
  };
```

This class will simply store `key` and `value` in an `Object` instance. We will also override the `toString` method to help us later in outputting the results on the browser console.

The put method

Let's implement the first method, the `put` method, as follows:

```
  this.put = function(key, value){
    var position = loseloseHashCode(key);

    if (table[position] == undefined) { //{1}
      table[position] = new LinkedList();
    }
    table[position].append(new ValuePair(key, value)); //{2}
  };
```

In this method, we will verify that the position we are trying to add the element to already has something in it (line {1}). If this is the first time we are adding an element in this position, we will initialize it with an instance of the `LinkedList` class (which you learned about in `Chapter 5`, *Linked Lists*). Then, we will add the `ValuePair` instance (`key` and `value`) to the `LinkedList` instance using the `append` method (line {2}) we implemented in `Chapter 5`, *Linked Lists*.

The get method

Next, we will implement the `get` method to retrieve a specified value via the following code:

```
  this.get = function(key) {
    var position = loseloseHashCode(key);

    if (table[position] !== undefined){ //{3}

      //iterate linked list to find key/value
      var current = table[position].getHead(); //{4}

      while(current.next){ //{5}
        if (current.element.key === key){ //{6}
          return current.element.value; //{7}
        }
```

```
      current = current.next; //{8}
    }

    //check in case first or last element
    if (current.element.key === key){ //{9}
      return current.element.value;
    }
  }
  return undefined; //{10}
};
```

The first verification we need to do is to check whether there is any element at the desired position (line {3}). If not, we return `undefined` to represent that the value was not found in the `HashTable` instance (line {10}). If there is a value in the position, we know that the instance is a `LinkedList` instance. Now, all we have to do is search for the element we want to find by iterating through the list. To do so, we need to get the reference of the head of the list (line {4}), and then we can iterate through it until we find the end of the list (line {5}, `current.next`, will be `null`).

The `Node` list contains the `next` pointer and the `element` attribute. The `element` attribute is an instance of `ValuePair`, so it has the `value` and `key` attributes. To access the `key` attribute of the `Node` list, we can use `current.element.key` and compare it to see whether it is `key` we are searching for (line {6}). (This is the reason we are using the `helper` class `ValuePair` to store the elements. We cannot simply store the value itself, as we would not know which value corresponds to a particular key.) If it is the same `key` attribute, we must return the `Node` value (line {7}), and if not, we should continue iterating through the list by going to the next element of the list (line {8}).

If the element we are looking for is the first or last element of the list, it will not go inside the `while` loop. For this reason, we also need to handle this special case in line {9}.

The remove method

Removing an element from the `HashTable` instance using the separate chaining technique is a little bit different from the `remove` method we implemented earlier in this chapter. Now that we are using `LinkedList`, we need to remove the element from `LinkedList`. Let's take a look at the `remove` method implementation:

```
this.remove = function(key){
  var position = loseloseHashCode(key);

  if (table[position] !== undefined){

    var current = table[position].getHead();
```

```
      while(current.next){
        if (current.element.key === key){ //{11}
          table[position].remove(current.element); //{12}
          if (table[position].isEmpty()){ //{13}
            table[position] = undefined; //{14}
          }
          return true; //{15}
        }
        current = current.next;
      }

      //check in case first or last element
      if (current.element.key === key){ //{16}
        table[position].remove(current.element);
        if (table[position].isEmpty()){
          table[position] = undefined;
        }
        return true;
      }
    }

  return false; //{17}
};
```

In the `remove` method, we will do the same thing we did in the `get` method to find the element we are looking for. When iterating through the `LinkedList` instance, if the `current` element in the list is the element we are looking for (line {11}), we will use the `remove` method to remove it from `LinkedList` (line {12}). Then, we will perform an extra validation: if the list is empty (line {13}, there are no elements in it anymore), we will set the table `position` as `undefined` (line {14}), so we can skip this position whenever we look for an element or try to print its contents. At last, we will return `true` to indicate that the element was removed (line {15}), or we will return `false` at the end to indicate that the element was not present in `HashTable` (line {17}). Also, we need to handle the special case of the first or last element (line {16}), as we did for the `get` method.

Overwriting these three methods, we have a `HashMap` instance with a separate chaining technique to handle collisions.

Linear probing

Another technique of collision resolution is linear probing. When we try to add a new element, if the position index is already occupied, then we will try index +1. If index +1 is occupied, then we will try index + 2, and so on.

The put method

Let's go ahead and implement the three methods we need to overwrite. The first one will be the put method, as follows:

```
this.put = function(key, value){
  var position = loseloseHashCode(key); // {1}

  if (table[position] == undefined) { // {2}
    table[position] = new ValuePair(key, value); // {3}
  } else {
    var index = ++position; // {4}
    while (table[index] != undefined){ // {5}
      index++; // {6}
    }
    table[index] = new ValuePair(key, value); // {7}
  }
};
```

As usual, we will start by getting the position generated by the hash function (line {1}). Next, we will verify that the position has an element in it (if it is already occupied, it will be line {2}). If not, we will add the element to it (line {3}, an instance of the ValuePair class).

If the position is already occupied, we need to find the next position that is not (position is undefined), so we will create an index variable and assign position + 1 to it (line {4}, the increment operator ++ before the variable will increment the variable first and then assign it to index). Then, we will verify whether the position is occupied (line {5}), and if it is, we will increment index (line {6}) until we find a position that is not occupied. Then, all we have to do is assign the value we want to this position (line {7}).

In some languages, we need to define the size of the array. One of the concerns of using linear probing is when the array is out of available positions. We do not need to worry about this in JavaScript as we do not need to define a size for the array, and it can grow as needed automatically. This is part of JavaScript's built-in functionality.

If we run the inserts from the *Handling collisions* section again, this will be the result for the hash table using linear probing:

Hash Table	
[...]	
[5]	Jonathan | jonathan@email.com
[6]	Jamie | jamie@email.com
[7]	Sue | sue@email.com
[...]	
[10]	Nathan | nathan@email.com
[...]	
[13]	Donnie | donnie@email.com
[14]	Ana | ana@email.com
[...]	
[16]	Tyrion | tyrion@email.com
[17]	Aaron | aaron@email.com
[18]	
[19]	Gandalf | gandalf@email.com
[...]	
[29]	John | johnsnow@email.com
[...]	

Let's simulate the insertions in the hash table:

1. We will try to insert **Gandalf**. The hash value is **19**, and as the hash table was just created, position **19** is empty. So, we can insert the name here.
2. We will try to insert **John** at position **29**. It is also empty, so we can insert the name.
3. We will try to insert **Tyrion** at position **16**. It is empty, so we can insert the name.

4. We will try to insert **Aaron**, which also has a hash value of **16**. Position **16** is already occupied by **Tyrion**, so we need to go to *position + 1* (16 +1). Position **17** is free, so we can insert **Aaron** at **17**.

5. Next, we will try to insert **Donnie** at position **13**. It is empty, so we can insert it.

6. We will try to insert **Ana** also at position **13**, but this position is occupied. So we try position **14**, which is empty; so, we can insert the name here.

7. Next, we will insert **Jonathan** at position **5**, which is empty; so, we can insert the name.

8. We will try to insert **Jamie** at position **5**, but this position is occupied. So, we will go to position **6**, which is empty, and we can insert the name.

9. We will try to insert **Sue** at position **5** as well, but this is occupied. So, we will go to position **6**, which is also occupied. Then, we will go to position **7**, which is empty; so, we can insert the name, and so on.

The get method

Now that we have added our elements, let's implement the `get` function so that we can retrieve their values, as follows:

```
this.get = function(key) {
  var position = loseloseHashCode(key);

  if (table[position] !== undefined){ //{8}
    if (table[position].key === key) { //{9}
      return table[position].value; //{10}
    } else {
      var index = ++position;
      while (table[index] === undefined
      || table[index].key !== key){ //{11}
        index++;
      }
      if (table[index].key === key) { //{12}
        return table[index].value; //{13}
      }
    }
  }
  return undefined; //{14}
};
```

To retrieve a key's value, we first need to verify that the key exists (line {8}). If it does not exist, it means that the value is not in the hash table, so we can return `undefined` (line {14}). If it does exist, we need to check whether the value we are looking for is the one at the specified position (line {9}). If positive, we will simply return its value (line {10}).

If not, we will continue searching the following positions in the `HashTable` instance until we find a position that contains an element, and this element's key matches the key we are searching for (line {11}). Then, we will verify that the item is the one we want (line {12}, just to make sure), and then we will return its value (line {13}).

This is the reason we will continue using the `ValuePair` class to represent the `HashTable` element, because we do not know at which position the element will actually be.

The remove method

The `remove` method is exactly the same as the `get` method. The difference will be in lines {10} and {13}, which will be replaced with the following code:

```
table[index] = undefined;
```

To remove an element, we will simply assign the value `undefined` to represent that the position is no longer occupied and that it is free to receive a new element if needed.

Creating better hash functions

The lose lose hash function we implemented is not a good hash function, as we have concluded (too many collisions). We would have multiple collisions if we use this function. A good hash function is composed of certain factors: time to insert and retrieve an element (performance) and also a low probability of collisions. We can find several different implementations on the Internet, or we can create our own.

Another simple hash function that we can implement and which is better than the lose lose hash function is **djb2**, which is as follows:

```
var djb2HashCode = function (key) {
  var hash = 5381; //{1}
  for (var i = 0; i < key.length; i++) { //{2}
    hash = hash * 33 + key.charCodeAt(i); //{3}
  }
  return hash % 1013; //{4}
};
```

This consists of initializing the `hash` variable with a prime number (line {1}, most implementations use `5381`); then, we will iterate the `key` parameter (line {2}), multiply the `hash` value by `33` (used as a magical number), and sum it with the ASCII value of the character (line {3}).

Finally, we will use the rest of the division of the total by another random prime number (greater than the size we think the `HashTable` instance can have in our case; let's consider 1000 as the size).

If we run the inserts from the *Handling collisions* section again, this will be the result we will get using `djb2HashCode` instead of `loseloseHashCode`:

```
798 - Gandalf
838 - John
624 - Tyrion
215 - Aaron
278 - Donnie
925 - Ana
288 - Jonathan
962 - Jamie
502 - Sue
804 - Mindy
54 - Paul
223 - Nathan
```

No collisions!

This is not the best hash function there is, but it is one of the most highly recommended hash functions by the community.

> There are also a few techniques to create a hash function for numeric keys. You can find a list and implementations at `http://goo.gl/VtdN2x`.

The ES6 Map class

ECMAScript 2015 introduced a `Map` class as part of the JavaScript API. We developed our `Dictionary` class based on the **ES6** `Map` class.

> You can take a look at the details of the ECMAScript 6 `Map` class implementation at `https://developer.mozilla.org/en-US/docs/Web/JavaScript/Reference/Global_Objects/Map` (or `http://goo.gl/dm8VP6`).

Now, let's consider how we can use the native `Map` class, as well.

Let's use the same examples we used to test our Dictionary class:

```
var map = new Map();

map.set('Gandalf', 'gandalf@email.com');
map.set('John', 'johnsnow@email.com');
map.set('Tyrion', 'tyrion@email.com');

console.log(map.has('Gandalf'));    //outputs true
console.log(map.size);    //outputs 3
console.log(map.keys()); //outputs ["Gandalf", "John", "Tyrion"]
console.log(map.values()); //outputs ["gandalf@email.com",
"johnsnow@email.com", "tyrion@email.com"]
console.log(map.get('Tyrion')); //outputs tyrion@email.com
```

The difference between our `Dictionary` class and the ES6 `Map` class is that the `values` and `keys` methods return an `Iterator` (which you learned in `Chapter 2, Arrays`) instead of the array with the values or the keys. Another difference is that we developed a `size` method to return the number of values the map is storing. The ES6 `Map` class has a property named `size`.

We can also call the `delete` method to remove an element from the map, as follows:

```
map.delete('John');
```

The `clear` method also resets the `map` data structure. This is the same functionality we implemented in the `Dictionary` class.

The ES6 WeakMap and WeakSet classes

Along with the two new data structures `Set` and `Map`, ES6 also introduced a weak type version of these classes: `WeakMap` and `WeakSet`.

Basically, the only difference between the `Map` or `Set` classes and their *Weak* versions are:

- The `WeakSet` or `WeakMap` classes do not have the `entries`, `keys`, and `values` methods
- It is only possible to use 0bjects as a key

The reason for creating and using these two classes is performance related. As WeakSet and WeakMap are weakly typed (using object as a key), there is no strong reference to the keys. This behavior allows the JavaScript garbage collector to clean an entire entry from the map or set.

Another advantage is that you can only retrieve a value if you have its key. As these classes do not have the iterator methods (entries, keys, and values), there is no way to retrieve a value unless you know what the key is. This confirms our choice in using the WeakMap class to encapsulate the private properties of the ES6 classes, as you learned in Chapter 3, *Stacks*.

The following is an example of what we can do with the WeakMap class:

```
var map = new WeakMap();

var ob1 = {name:'Gandalf'}, //{1}
    ob2 = {name:'John'},
    ob3 = {name:'Tyrion'};

map.set(ob1, 'gandalf@email.com'); //{2}
map.set(ob2, 'johnsnow@email.com');
map.set(ob3, 'tyrion@email.com');

console.log(map.has(ob1));  //{3} outputs true
console.log(map.get(ob3)); //{4} outputs tyrion@email.com
map.delete(ob2); //{5}
```

We can still use the set method of the WeakMap class. However, as it does not allow us to use String or any other primitive datatype (numeric, String, or Boolean values), we need to transform the name into an object (lines {1} and {2}).

To search value (line {3}), retrieve its value (line {4}), and also delete (line {5}), we need to pass the object created as a key.

The same logic is applied to the WeakSet class.

Summary

In this chapter, you learned about dictionaries and how to add, remove, and get elements among other methods. You also learned the difference between a dictionary and a set.

We covered hashing, how to create a hash table (or hash map) data structure, how to add, remove, and get elements, and also how to create hash functions. You learned how to handle collision in a hash table using two different techniques.

We also covered how to use the ES6 `Map` class and also the `WeakMap` and `WeakSet` classes.

In the next chapter, you will learn a new data structure called `tree`.

8
Trees

So far in this book, we have covered some sequential data structures. The first non-sequential data structure we covered in this book was the **Hash Table**. In this chapter, you will learn about another non-sequential data structure called a **tree**, which is very useful for storing information that needs to be found easily.

In this chapter, we will cover:

- Tree terminology
- Creating a tree data structure
- Traversing a tree
- Adding and removing nodes
- The AVL tree

The tree data structure

A tree is an abstract model of a hierarchical structure. The most common example of a tree in real life would be a family tree or a company organizational chart, as we can see in the following figure:

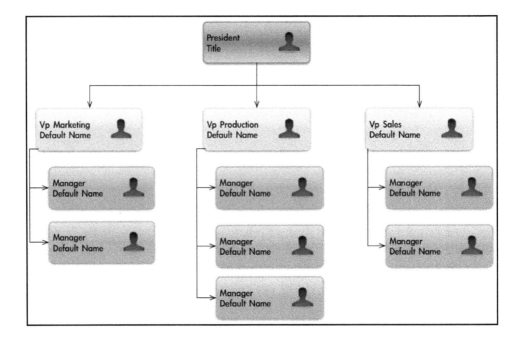

Tree terminology

A tree consists of nodes with a parent-child relationship. Each node has a parent (except for the first node at the top) and zero or more children, as in the following figure:

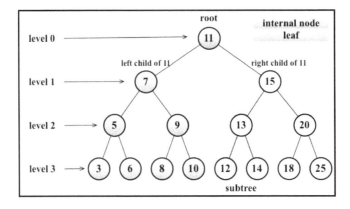

The top node of a tree is called the **root** (**11**). It is the node that does not have a parent. Each element of the tree is called a node. There are **internal nodes** and **external nodes**. An internal node is a node with at least one child (**7,5,9,15,13**, and **20** are internal nodes). A node that does not have children is called an external node or leaf (**3,6,8,10,12,14,18**, and **25** are leaves).

A node can have ancestors and descendants. The ancestors of a node (except the root) are parent, grandparent, great-grandparent, and so on. The descendants of a node are children (child), grandchildren (grandchild), great-grandchildren (great-grandchild), and so on. For example, node **5** has **7** and **11** as its ancestors and **3** and **6** as its descendants.

Another terminology used with trees is the subtree. A subtree consists of a node and its descendants. For example, the nodes **13**, **12**, and **14** constitute a subtree from the tree of the preceding diagram.

The depth of a node consists of the number of ancestors. For example, node **3** has a depth of 3 because it has three ancestors (**5,7**, and **11**).

The height of a tree consists of the maximum depth of any node. A tree can also be broken down into levels. The root is on **level 0**, its children are on **level 1**, and so on. The tree from the preceding diagram has a height of 3 (the maximum depth is 3, as shown in the preceding figure **level 3**).

Now that we know the most important terms related to trees, we can start learning more about trees.

The binary and binary search trees

A node in a binary tree has two children at most: one left child and one right child. This definition allows us to write more efficient algorithms to insert, search, and delete nodes to/from a tree. Binary trees are largely used in computer science.

A binary search tree is a binary tree, but it only allows you to store nodes with lesser values on the left-hand side and nodes with greater values on the right-hand side. The diagram in the previous topic exemplifies a binary search tree.

This will be the data structure that we will work on in this chapter.

Creating the BinarySearchTree class

Let's start by creating our `BinarySearchTree` class. First, let's declare its skeleton via the following code:

```
function BinarySearchTree() {

  var Node = function(key){ //{1}
    this.key = key;
    this.left = null;
    this.right = null;
  };

  var root = null; //{2}
}
```

The following diagram exemplifies how a **Binary Search Tree (BST)** is organized in terms of the data structure:

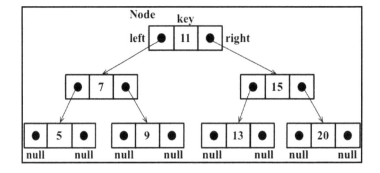

Just as in linked lists, we will work with pointers again to represent the connection between the nodes (called **edges** in tree terminology). When we worked with double linked lists, each node had two pointers: one to indicate the next node and another one to indicate the previous node. Working with trees, we will use the same approach (we will also work with two pointers). However, one pointer will point to the left child, and the other one will point to the right child. For this reason, we will declare a `Node` class that will represent each node of the tree (line {1}). A small detail that is worth noting is that instead of calling the node itself as a node or item, as we did in the previous chapters, we will call it a **key**. A key is how a tree node is known in tree terminology.

We will follow the same pattern we used in the `LinkedList` class (from `Chapter 5`, *Linked Lists*). This means that we will also declare a variable so that we can control the first node of the data structure. In the case of a tree, instead of the head, we have the root (line {2}).

Next, we need to implement some methods. The following are the methods we will implement in our tree class:

- `insert(key)`: This inserts a new key in the tree
- `search(key)`: This searches for the key in the tree and returns `true` if it exists and `false` if the node does not exist
- `inOrderTraverse`: This visits all nodes of the tree using in-order traverse
- `preOrderTraverse`: This visits all nodes of the tree using pre-order traverse
- `postOrderTraverse`: This visits all the nodes of the tree using post-order traverse
- `min`: This returns the minimum value/key in the tree
- `max`: This returns the maximum value/key in the tree
- `remove(key)`: This removes the key from the tree

We will implement each of these methods in the subsequent sections.

Inserting a key into a tree

The methods we will be implementing in this chapter are a little bit more complex than the ones we implemented in previous chapters. We will use a lot of recursion in our methods. If you are not familiar with recursion, refer to the *Recursion* section in Chapter 11, *Patterns of Algorithm*.

The following code is the first piece of the algorithm used to insert a new key in a tree:

```
this.insert = function(key){

  var newNode = new Node(key); //{1}

  if (root === null){ //{2}
    root = newNode;
  } else {
    insertNode(root,newNode); //{3}
  }
};
```

To insert a new node (or item) into a tree, there are three steps we need to follow.

The first step is to create the instance of the `Node` class that will represent the new node (line {1}). Because of its constructor properties, we only need to pass the value we want to add to the tree, and its `left` and `right` pointers will have a `null` value automatically.

Second, we need to verify that the insertion is a special case. A special case would be if the node we are trying to add is the first one in the tree (line {2}). If it is, all we have to do is point the root to this new node.

The third step is to add a node to a different position than the root. In this case, we will need a `helper` (line {3}) private function to help us to do this, which is declared as follows:

```
var insertNode = function(node, newNode){
  if (newNode.key < node.key){  //{4}
    if (node.left === null){    //{5}
      node.left = newNode;      //{6}
    } else {
      insertNode(node.left, newNode); //{7}
    }
  } else {
    if (node.right === null){   //{8}
      node.right = newNode;     //{9}
    } else {
      insertNode(node.right, newNode); //{10}
    }
  }
};
```

The `insertNode` function will help us find out where the correct place to insert a new node is. The following list describes what this function does:

- If the tree is not empty, we need to find a place to add a new node. For this reason, we will call the `insertNode` function by passing the root and the node as parameters (line {3}).
- If the node's key is less than the current node key (in this case, it is the root (line {4})), then we need to check the left child of the node. If there is no left node (line {5}), then we will insert the new node there (line {6}). If not, we need to descend a level in the tree by calling `insertNode` recursively (line {7}). In this case, the node we will compare next time will be the left child of the current node.
- If the node's key is greater than the current node key and there is no right child (line {8}), then we will insert the new node there (line {9}). If not, we will also need to call the `insertNode` function recursively, but the new node to be compared will be the right child (line {10}).

Let's use an example so that we can understand this process better.

Consider the following scenario: we have a new tree, and we are trying to insert its first key. In this case, we will run the following code:

```
var tree = new BinarySearchTree();
tree.insert(11);
```

In this case, we will have a single node in our tree, and the root pointer will be pointing to it. The code that will be executed is in line {2} of our source code.

Now, let's consider that we already have the following tree:

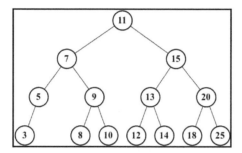

The code to create the tree seen in the preceding diagram is a continuation of the previous code (in which we inserted the 11 key), as follows:

```
tree.insert(7);
tree.insert(15);
tree.insert(5);
tree.insert(3);
tree.insert(9);
tree.insert(8);
tree.insert(10);
tree.insert(13);
tree.insert(12);
tree.insert(14);
tree.insert(20);
tree.insert(18);
tree.insert(25);
```

Also, we would like to insert a new key with the value 6, so we will execute the following code:

```
tree.insert(6);
```

The following steps will be executed:

1. The tree is not empty, so the code from line {3} will be executed. The code will call the `insertNode` method (`root`, `key[6]`).

2. The algorithm will check line {4} (`key[6] < root[11]` is `true`), then it will check line {5} (`node.left[7]` is not `null`), and finally, it will go to line {7} by calling `insertNode(node.left[7], key[6])`.

3. We will go inside the `insertNode` method again, but with different parameters. It will check line {4} again (`key[6] < node[7]` is `true`), then it will check line {5} (`node.left[5]` is not `null`), and finally, it will go to line {7} by calling `insertNode(node.left[5], key[6])`.

4. We will go once more inside the `insertNode` method. It will check line {4} again (`key[6] < node[5]` is `false`), then it will go to line {8} (`node.right` is `null`—node **5** does not have any right child descendents), and finally, it will execute line {9} by inserting key 6 as the right child of node **5**.

5. After this, the stack of method calls will pop up, and the execution will end.

This will be the result after key 6 is inserted in the tree:

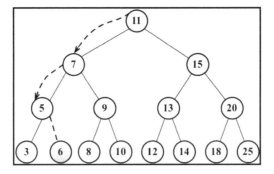

Tree traversal

Traversing (or walking) a tree is the process of visiting all the nodes of a tree and performing an operation at each node. However, how should we do this? Should we start from the top of the tree or from the bottom? From the left-hand or the right-hand side? There are three different approaches that can be used to visit all the nodes in a tree: in-order, pre-order, and post-order.

In the following sections, we will dive deeply into the uses and implementations of these three types of tree traversals.

In-order traversal

An **in-order** traversal visits all the nodes of a BST in an ascending order, meaning it will visit the nodes from the smallest to the largest. An application of in-order traversal would be to sort a tree. Let's check out its implementation:

```
this.inOrderTraverse = function(callback){
  inOrderTraverseNode(root, callback); //{1}
};
```

The `inOrderTraverse` method receives a `callback` function as a parameter. This function can be used to perform the action we want to execute when the node is visited (this is known as the visitor pattern; for more information on this, refer to `http://en.wikipedia.org/wiki/Visitor_pattern`). As most algorithms we are implementing for the BST are recursive, we will use a private `helper` function that will receive `node` and the `callback` function to help us with it (line {1}). Execute the following code:

```
var inOrderTraverseNode = function (node, callback) {
  if (node !== null) { //{2}
    inOrderTraverseNode(node.left, callback);   //{3}
    callback(node.key);                         //{4}
    inOrderTraverseNode(node.right, callback);  //{5}
  }
};
```

To traverse a tree using the in-order method, we need to first check whether the tree `node` that was passed as a parameter is `null` (this is the point where the recursion stops being executed, line {2}, which is the base case of the recursion algorithm).

Next, we will visit the left node (line {3}) by calling the same function recursively. Then, we will visit the root node (line {4}) by performing an action with it (`callback`), and then we will visit the right node (line {5}).

Let's try to execute this method using the tree from the previous topic as an example, as follows:

```
function printNode(value){ //{6}
  console.log(value);
}
tree.inOrderTraverse(printNode); //{7}
```

However, first, we need to create a callback function (line {6}). All we will do is print the node's value on the browser's console. Then, we can call the `inOrderTraverse` method by passing our callback function as a parameter (line {7}). When we execute this code, the following will be the output in the console (each number will be output on a different line):

```
3  5  6  7  8  9  10  11  12  13  14  15  18  20  25
```

The following diagram illustrates the path that the `inOrderTraverse` method followed:

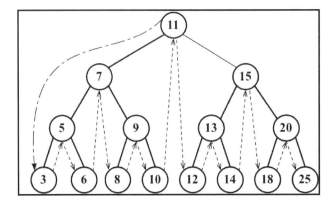

Pre-order traversal

A **pre-order** traversal visits the node prior to its descendants. An application of pre-order traversal could be to print a structured document.

Let's take a look at its implementation:

```
this.preOrderTraverse = function(callback){
    preOrderTraverseNode(root, callback);
};
```

The `preOrderTraverseNode` method implementation is as follows:

```
var preOrderTraverseNode = function (node, callback) {
  if (node !== null) {
    callback(node.key); //{1}
    preOrderTraverseNode(node.left, callback); //{2}
    preOrderTraverseNode(node.right, callback); //{3}
  }
};
```

The difference between the in-order and pre-order traversals is that the pre-order one visits the root node first (line {1}), then the left node (line {2}), and finally the right node (line {3}), while the in-order traversal executes the lines in the following order: lines {2}, {1}, and {3}.

The following will be the output in the console (each number will be output on a different line):

11 7 5 3 6 9 8 10 15 13 12 14 20 18 25

The following diagram illustrates the path followed by the `preOrderTraverse` method:

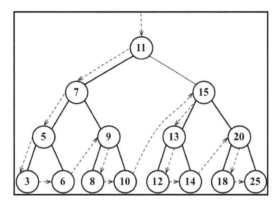

Post-order traversal

A **post-order** traversal visits the node after it visits its descendants. An application of post-order traversal could be computing the space used by a file in a directory and its subdirectories.

Let's take a look at its implementation:

```
this.postOrderTraverse = function(callback){
  postOrderTraverseNode(root, callback);
};
```

The `postOrderTraverseNode` implementation is as follows:

```
var postOrderTraverseNode = function (node, callback) {
  if (node !== null) {
    postOrderTraverseNode(node.left, callback);   //{1}
    postOrderTraverseNode(node.right, callback);  //{2}
```

```
    callback(node.key);                                   //{3}
   }
};
```

In this case, the post-order traversal will visit the left node (line {1}), then the right node (line {2}), and at last, the root node (line {3}).

As you can see, the algorithms for the in-order, pre-order, and post-order approaches are very similar; the only thing that changes is the order in which lines {1}, {2}, and {3} are executed in each method.

This will be the output in the console (each number will be output on a different line):

3 6 5 8 10 9 7 12 14 13 18 25 20 15 11

The following diagram illustrates the path the `postOrderTraverse` method followed:

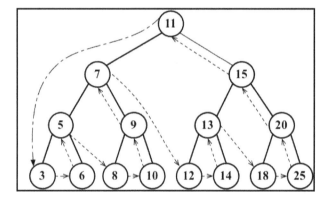

Searching for values in a tree

There are three types of searches that are usually performed in trees:

- Searching for minimum values
- Searching for maximum values
- Searching for a specific value

Let's take a look at each one.

Searching for minimum and maximum values

Let's use the following tree for our examples:

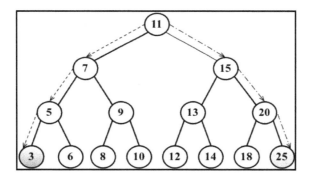

Just looking at the preceding figure, could you easily find the minimum and maximum values of the tree?

If you take a look at the leftmost node in the last level of the tree, you will find the value **3**, which is the lowest key from this tree. And if you take a look at the node that is furthest to the right (also in the last level of the tree), you will find the key **25**, which is the highest key in this tree. This information helps us a lot when implementing methods that will find the minimum and maximum nodes of the tree.

First, let's take a look at the method that will find the minimum key of the tree, as follows:

```
this.min = function() {
    return minNode(root);  //{1}
};
```

The `min` method will be the method exposed to the user. This method calls the `minNode` method (line {1}), as follows:

```
var minNode = function (node) {
    if (node){
        while (node && node.left !== null) { //{2}
            node = node.left;                //{3}
        }

        return node.key;
    }
    return null;   //{4}
};
```

The `minNode` method allows us to find the minimum key from any node of the tree. We can use it to find the minimum key from a subtree or from the tree itself. For this reason, we will call the `minNode` method by passing the tree root (line {1}) because we want to find the minimum key of the whole tree.

Inside the `minNode` method, we will traverse the `left` edge of the tree (lines {2} and {3}) until we find the node at the highest level of the tree (the leftmost end).

In a similar way, we also have the `max` method, which looks similar to the following:

```
this.max = function() {
    return maxNode(root);
};

var maxNode = function (node) {
    if (node){
        while (node && node.right !== null) { //{5}
            node = node.right;
        }

        return node.key;
    }
    return null;
};
```

To find the maximum key, we will traverse the right edge of the tree (line {5}) until we find the last node at the right-hand end of the tree.

So, for the minimum value, we will always go to the left-hand side of the tree, and for the maximum value, we will always navigate to the right-hand side of the tree.

Searching for a specific value

In previous chapters, we also implemented the `find`, `search`, and `get` methods to find a specific value in the data structure (which is similar to the `has` method we implemented in previous chapters). We will implement the `search` method for the BST as well. Let's take a look at its implementation:

```
this.search = function(key){
    return searchNode(root, key); //{1}
};

var searchNode = function(node, key){
```

```
  if (node === null){ //{2}
    return false;
  }
  if (key < node.key){ //{3}
    return searchNode(node.left, key); //{4}

  } else if (key > node.key){ //{5}
    return searchNode(node.right, key); //{6}

  } else {
    return true; //{7}
  }
};
```

The first thing we need to do is declare the `search` method. Following the pattern of other methods declared for BST, we will use a `helper` function to help us (line {1}).

The `searchNode` method can be used to find a specific key in the tree or any of its subtrees. This is the reason we will call this method in line {1} by passing the `root` tree as a parameter.

Before we start the algorithm, we will validate that the `node` passed as a parameter is valid (is not `null`). If it is, it means that the key was not found, and we will return `false`.

If the node is not `null`, we need to continue the verification. If the key we are looking for is lower than the current node (line {3}), then we will continue the search using the left child subtree (line {4}). If the value we are looking for is greater than the current node (line {5}), then we will continue the search from the right child of the current node (line {6}). Otherwise, it means that the key we are looking for is equal to the current node's key, and we will return `true` to indicate that we found the key (line {7}).

We can test this method using the following code:

```
console.log(tree.search(1) ? 'Key 1 found.' : 'Key 1 not found.');
console.log(tree.search(8) ? 'Key 8 found.' : 'Key 8 not found.');
```

It will output the following:

```
Value 1 not found.
Value 8 found.
```

Let's go into more detail on how the method was executed to find key 1:

1. We called the `searchNode` method, passing the root as a parameter (line {1}). The `node[root[11]]` is not `null` (line {2}), so we will go to line {3}.

2. The `key[1] < node[11]` is `true` (line {3}), so we will go to line {4} and call the `searchNode` method again, passing `node[7], key[1]` as a parameters.

3. The `node[7]` is not `null` (line {2}), so we will go to line {3}.

4. The `key[1] < node[7]` is `true` (line {3}), so we will go to line {4} and call the `searchNode` method again, passing `node[5], key[1]` as a parameters.

5. The `node[5]` is not `null` (line {2}), so we will go to line {3}.

6. The `key[1] < node[5]` is `true` (line {3}), so we will go to line {4} and call the `searchNode` method again, passing `node[3], key[1]` as a parameters.

7. The `node[3]` is not `null` (line {2}), so we will go to line {3}.

8. The `key[1] < node[3]` is `true` (line {3}), so we will go to line {4} and call the `searchNode` method again, passing `null, key[1]` as a parameters. The `null` was passed as a parameter because `node[3]` is a leaf (it does not have children, so the left child will have the value `null`).

9. The `node` is `null` (in line {2}, the `node` to search in this case is `null`), so we will return `false`.

10. After this, the stack of method calls will pop up, and the execution will end.

Let's do the same exercise to search value 8, as follows:

1. We called the `searchNode` method, passing `root` as a parameter (line {1}). The `node[root[11]]` is not `null` (line {2}), so we will go to line {3}.

2. The `key[8] < node[11]` is `true` (line {3}), so we will go to line {4} and call the `searchNode` method again, passing `node[7], key[8]` as a parameters.

3. The `node[7]` is not `null` (line {2}), so we will go to line {3}.

4. The `key[8] < node[7]` is `false` (line {3}), so we will go to line {5}.

5. The `key[8] > node[7]` is `true` (line {5}), so we will go to line {6} and call the `searchNode` method again, passing `node[9], key[8]` as a parameters.

6. The `node[9]` is not `null` (line {2}), so we will go to line {3}.

7. The `key[8] < node[9]` is `true` (line {3}), so we will go to line {4} and call the `searchNode` method again, passing `node[8], key[8]` as a parameters.

8. The `node[8]` is not `null` (line {2}), so we will go to line {3}.

9. The `key[8] < node[8]` is `false` (line {3}), so we will go to line {5}.

10. The `key[8] > node[8]` is `false` (line {5}), so we will go to line {7} and return `true` because `node[8]` is the key we were looking for.

11. After this, the stack of method calls will pop up, and the execution will end.

Removing a node

The next and final method we will implement for our BST is the `remove` method. This is the most complex method we will implement in this book. Let's start with the method that will be available to be called from a tree instance, as follows:

```
this.remove = function(key){ root = removeNode(root, key); //{1} };
```

This method receives the desired `key` to be removed, and it also calls `removeNode`, passing `root` and `key` to be removed as parameters (line {1}). One very important thing to note is that the root receives the return of the method `removeNode`. We will understand why in a second.

The complexity of the `removeNode` method is due to the different scenarios that we need to handle and also because it is recursive.

Let's take a look at the `removeNode` implementation, as follows:

```
var removeNode = function(node, key){

  if (node === null){ //{2}
    return null;
  }
  if (key < node.key){ //{3}
    node.left = removeNode(node.left, key); //{4}
    return node; //{5}

  } else if (key > node.key){ //{6}
    node.right = removeNode(node.right, key); //{7}
    return node; //{8}

  } else { // key is equal to node.key

    //case 1 - a leaf node
    if (node.left === null && node.right === null){ //{9}
      node = null; //{10}
      return node; //{11}
    }

    //case 2 - a node with only 1 child
    if (node.left === null){ //{12}
      node = node.right; //{13}
      return node; //{14}

    } else if (node.right === null){ //{15}
      node = node.left; //{16}
      return node; //{17}
```

```
        }

        //case 3 - a node with 2 children
        var aux = findMinNode(node.right); //{18}
        node.key = aux.key; //{19}
        node.right = removeNode(node.right, aux.key); //{20}
        return node; //{21}
    }
};
```

As a stop point we have line `{2}`. If the node we are analyzing is `null`, it means the key does not exist in the tree, and for this reason, we will return `null`.

Then, the first thing we need to do is to find the node in the tree. So, if the key we are looking for has a lower value than the current node (line `{3}`), then we will go to the next node at the left-hand side edge of the tree (line `{4}`). If the key is greater than the current node (line `{6}`), then we will go the next node at the right-hand side edge of the tree (line `{7}`).

If we find the key we are looking for (`key is equal to node.key`), then we will have three different scenarios to handle.

The `findMinNode` function is presented as follows:

```
var findMinNode = function(node){
  while (node && node.left !== null) {
    node = node.left;
  }
  return node;
};
```

Removing a leaf node

The first scenario is a leaf node that does not have a left or right child line `{9}`. In this case, all we have to do is get rid of this node by assigning `null` to it (line `{9}`). However, as you learned during the implementation of linked lists, we know that assigning `null` to the node is not enough, and we also need to take care of the pointers. In this case, the node does not have any children, but it has a parent node. We need to assign `null` to its parent node, and this can be done by returning `null` (line `{11}`).

As the node already has the value `null`, the parent pointer to the node will receive this value as well. And this is the reason we are returning the node value as the return function. The parent node will always receive the value returned from the function. An alternative to this approach could be passing the parent and the node as a parameter of the method.

If we take a look back at the first lines of the code of this method, we will notice that we are updating the pointer values of the left and right pointers of the nodes in lines {4} and {7}, and we are also returning the updated node in lines {5} and {8}.

The following diagram exemplifies the removal of a leaf node:

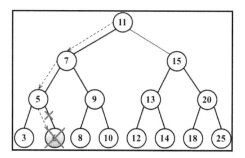

Removing a node with a left or right child

Now, let's take a look at the second scenario, which is a node that has a left or right child. In this case, we need to skip this node and assign the parent pointer to the child node.

If the node does not have a left child (line {12}), it means it has a right child. So, we will change the reference of the node to its right child (line {13}) and return the updated node (line {14}). We will do the same if the node does not have the right child (line {15}); we will update the node reference to its left child (line {16}) and return the updated value (line {17}).

The following diagram exemplifies the removal of a node with only a left or right child:

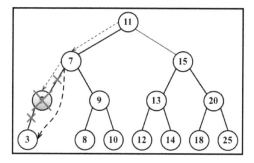

Removing a node with two children

Now comes the third scenario and the most complex one, which is the scenario where the node we are trying to remove has two children: the right and left one. To remove a node with children, there are four steps that need to be performed, as follows:

1. Once we find the node we want to remove, we need to find the minimum node from its right-hand side edge subtree (its successor line {18}).
2. Then, we will update the value of the node with the key of the minimum node from its right-hand side subtree (line {19}). With this action, we are replacing the key of the node, which means it was removed.
3. However, now we have two nodes in the tree with the same key, and this cannot happen. What we need to do now is remove the minimum node from the right subtree as we moved it to the place of the removed node (line {20}).
4. Finally, we will return the updated node reference to its parent (line {21}).

The implementation of the `findMinNode` method is exactly the same as the `min` method. The only difference is that in the `min` method, we are returning only the key, and in the `findMinNode` method, we are returning the node.

The following diagram exemplifies the removal of a node with only a left child and a right child:

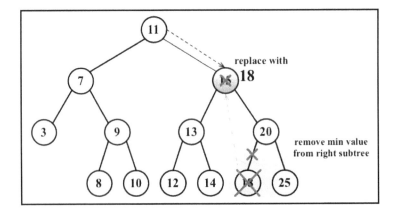

Self-balancing trees

Now that you know how to work with BST, you can dive into the study of trees if you want to.

BST has a problem: depending on how many nodes you add, one of the edges of the tree can be very deep, meaning a branch of the tree can have a high level and another branch can have a low level, as shown in the following diagram:

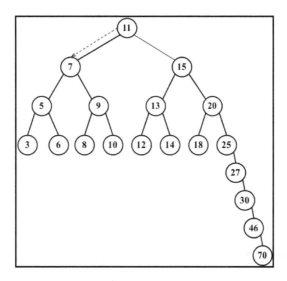

This can cause performance issues when adding, removing, and searching for a node on a particular edge of the tree. For this reason, there is a tree called the **Adelson-Velskii and Landi's tree** (**AVL tree**). The AVL tree is a self-balancing BST tree, which means the height of both the left and right subtrees of any node differs by 1 at most. You will learn more about the AVL tree in the next topic.

Adelson-Velskii and Landi's tree (AVL tree)

The AVL tree is a self-balancing tree, meaning the tree tries to self-balance whenever a node is added to it or removed from it. The height of the left or right subtree of any node (and any level) differs by 1 at most. This means the tree will try to become a complete tree whenever possible while adding or removing a node.

Inserting a node in the AVL tree

Inserting and removing nodes in an AVL tree works the same way as in BST. However, the difference in the AVL tree is that we will need to verify its **balance factor**, and if needed, we will apply the logic to self-balance the tree.

The following code inserts a new node in an ALV tree:

```
var insertNode = function(node, element) {
  if (node === null) {
    node = new Node(element);
  } else if (element < node.key) {
    node.left = insertNode(node.left, element);

    if (node.left !== null) {
      //verify if balancing is needed {1}
    }
  } else if (element > node.key) {
    node.right = insertNode(node.right, element);

    if (node.right !== null) {
      //verify if balancing is needed {2}
    }
  }
  return node;
};
```

However, whenever we insert a new node, we need to check whether the tree needs to be balanced (lines {1} and {2}).

Calculating the balance factor

In an AVL tree, for every node, we need to calculate the difference between the height of the right-hand side subtree (hr) and the left-hand side subtree (hl). The result of $hr - hl$ needs to be 0, 1, or -1. If the result is different from these values, it means the tree needs to be balanced. This concept is called the balance factor.

The following diagram exemplifies the balance factor of some trees (all trees are balanced):

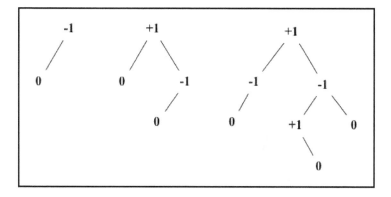

The code to calculate the height of a node is given as follows:

```
var heightNode = function(node) {
  if (node === null) {
    return -1;
  } else {
    return Math.max(heightNode(node.left),
    heightNode(node.right)) + 1;
  }
};
```

So, if we are inserting a new node in a left-hand side subtree, we will calculate the height, and if it is larger than 1 (meaning it is not -1, 0 or 1), then we will balance the left-hand side subtree, as follows:

```
//this code replaces line {1} from insertNode method
if ((heightNode(node.left) - heightNode(node.right)) > 1){
  // do rotations {3}
}
```

We will apply the same logic if we are inserting a node in a right-hand side subtree via the following code:

```
//this code replaces line {2} from insertNode method
if ((heightNode(node.right) - heightNode(node.left)) > 1){
  // do rotations {4}
}
```

AVL rotations

When inserting nodes to an AVL tree, there are two balancing processes that can be used: simple rotation or double rotation. Between simple rotation and double rotation, there are four scenarios:

- **Right-Right (RR)**: This is a single rotation to the left
- **Left-Left (LL)**: This is a single rotation to the right
- **Left-Right (LR)**: This is a double rotation to the right
- **Right-Left (RL)**: This is a double rotation to the left

Let's consider how each one works.

Right-Right (RR): A single rotation to the left

Consider the following diagram:

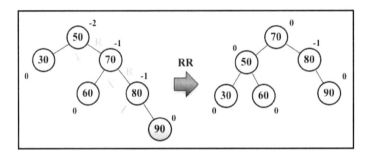

Suppose node **90** was the last one inserted in the AVL tree. This would make the tree unbalanced (node **50** –Y has height -2), so we would need to balance it. These are the steps we will perform to balance the tree:

- Node **X**, which is in the middle of the three nodes involved in the balancing (**X**, **Y**, and **Z**), will take place of the node **Y**, which has a balance factor of **-2** (line {1})
- Node **X**, the right-hand side subtree, will not be changed
- Node **X**, the left-hand side subtree (node **Z**), will be placed as the right-hand side subtree of node **Y** (line {2})
- Node **X**, the left-hand side child, will reference node **Y** (line {3})

The following code exemplifies this process:

```
var rotationRR = function(node) {
    var tmp = node.right;   //{1}
```

```
    node.right = tmp.left;  //{2}
    tmp.left = node;        //{3}
    return tmp;
};
```

Left-Left (LL): a single rotation to the right

Consider the following diagram:

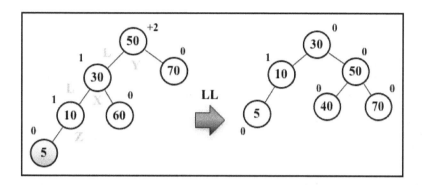

Suppose node **5** was the last one inserted in the AVL tree. This would make the tree unbalanced (node **50 –Y** has height **+2**), so we would need to balance it. These are the steps we will perform to balance the tree:

- Node **X**, which is in the middle of the three nodes involved in the balancing (**X**, **Y**, and **Z**), will take the place of node **Y**, which has a balance factor of **+2** (line {1})
- Node **X**, the left-hand side subtree, will not be changed
- Node **X**, the right-hand side subtree (node **Z**), will be placed as the left-hand side subtree of node **Y** (line {2})
- Node **X**, the right-hand side child, will reference node **Y** (line {3})

The following code exemplifies this process:

```
var rotationLL = function(node) {
  var tmp = node.left;    //{1}
  node.left = tmp.right;  //{2}
  tmp.right = node;       //{3}
  return tmp;
};
```

Left-Right (LR): a double rotation to the right

Consider the following diagram:

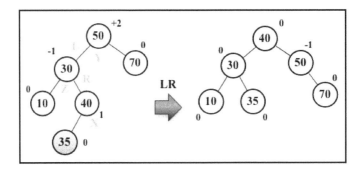

Suppose node **35** was the last one inserted in the AVL tree. This would make the tree unbalanced (node **50 –Y** has height **+2**), so we would need to balance it. These are the steps we will perform to balance the tree:

- Node **X** will take place of node **Y**, which has a balance factor of **+2**
- Node **X**, the right-hand side subtree (node **Z**), will be placed as the left-hand side subtree of node **Y**
- Node **X**, the left-hand side subtree, will be placed as the right-hand side subtree of node **Z**
- Node **X**, the right-hand side child, will reference node **Y**
- Node **X**, the left-hand side child, will reference node **Z**

So basically, we are doing an RR rotation first and then an LL rotation.

The following code exemplifies this process:

```
var rotationLR = function(node) {
  node.left = rotationRR(node.left);
  return rotationLL(node);
};
```

Right-Left (RL): a double rotation to the left

Consider the following diagram:

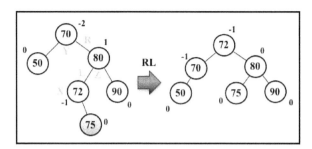

Suppose node **75** was the last one inserted in the AVL tree. This would make the tree unbalanced (node **70 –Y** has height **-2**), so we would need to balance it. These are the steps we will perform to balance the tree:

- Node **X** will take the place of node **Y**, which has a balance factor of **-2**
- Node **X**, the right-hand side subtree (node **Z**), will be placed as the left-hand side subtree of node **Z**
- Node **X**, the left-hand side subtree, will be placed as the right-hand side subtree of node **Y**
- Node **X**, the right-hand side child, will reference node **Y**
- Node **X**, the left-hand side child, will reference node **Z**

So basically, we are doing an LL rotation first and then an RR rotation.

The following code exemplifies this process:

```
var rotationRL = function(node) {
  node.right = rotationLL(node.right);
  return rotationRR(node);
};
```

Completing the insertNode method

After verifying that the tree needs to be balanced, we just need to apply the correct rotation for each case.

If we are inserting a node in the left-hand side subtree and the value of the node is smaller than the value of its left-hand side child, we will do an LL rotation. Otherwise, we will do an LR rotation. The code that exemplifies this process is given here:

```
//this code replaces line {1} from insertNode method
if ((heightNode(node.left) - heightNode(node.right)) > 1){
```

```
      // do rotations {3}
      if (element < node.left.key){
        node = rotationLL(node);
      } else {
        node = rotationLR(node);
      }
   }
```

If we are inserting a node in the right-hand side subtree and the value of the node is bigger than the value of its right-hand side child, we will do an RR rotation. Otherwise, we will do an RL rotation. The code that exemplifies this process is given as follows:

```
   //this code replaces line {2} from insertNode method
   if ((heightNode(node.right) - heightNode(node.left)) > 1){
     // do rotations {4}
     if (element > node.right.key){
       node = rotationRR(node);
     } else {
       node = rotationRL(node);
     }
   }
```

More about binary trees

Although the AVL tree is a self-balanced tree, sometimes its performance in inserting or removing nodes is not the best one. A better option would be using the **Red-Black** tree.

The Red-Black tree allows an efficient in-order traversal of its nodes (http://goo.gl/0xED8K). Although we will not cover this tree in this book, you can find its source code within the book's code bundle.

You should also check out the Heap tree (http://goo.gl/SF1hW6) if you want to learn more about trees.

Summary

In this chapter, we covered the algorithms to add, search, and remove items from a binary search tree, which is the basic tree data structure largely used in computer science. We covered three traversal approaches to visit all the nodes of a tree. You also learned how to develop a self-balanced tree named the AVL tree.

In the next chapter, we will study the basic concepts of graphs, which are also a nonlinear data structure.

9
Graphs

In this chapter, you will learn about another nonlinear data structure called graph. This will be the last data structure we will cover before diving into sorting and searching algorithms.

This chapter will cover a considerable part of the wonderful applications of graphs. Since this is a vast topic, we could write a book like this just to dive into the amazing world of graphs.

Graph terminology

A **graph** is an abstract model of a network structure. A graph is a set of **nodes** (or **vertices**) connected by **edges**. Learning about graphs is important because any binary relationship can be represented by a graph.

Any social network, such as Facebook, Twitter, and Google+, can be represented by a graph.

We can also use graphs to represent roads, flights, and communications, as shown in the following image:

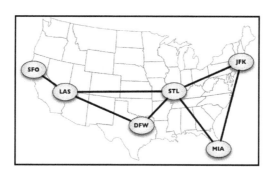

Let's learn more about the mathematical and technical concepts of graphs.

A graph $G = (V, E)$ is composed of:

- **V**: A set of vertices
- **E**: A set of edges connecting the vertices in V

The following diagram represents a graph:

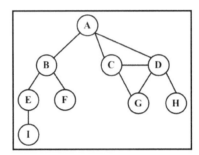

Let's cover some graph terminology before we start implementing any algorithms.

Vertices connected by an edge are called **adjacent vertices**. For example, **A** and **B** are adjacent, **A** and **D** are adjacent, **A** and **C** are adjacent, and **A** and **E** are *not* adjacent.

A degree of a vertex consists of the number of adjacent vertices. For example, **A** is connected to other three vertices, therefore, **A** has degree 3; **E** is connected to other two vertices, therefore, **E** has degree 2.

A path is a sequence of consecutive vertices, such as $v1, v2, ..., vk$, where vi and $vi+1$ are adjacent. Using the graph from the previous diagram as an example, we have the paths **A B E I** and **A C D G**, among others.

A simple path does not contain repeated vertices. As an example, we have the path **A D G**. A **cycle** is a simple path, except for the last vertex, which is the same as the first vertex: **A D C A** (back to **A**).

A graph is **acyclic** if it does not have cycles. A graph is connected if there is a path between every pair of vertices.

Directed and undirected graphs

Graphs can be **undirected** (where edges do not have a direction) or **directed** (**digraph**), where edges have a direction, as demonstrated here:

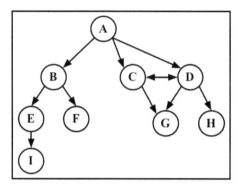

A graph is **strongly connected** if there is a path in both directions between every pair of vertices. For example, **C** and **D** are strongly connected, while **A** and **B** are not strongly connected.

Graphs can also be **unweighted** (as we have noted so far) or **weighted** (in which the edges have weights), as shown in the following diagram:

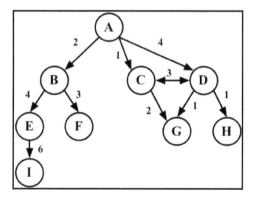

We can solve many problems in the computer science world using graphs, such as searching a graph for a specific vertex or searching for a specific edge, finding a path in the graph (from one vertex to another), finding the shortest path between two vertices, and cycle detection.

Representing a graph

There are a few ways in which we can represent graphs when it comes to data structures. There is no correct way of representing a graph among the existing possibilities. It depends on the type of problem you need to resolve and the type of graph as well.

The adjacency matrix

The most common implementation is the adjacency matrix. Each node is associated with an integer, which is the array index. We will represent the connectivity between vertices using a two-dimensional array, as *array[i][j]* = = = *1* if there is an edge from the node with index *i* to the node with index *j* or as *array[i][j]* = = = *0* otherwise, as demonstrated by the following diagram:

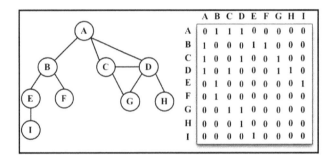

Graphs that are not strongly connected (**sparse graphs**) will be represented by a matrix with many zero entries in the adjacency matrix. This means we would waste space in the computer memory to represent edges that do not exist; for example, if we need to find the adjacent vertices of a given vertex, we will have to iterate through the whole row even if this vertex has only one adjacent vertex. Another reason this might not be a good representation is that the number of vertices in the graph may change, and a two-dimensional array is inflexible.

The adjacency list

We can use a dynamic data structure to represent graphs as well, called an **adjacency list**. This consists of a list of adjacent vertices for every vertex of the graph. There are a few different ways we can represent this data structure. To represent the list of adjacent vertices, we can use a list (array), a linked list, or even a hash map or dictionary. The following diagram exemplifies the adjacency list data structure:

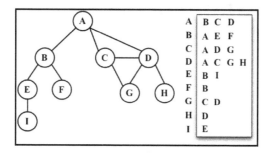

Both representations are very useful and have different properties (for example, finding out whether the vertices *v* and *w* are adjacent is faster using an adjacent matrix), although adjacency lists are probably better for most problems. We will use the adjacency list representation for the examples in this book.

The incidence matrix

We can also represent a graph using an **incidence matrix**. In an incidence matrix, each row of the matrix represents a vertex, and each column represents an edge. We will represent the connectivity between two objects using a two-dimensional array, as *array[v][e]* = = = *1* if the vertex *v* is incident upon edge *e* or as *array[v][e]* = = = *0* otherwise, as demonstrated in the following diagram:

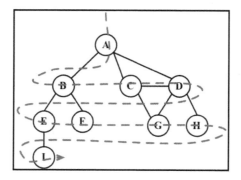

An incidence matrix is usually used to save space and memory when we have more edges than vertices.

Creating the Graph class

As usual, we will declare the skeleton of our class:

```
function Graph() {
  var vertices = []; //{1}
  var adjList = new Dictionary(); //{2}
}
```

We will use an array to store the names of all the vertices of the graph (line {1}), and we will use a dictionary (implemented in Chapter 7, *Dictionaries and Hashes*) to store the adjacent list (line {2}). The dictionary will use the name of the vertex as a key and the list of adjacent vertices as a value. Both the vertices array and the adjList dictionary are private attributes of our Graph class.

Next, we will implement two methods: one to add a new vertex to the graph (because when we instantiate the graph, it will create an empty one) and another method to add edges between the vertices. Let's implement the addVertex method first, as follows:

```
this.addVertex = function(v){
  vertices.push(v); //{3}
  adjList.set(v, []); //{4}
};
```

This method receives a vertex v as a parameter. We will add this vertex to the list of vertices (line {3}), and we will also initialize the adjacent list with an empty array by setting the dictionary value of the vertex v key with an empty array (line {4}).

Now, let's implement the addEdge method via the following code:

```
this.addEdge = function(v, w){
  adjList.get(v).push(w); //{5}
  adjList.get(w).push(v); //{6}
};
```

This method receives two vertices as parameters. First, we will add an edge from vertex v to vertex w (line {5}) by adding w to the adjacent list of v. If you want to implement a directed graph, line {5} is enough. As we are working with undirected graphs in most examples in this chapter, we also need to add an edge from w to v (line {6}).

 Note that we are only adding new elements to the array as we have already initialized it in line {4}.

Let's test this code, as follows:

```
var graph = new Graph();
var myVertices = ['A','B','C','D','E','F','G','H','I']; //{7}
for (var i=0; i<myVertices.length; i++){ //{8}
  graph.addVertex(myVertices[i]);
}
graph.addEdge('A', 'B'); //{9}
graph.addEdge('A', 'C');
graph.addEdge('A', 'D');
graph.addEdge('C', 'D');
graph.addEdge('C', 'G');
graph.addEdge('D', 'G');
graph.addEdge('D', 'H');
graph.addEdge('B', 'E');
graph.addEdge('B', 'F');
graph.addEdge('E', 'I');
```

To make our lives easier, let's create an array with all the vertices we want to add to our graph (line {7}). Then, we only need to iterate through the vertices array and add the values one by one to our graph (line {8}). Finally, we will add the desired edges (line {9}). This code will create the graph we used in the diagrams presented so far in this chapter.

To make our lives even easier, let's also implement the toString method for this Graph class so that we can output the graph on the console:

```
this.toString = function(){
  var s = '';
  for (var i=0; i<vertices.length; i++){ //{10}
    s += vertices[i] + ' -> ';
    var neighbors = adjList.get(vertices[i]); //{11}
    for (var j=0; j<neighbors.length; j++){ //{12}
      s += neighbors[j] + ' ';
    }
    s += '\n'; //{13}
  }
  return s;
};
```

We will build a string with the adjacent list representation. First, we will iterate the list of vertices arrays (line {10}) and add the name of the vertex to our string. Then, we will get the adjacent list for this vertex (line {11}), and we will also iterate it (line {12}) to get the name of the adjacent vertex and add it to our string. After we iterate the adjacent list, we will add a new line to our string (line {13}) so that we can see a pretty output on the console. Let's try this code:

```
console.log(graph.toString());
```

This will be the output:

```
A -> B C D
B -> A E F
C -> A D G
D -> A C G H
E -> B I
F -> B
G -> C D
H -> D
I -> E
```

A pretty adjacent list! From this output, we know that vertex A has the following adjacent vertices: B, C, and D.

Graph traversals

Similar to the tree data structure, we can also visit all the nodes of a graph. There are two algorithms that can be used to traverse a graph, called **breadth-first search** (**BFS**) and **depth-first search** (**DFS**). Traversing a graph can be used to find a specific vertex or a path between two vertices, to check whether the graph is connected, to check whether it contains cycles, and so on.

Before we implement the algorithms, let's try to better understand the idea of traversing a graph.

The idea of graph traversal algorithms is that we must track each vertex when we first visit it and keep track of which vertices have not yet been completely explored. For both traversal graph algorithms, we need to specify which will be the first vertex to be visited.

To completely explore a vertex, we need to look at each edge of this vertex. For each edge connected to a vertex that has not been visited yet, we will mark it as discovered and add it to the list of vertices to be visited.

In order to have efficient algorithms, we must visit each vertex twice at the most when each of its endpoints is explored. Every edge and vertex in the connected graph will be visited.

The BFS and DFS algorithms are basically the same with only one difference, which is the data structure used to store the list of vertices to be visited. Take a look at the following table:

Algorithm	Data structure	Description
DFS	Stack	By storing the vertices in a stack (learned in Chapter 3, *Stacks*), the vertices are explored by lurching along a path, visiting a new adjacent vertex if there is one available.
BFS	Queue	By storing the vertices in a queue (learned in Chapter 4, *Queues*), the oldest unexplored vertices are explored first.

When marking the vertices that we have already visited, we will use three colors to reflect their status:

- **White**: This represents that the vertex has not been visited
- **Grey**: This represents that the vertex has been visited but not explored
- **Black**: This represents that the vertex has been completely explored

This is why we must visit each vertex twice at the most, as mentioned earlier.

Breadth-first search (BFS)

The BFS algorithm starts traversing the graph from the first specified vertex and visits all its neighbors (adjacent vertices) first, one layer of the graph at a time. In other words, it visits the vertices first widely and then deeply, as demonstrated by the following diagram:

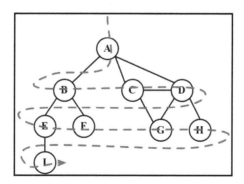

These are the steps followed by the BFS algorithm, starting at vertex *v*:

1. Create a queue *Q*.
2. Mark *v* as discovered (grey) and enqueue *v* into *Q*.
3. While *Q* is not empty, perform the following steps:
    1. Dequeue *u* from *Q*.
    2. Mark *u* as discovered (grey).
    3. Enqueue all the unvisited (white) neighbors *w* of *u*.
    4. Mark *u* as explored (black).

Let's implement the BFS algorithm as follows:

```
var initializeColor = function(){
  var color = [];
  for (var i=0; i<vertices.length; i++){
    color[vertices[i]] = 'white'; //{1}
  }
  return color;
};

this.bfs = function(v, callback){

  var color = initializeColor(), //{2}
  queue = new Queue();        //{3}
  queue.enqueue(v);              //{4}

  while (!queue.isEmpty()){        //{5}
    var u = queue.dequeue(),          //{6}
    neighbors = adjList.get(u); //{7}
    color[u] = 'grey';                        //{8}
    for (var i=0; i<neighbors.length; i++){ //{9}
      var w = neighbors[i];                //{10}
      if (color[w] === 'white'){            //{11}
        color[w] = 'grey';                  //{12}
        queue.enqueue(w);                   //{13}
      }
    }
    color[u] = 'black'; //{14}
    if (callback) {     //{15}
      callback(u);
    }
  }
};
```

For both BFS and DFS, we need to mark the vertices visited. To do so, we will use a `helper` array called `color`. As and when we start executing the BFS or DFS algorithms, all the vertices have the color `white` (line {1}), so we can create a `helper` function called `initializeColor`, which will do this for us for both the algorithms that we are implementing.

Let's dive into the BFS method implementation. The first thing we will do is use the `initializeColor` function to initialize the `color` array with the `white` color (line {2}). We also need to declare and create a `Queue` instance (line {3}) that will store the vertices that need to be visited and explored.

Following the steps we explained at the beginning of this chapter, the `bfs` method receives a vertex that will be used as the point of origin for our algorithm. As we need a starting point, we will `enqueue` this vertex into the queue (line {4}).

If the queue is not empty (line {5}), we will remove a vertex from the queue by dequeuing it (line {6}), and we will get its adjacency list that contains all its neighbors (line {7}). We will also mark this vertex as `grey`, meaning we have discovered it (but have not finished exploring it yet).

For each neighbor of u (line {9}), we will obtain its value (the name of the vertex, line {10}), and if it has not been visited yet (the color set to `white`, line {11}), we will mark that we have discovered it (the color is set to `grey`, line {12}) and will add this vertex to the queue (line {13}) so that it can be finished exploring when we `dequeue` it from the queue.

When we finish exploring the vertex and its adjacent vertices, we will mark it is as explored (the color is set to `black`, line {14}).

The `bfs` method we are implementing also receives a callback (we used a similar approach in *Chapter 8*, *Trees*, for tree traversals). This parameter is optional, and if we pass any `callback` function (line {15}), we will use it.

Let's test this algorithm by executing the following code:

```
function printNode(value){ //{16}
  console.log('Visited vertex: ' + value); //{17}
}
graph.bfs(myVertices[0], printNode); //{18}
```

First, we declared a `callback` function (line {16}) that will simply output in the browser's console or the name (line {17}) of the vertex that was completely explored by the algorithm. Then, we called the `bfs` method, passing the first vertex (`A` from the `myVertices` array that we declared at the beginning of this chapter) and the `callback` function. When we execute this code, the algorithm will output the following result in the browser's console:

```
Visited vertex: A
Visited vertex: B
Visited vertex: C
Visited vertex: D
Visited vertex: E
Visited vertex: F
Visited vertex: G
Visited vertex: H
Visited vertex: I
```

As you can note, the order of the vertices visited is the same as shown by the diagram at the beginning of this section.

Finding the shortest paths using BFS

So far, we have only demonstrated how the BFS algorithm works. We can use it for more things than just outputting the order of vertices visited. For example, how would we solve the following problem?

Given a graph G and the source vertex v, find the distance (in number of edges) from v to each vertex u Î G along the shortest path between v and u.

Given a vertex v, the BFS algorithm visits all the vertices with distance 1, then distance 2, and so on. So, we can use the BFS algorithm to solve this problem. We can modify the `bfs` method to return some information for us:

- The distances $d[u]$ from v to u
- The predecessors $pred[u]$, which are used to derive a shortest path from v to every other vertex u

Let' take a look at the implementation of an improved BFS method:

```
this.BFS = function(v){

  var color = initializeColor(),
  queue = new Queue(),
  d = [],     //{1}
  pred = []; //{2}
  queue.enqueue(v);

  for (var i=0; i<vertices.length; i++){ //{3}
    d[vertices[i]] = 0;                   //{4}
    pred[vertices[i]] = null;             //{5}
  }

  while (!queue.isEmpty()){
    var u = queue.dequeue(),
    neighbors = adjList.get(u);
    color[u] = 'grey';
    for (i=0; i<neighbors.length; i++){
      var w = neighbors[i];
      if (color[w] === 'white'){
        color[w] = 'grey';
        d[w] = d[u] + 1;                  //{6}
        pred[w] = u;                      //{7}
        queue.enqueue(w);
      }
    }
    color[u] = 'black';
  }
  return { //{8}
  distances: d,
  predecessors: pred
  };
};
```

What has changed in this version of the BFS method?

The source code of this chapter contains two bfs methods: bfs (the first one we implemented) and BFS (the improved one).

We also need to declare the d array (line {1}), which represents the distances, and the pred array (line {2}), which represents the predecessors. The next step would be initializing the d array with (zero-line {4}) and the pred array with null (line {5}) for every vertex of the graph (line {3}).

When we discover the neighbor w of a vertex u, we will set the predecessor value of w as u (line {7}) and also increment the distance (line {6}) between v and w by adding 1 and the distance of u (as u is a predecessor of w, we have the value of d[u] already).

At the end of the method, we can return an object with d and pred (line {8}).

Now, we can execute the BFS method again and store its return value in a variable, as follows:

```
var shortestPathA = graph.BFS(myVertices[0]);
console.log(shortestPathA);
```

As we executed the BFS method for the vertex A, this will be the output on the console:

```
distances: [A: 0, B: 1, C: 1, D: 1, E: 2, F: 2, G: 2, H: 2 , I: 3],
predecessors: [A: null, B: "A", C: "A", D: "A", E: "B", F: "B", G: "C", H:
"D", I: "E"]
```

This means that vertex A has a distance of 1 edge from vertices B, C, and D; a distance of 2 edges from vertices E, F, G, and H; and a distance of 3 edges from vertex I.

With the predecessor's array, we can build the path from vertex A to the other vertices using the following code:

```
var fromVertex = myVertices[0]; //{9}
for (var i=1; i<myVertices.length; i++){ //{10}
  var toVertex = myVertices[i], //{11}
  path = new Stack();        //{12}
  for (var v=toVertex; v!== fromVertex;
  v=shortestPathA.predecessors[v]) { //{13}
    path.push(v);                       //{14}
  }
  path.push(fromVertex);       //{15}
  var s = path.pop();          //{16}
  while (!path.isEmpty()){      //{17}
    s += ' - ' + path.pop(); //{18}
  }
  console.log(s); //{19}
}
```

We will use the vertex A as the source vertex (line {9}). For every other vertex (except vertex A, line {10}), we will calculate the path from vertex A to it. To do so, we will get the value of the toVertex method from the vertices array (line {11}), and we will create a stack to store the path values (line {12}).

Next, we will follow the path from `toVertex` to `fromVertex` (line {13}). The v variable will receive the value of its predecessor, and we will be able to take the same path backwards. We will add the v variable to the stack (line {14}). Finally, we will add the origin vertex to the stack as well (line {15}) to have the complete path.

After this, we will create an s string, and we will assign the origin vertex to it (this will be the last vertex added to the stack, so it is the first item to be popped out, line {16}). While the stack is not empty (line {17}), we will remove an item from the stack and concatenate it to the existing value of the s string (line {18}). Finally (line {19}), we simply output the path on the browser's console.

After executing the previous code, we will get the following output:

```
A - B
A - C
A - D
A - B - E
A - B - F
A - C - G
A - D - H
A - B - E - I
```

Here, we have the shortest path (in number of edges) from A to the other vertices of the graph.

Further study on the shortest paths algorithms

The graph we used in this example is not a weighted graph. If we want to calculate the shortest path in weighted graphs (for example, what the shortest path is between city A and city B, an algorithm used in GPS and Google Maps), BFS is not the indicated algorithm.

There is **Dijkstra's algorithm**, which solves the single-source shortest path problem, for example. The **Bellman-Ford algorithm** solves the single-source problem if edge weights are negative. The **A* search algorithm** provides the shortest path for a single pair of vertices using heuristics to try to speed up the search. The **Floyd-Warshall algorithm** provides the shortest path for all pairs of vertices.

As mentioned on the first page of this chapter, the subject of graphs is an extensive topic, and we have many solutions for the shortest path problem and its variations. However, before we start studying these other solutions, you need to learn the basic concepts of graphs, which we covered in this chapter. These other solutions will not be covered in the book, but you can have an adventure of your own exploring the amazing graph world.

Depth-first search (DFS)

The DFS algorithm will start traversing the graph from the first specified vertex, will follow a path until the last vertex of this path is visited, will then backtrack, and will finally follow the next path. In other words, it visits the vertices first deeply and then widely, as demonstrated in the following diagram:

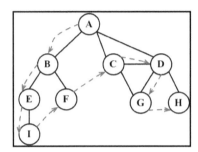

The DFS algorithm does not need a source vertex. In the DFS algorithm, for each unvisited vertex v in graph G, visit the vertex v.

To visit vertex v, perform the following:

1. Mark v as discovered (grey).
2. For all unvisited (white) neighbors w of v, visit vertex w and mark v as explored (black).

As you can note, the DFS steps are recursive, meaning the DFS algorithm uses a stack to store the calls (a stack created by the recursive calls).

Let's implement the DFS algorithm as follows:

```
this.dfs = function(callback){
  var color = initializeColor(); //{1}

  for (var i=0; i<vertices.length; i++){ //{2}
    if (color[vertices[i]] === 'white'){ //{3}
      dfsVisit(vertices[i], color, callback); //{4}
    }
  }
};

var dfsVisit = function(u, color, callback){
  color[u] = 'grey'; //{5}
  if (callback) {      //{6}
```

```
      callback(u);
  }
  var neighbors = adjList.get(u);          //{7}
  for (var i=0; i<neighbors.length; i++){  //{8}
    var w = neighbors[i];                  //{9}
    if (color[w] === 'white'){             //{10}
      dfsVisit(w, color, callback);        //{11}
    }
  }
  color[u] = 'black'; //{12}
};
```

The first thing we need to do is create and initialize the `color` array (line {1}) with the value `white` for each vertex of the graph. We did the same thing for the BFS algorithm. Then, for each nonvisited vertex (lines {2} and {3}) of the `Graph` instance, we will call the recursive private function `dfsVisit`, passing the vertex, the `color` array, and the `callback` function (line {4}).

Whenever we visit the u vertex, we will mark it as discovered (`grey`, line {5}). If there is a `callback` function (line {6}), we will execute it to output the vertex visited. Then, the next step is getting the list of neighbors of the vertex u (line {7}). For each unvisited (the color `white`, lines {10} and {8}) neighbor w (line {9}) of u, we will call the `dfsVisit` function, passing w and the other parameters (line {11}, add the vertex w to the stack so it can be visited next). At the end, after the vertex and its adjacent vertices are visited deeply, we will **backtrack**, meaning the vertex is completely explored and is marked `black` (line {12}).

Let's test the `dfs` method by executing the following code:

```
graph.dfs(printNode);
```

This will be its output:

```
Visited vertex: A
Visited vertex: B
Visited vertex: E
Visited vertex: I
Visited vertex: F
Visited vertex: C
Visited vertex: D
Visited vertex: G
Visited vertex: H
```

The order is the same as demonstrated by the diagram at the beginning of this section. The following diagram demonstrates the step-by-step process of the algorithm:

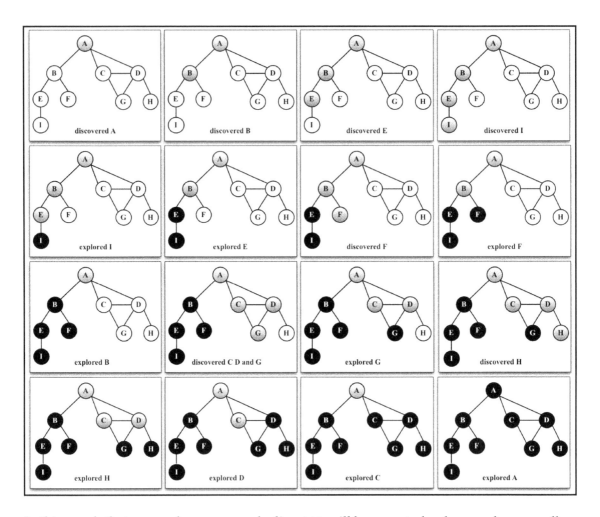

In this graph that we used as an example, line {4} will be executed only once, because all the other vertices have a path to the first one that is called the `dfsVisit` function (vertex A). If vertex B is the first one to call the function, then line {4} would be executed again for another vertex (for example, vertex A).

Exploring the DFS algorithm

So far, we have only demonstrated how the DFS algorithm works. We can use it for more functions than just outputting the order of vertices visited.

Given a graph G, the DFS algorithm traverses all the vertices of G and constructs a forest (a collection of **rooted trees**) together with a set of source vertices (**roots**) and outputs two arrays: the discovery time and finish explorer time. We can modify the dfs method to return some information for us, such as the following:

- The discovery time $d[u]$ of u
- The finish time $f[u]$ when u is marked black
- The predecessors $p[u]$ of u

Let's take a look at the implementation of the improved BFS method:

```
var time = 0; //{1}
this.DFS = function(){
  var color = initializeColor(), //{2}
  d = [],
  f = [],
  p = [];
  time = 0;

  for (var i=0; i<vertices.length; i++){ //{3}
    f[vertices[i]] = 0;
    d[vertices[i]] = 0;
    p[vertices[i]] = null;
  }
  for (i=0; i<vertices.length; i++){
    if (color[vertices[i]] === 'white'){
      DFSVisit(vertices[i], color, d, f, p);
    }
  }
  return {             //{4}
    discovery: d,
    finished: f,
    predecessors: p
  };
};

var DFSVisit = function(u, color, d, f, p){
  console.log('discovered ' + u);
  color[u] = 'grey';
  d[u] = ++time;       //{5}
  var neighbors = adjList.get(u);
```

```
    for (var i=0; i<neighbors.length; i++){
      var w = neighbors[i];
      if (color[w] === 'white'){
        p[w] = u;                          //{6}
        DFSVisit(w,color, d, f, p);
      }
    }
    color[u] = 'black';
    f[u] = ++time;        //{7}
    console.log('explored ' + u);
  };
```

As we want to track the time of discovery and the time when we finished exploring, we need to declare a variable to do this (line {1}). We cannot pass time as a parameter because variables that are not objects and cannot be passed as a reference to other JavaScript methods (passing a variable as a reference means that if this variable is modified inside the other method, the new values will also be reflected in the original variable). Next, we will declare the d, f, and p arrays, too (line {2}). We also need to initialize these arrays for each vertex of the graph (line {3}). At the end of the method, we will return these values (line {4}) so that we can work with them later.

When a vertex is first discovered, we will track its discovery time (line {5}). When it is discovered as an edge from u, we also keep track of its predecessor (line {6}). At the end, when the vertex is completely explored, we will track its finish time (line {7}).

What is the idea behind the DFS algorithm? The edges are explored out of the most recently discovered vertex *u*. Only the edges to nonvisited vertices are explored. When all the edges of *u* are explored, the algorithm backtracks to explore other edges where the vertex *u* was discovered. The process continues until we discover all the vertices that are reachable from the original source vertex. If any undiscovered vertices remain, we will repeat the process for a new source vertex. We will repeat the algorithm until all the vertices from the graph are explored.

There are two things that we need to check for the improved DFS algorithm:

- The time variable can only have values from one to two times the number of vertices of the graph $(2|V|)$
- For all the vertices u, d[u] < f[u] (meaning the discovered time needs to have a lower value than the finish time, which would in turn mean that all the vertices are explored)

With these two assumptions, we have the following rule:

```
1 ≤ d[u] < f[u] ≤ 2|V|
```

If we run the new DFS method for the same graph again, we will get the following discovery/finish time for each vertex of the graph:

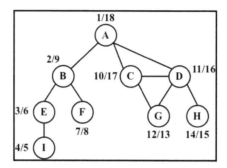

However, what can we do with this information? Let's consider this in the following section.

Topological sorting using DFS

Given the following graph, let's suppose each vertex is a task that you need to execute:

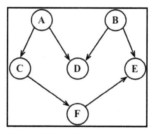

 This is a directed graph, meaning there is an order that the tasks need to be executed. For example, task **F** cannot be executed before task **A**. Note that the previous graph also does not have a cycle, meaning it is an acyclic graph. So, we can say that the previous graph is a **directed acyclic graph (DAG)**.

When we need to specify the order that some tasks or steps need to be executed in, it is called **topological sorting** (or **topsort** or even **toposort**). This problem is present in different scenarios of our lives. For example, when we start a computer science course, there is an order of disciplines that we can take before taking any other discipline (you cannot take Algorithms II before taking Algorithms I). When we are working in a development project, there are some steps that need to be executed in order; for example, first we need to get the requirements from the client, then develop what is asked for by the client, and then deliver the project. You cannot deliver the project and gather the requirements after.

Topological sorting can only be applied to DAGs. So, how can we use topological sorting using DFS? Let's execute the DFS algorithm for the diagram presented at the beginning of this topic:

```
graph = new Graph();
myVertices = ['A','B','C','D','E','F'];
for (i=0; i<myVertices.length; i++){
  graph.addVertex(myVertices[i]);
}
graph.addEdge('A', 'C');
graph.addEdge('A', 'D');
graph.addEdge('B', 'D');
graph.addEdge('B', 'E');
graph.addEdge('C', 'F');
graph.addEdge('F', 'E');
var result = graph.DFS();
```

This code will create the graph, apply the edges, execute the improved DFS algorithm, and store the results inside the `result` variable. The following diagram demonstrates the discovery and finish time of the graph after DFS is executed:

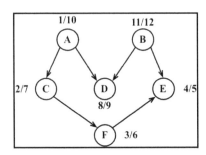

Now, all we have to do is sort the finishing time array and the decreasing order of finishing time, and we will have the topological sorting for the graph, as follows:

B – A – D – C – F – E

Note that the previous toposort result is only one of the possibilities. There might be different results if we modify the algorithm a little bit. For example, the following result is one of many other possibilities:

```
A - B - C - D - F - E
```

This could also be an acceptable result.

Shortest path algorithms

Given a map of streets, consider you want to get from point A to point B using the shortest path possible. We can use, as an example for this problem, the way from **Santa Monica Blvd** to **Hollywood Blvd** in Los Angeles, as demonstrated by the following image:

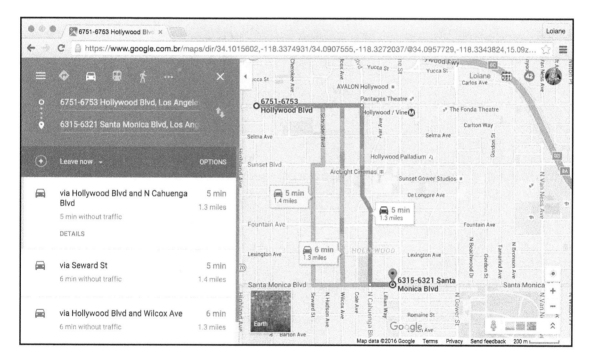

This is a very common problem in our lives, and we will use apps such as *Apple* or *Google Maps* and *Waze* to try to solve it, especially if you live in a big city. Of course, we also have other constraints involved, such as time or car traffic, but the original problem remains: how do we get from A to B using the shortest path?

We can use graphs to solve this problem for us, and the algorithm is called the shortest path. There are two algorithms that are very famous, which are **Dijkstra's algorithm** and **Floyd-Warshall algorithm**, which we will cover in the next topics.

Dijkstra's algorithm

Dijkstra's algorithm is a **greedy algorithm** (you will learn more about greedy algorithms in Chapter 11, *Patterns of Algorithm*) to calculate the shortest path between a single source and all the other sources, meaning we can use it to calculate the shortest path from a graph vertex to all the other vertices.

Consider the following graph:

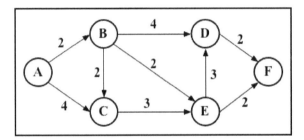

Let's take a look at how we can find the shortest path between the vertex **A** and all the other vertices. But first, we need to declare the adjacent matrix that represents the preceding graph, as follows:

```
var graph = [[0, 2, 4, 0, 0, 0],
             [0, 0, 1, 4, 2, 0],
             [0, 0, 0, 0, 3, 0],
             [0, 0, 0, 0, 0, 2],
             [0, 0, 0, 3, 0, 2],
             [0, 0, 0, 0, 0, 0]];
```

Now, let's consider how Dijkstra's algorithm works using the following code:

```
this.dijkstra = function(src){
  var dist = [], visited = [],
  length = this.graph.length;

  for (var i = 0; i < length; i++) { //{1}
    dist[i] = INF;
    visited[i] = false;
  }
```

```
    dist[src] = 0;  //{2}

    for (var i = 0; i < length-1; i++){  //{3}

      var u = minDistance(dist, visited);  //{4}

      visited[u] = true;  //{5}

      for (var v = 0; v < length; v++){
        if (!visited[v] &&
        this.graph[u][v]!=0 && dist[u] != INF &&
        dist[u]+this.graph[u][v] < dist[v]){  //{6}
          dist[v] = dist[u] + this.graph[u][v];  //{7}
        }
      }
    }
    return dist;  //{8}
  };
```

The following is a description of how the algorithm works:

- Line {1}: First, we need to initialize all distances (dist) as infinite (JavaScript max number INF = Number.MAX_SAFE_INTEGER) and visited[] as false
- Line {2}: Second, we will set the distance of the source vertex from itself as
- Line {3}: Then, we will find the shortest path for all vertices
- Line {4}: To do so, we need to select the minimum distance vertex from the set of vertices that is not processed yet
- Line {5}: We need to mark the selected vertex as visited so that we do not calculate twice
- Line {6}: In case a shortest path is found, we will set the new value for the shortest path (line {7})
- Line {8}: After all the vertices are processed, we will return the result containing the shortest path value from the vertex source (src) to all the other vertices of the graph

To calculate the minDistance between, we will search for the minimum value in the dist array, as follows, and return the array index that contains the minimum value:

```
  var minDistance = function(dist, visited){
    var min = INF, minIndex = -1;

    for (var v = 0; v < dist.length; v++){
      if (visited[v] == false && dist[v] <= min){
        min = dist[v];
```

```
        minIndex = v;
      }
    }
    return minIndex;
  };
```

If we execute the preceding algorithm for the graph we presented at the beginning of the topic, we will have the following output:

```
0       0
1       2
2       3
3       6
4       4
5       6
```

 It is also possible to modify the algorithm to return the value of the shortest path and also the path.

The Floyd-Warshall algorithm

The Floyd-Warshall algorithm is a dynamic programming algorithm (you will learn more about dynamic programming in Chapter 11, *Patterns of Algorithm*) to calculate all the shortest paths on a graph. With this algorithm, we can find the shortest path from all the sources to all the vertices.

The Floyd-Warshall algorithm is given as follows:

```
this.floydWarshall = function(){
  var dist = [], length = this.graph.length, i, j, k;

  for (i = 0; i < length; i++){ //{1}
    dist[i] = [];
    for (j = 0; j < length; j++){
      dist[i][j] = this.graph[i][j];
    }
  }

  for (k = 0; k < length; k++){       //{2}
    for (i = 0; i < length; i++){
      for (j = 0; j < length; j++){
        if (dist[i][k] + dist[k][j] < dist[i][j]){ //{3}
          dist[i][j] = dist[i][k] + dist[k][j]; //{4}
```

```
            }
         }
       }
     }
   return dist;
};
```

The following is the description of how the algorithm works:

- Line {1}: First, we will initiate the distance array with the value of the weight between each vertex as the minimum possible distance between i and j is the weight of these vertices
- Line {2}: Using vertices 0...k as intermediate points, the shortest path between i and j is given through k
- Line {3}: The formula used to calculate the shortest path between i and j through vertex k is given in line {3}
- Line {4}: If a new value for the shortest path is found, we will use it

The formula on line {3} is the heart of the Floyd-Warshall algorithm. If we execute the preceding algorithm to the graph we exemplified at the beginning of the topic, we will have the following output:

```
0    2    3    6    4    6
INF  0    1    4    2    4
INF  INF  0    6    3    5
INF  INF  INF  0    INF  2
INF  INF  INF  3    0    2
INF  INF  INF  INF  INF  0
```

Here, INF means that there is no shortest path between vertex i and j.

Another way of obtaining the same result would be to run Dijkstra's algorithm for each vertex of the graph.

Minimum spanning tree (MST)

The minimum spanning tree (**MST**) problem is very common in network designing. Imagine you have a business with several offices and want to connect the office's phone lines with each other with a minimum total cost to save money. Which is the best way of doing this?

This can also be applied to the island bridge problem. Consider you have an *n* number of islands and want to build bridges to connect each of them with a minimum cost.

Both the preceding problems can be solved with an MST algorithm, in which each office or island can be represented as a vertex of a graph, and the edges represent the cost. Here, we have an example of a graph where the thicker edges are a solution to MST:

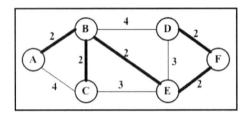

There are two main algorithms to find the minimal spanning trees: **Prim's algorithm** and **Kruskal's algorithm**, which you will learn in the following topics.

Prim's algorithm

Prim's algorithm is a greedy algorithm that finds an MST problem for a connected weighted undirected graph. It finds a subset of the edges that forms a tree that includes every vertex, where the total weight of all the edges in the tree is minimized.

Now, let's take a look at how Prim's algorithm works using the following code:

```
this.prim = function() {
    var parent = [], key = [], visited = [];
    length = this.graph.length, i;

    for (i = 0; i < length; i++){ //{1}
        key[i] = INF;
        visited[i] = false;
    }

    key[0] = 0;       //{1}
    parent[0] = -1;

    for (i = 0; i < length-1; i++) {   //{3}
        var u = minKey(key, visited); //{4}
        visited[u] = true;             //{5}

        for (var v = 0; v < length; v++){
            if (this.graph[u][v] && visited[v] == false
```

```
          && this.graph[u][v] <  key[v]){ //{6}
          parent[v]  = u;                 //{7}
          key[v] = this.graph[u][v]; //{8}
          }
      }
   }
   return parent; //{9}
};
```

The following is a description of how the algorithm works:

- Line {1}: First, we need to initialize all the `keys` vertices as infinite (JavaScript max number INF = `Number.MAX_SAFE_INTEGER`) and `visited[]` as `false`
- Line {2}: Second, we will set the first key as so that this vertex is picked as the first vertex and `parent[0] = -1` because the first node is always the root of MST
- Line {3}: Then, we will find MST for all vertices
- Line {4}: To do so, we need to select the minimum key vertex from the set of vertices that was not processed yet (the same function as we used in Dijkstra's algorithm but with a different name)
- Line {5}: We need to mark the selected vertex as `visited` so that we do not calculate it twice
- Line {6}: In case a minimum weight is found, we will store the MST path value (`parent`, line {7}) and set the new cost for the MST value (line {8})
- Line {9}: After all the vertices are processed, we will return the result containing the MST

If we compare Prim's algorithm with Dijkstra's algorithm, we will see that they are very similar, with the exception of lines {7} and {8}. Line {7} keeps the parent array, which is the array that stores the MST. Line {8} stores the minimum edge value, while in Dijkstra's algorithm, the distance array is used instead of the `key` array to store the distance. We can modify Dijkstra's algorithm to add to the `parent` array, and this way, we can track the path along with its distance value.

Let's now execute the preceding algorithm for the following graph:

```
var graph = [[0, 2, 4, 0, 0, 0],
             [2, 0, 2, 4, 2, 0],
             [4, 2, 0, 0, 3, 0],
             [0, 4, 0, 0, 3, 2],
             [0, 2, 3, 3, 0, 2],
             [0, 0, 0, 2, 2, 0]];
```

We will have the following output:

```
Edge    Weight
0 - 1    2
1 - 2    2
5 - 3    2
1 - 4    2
4 - 5    2
```

Kruskal's algorithm

Similarly to Prim's algorithm, Kruskal's algorithm is also a greedy algorithm that finds MST for a connected weighted undirected graph.

Let's consider how Kruskal's algorithm works using the following code:

```
this.kruskal = function(){
  var length = this.graph.length,
  parent = [], cost,
  ne = 0, a, b, u, v, i, j, min;
  cost = initializeCost(); //{1}

  while(ne<length-1) { //{2}

    for(i=0, min = INF;i < length; i++) { //{3}
      for(j=0;j < length; j++) {
        if(cost[i][j] < min) {
          min=cost[i][j];
          u = i;
          v = j;
        }
      }
    }

    u = find(u, parent); //{4}
    v = find(v, parent); //{5}

    if (union(u, v, parent)){ //{6}
      ne++;
    }

    cost[u][v] = cost[v][u] = INF; //{7}
  }
  return parent;
}
```

The following is a description of how the algorithm works:

- Line {1}: First, we will copy the adjacent matrix values to the cost array so that we can modify it without loosing the original values (line {7})
- Line {2}: While MST has fewer than total edges -1
- Line {3}: Find edge with minimum cost
- Lines {4} and {5}: To avoid cycles, verify that the edge is already in MST
- Line {6}: If edges u and v are not the same, then add it to MST
- Line {7}: Remove the edges from the list so that we do not calculate it twice
- Line {8}: Return MST

The find function is given as follows. It prevents cycles in MST:

```
var find = function(i, parent){
  while(parent[i]){
    i = parent[i];
  }
  return i;
};
```

The union function is also given here:

```
var union = function(i, j, parent){
  if(i != j) {
    parent[j] = i;
    return true;
  }
  return false;
};
```

There are a few variations of this algorithm that can be developed. It will depend on the data structure used to sort the weight the edges values (such as Priority Queue) and also how the graph is represented.

Summary

In this chapter, we covered the basic concepts of graphs. You learned the different ways we can represent this data structure, and we implemented an algorithm to represent a graph using an adjacency list. You also learned how to traverse a graph using BFS and DFS approaches. This chapter also covered two applications of BFS and DFS, which find the shortest path using BFS and topological sorting using DFS.

This chapter also covered some famous algorithms such as Dijkstra's algorithm and the Floyd-Warshall algorithm to calculate the shortest path. We also covered Prim's algorithm and Kruskal's algorithm to calculate the minimum spanning tree of the graph.

In the next chapter, you will learn the most common sorting algorithms used in computer science.

10
Sorting and Searching Algorithms

Suppose we have a telephone agenda (or a notebook) that does not have any sorting order. When you need to add a contact with telephone numbers, you simply write it down in the next available slot. Suppose you also have a high number of contacts in your contact list. On any ordinary day, you need to find a particular contact and his/her telephone number. However, as the contact list is not organized in any order, you have to check it contact by contact until you find the desired one. This approach is horrible, don't you agree? Imagine that you have to search for a contact in *Yellow Pages* and it is not organized! It could take forever!

For this reason, among others, we need to organize sets of information, such as the information we have stored in data structures. Sorting and searching algorithms are widely used in the daily problems we have to solve.

In this chapter, you will learn about the most commonly used sorting and searching algorithms, such as the bubble sort, selection sort, insertion sort, merge sort, quick sort, and heap sort as well as the sequential and binary search algorithms.

The sorting algorithms

From this introduction, you should understand that you need to learn how to sort first and then search for the information given. In this section, we will cover some of the most well-known sorting algorithms in computer science. We will start with the slowest one, and then we will cover some better algorithms.

Before we get started with the sorting algorithms, let's create an `array` (list) to represent the data structure that we want to sort and search, as follows:

```
function ArrayList(){

  var array = []; //{1}

  this.insert = function(item){ //{2}
    array.push(item);
  };

  this.toString= function(){ //{3}
    return array.join();
  };
}
```

As you can note, `ArrayList` is a simple data structure that stores the items in an array (line {1}). We only have an `insert` method to add elements to our data structure (line {2}), which simply uses the native `push` method of the JavaScript `Array` class that we covered in Chapter 2, *Arrays*. Finally, to help us verify the result, the `toString` method (line {3}) concatenates all the array's elements into a single string so that we can easily output the result in the browser's console using the `join` method from the native JavaScript `Array` class.

 The `join` method joins the elements of an array into a string and returns the string.

Note that this `ArrayList` class does not have any method to remove data or insert it into specific positions. We want to keep it simple so that we can focus on the sorting and searching algorithms. We will add all the sorting and searching methods to this class.

Now, we can get started!

The bubble sort

When people first start learning sorting algorithms, they usually learn the bubble sort algorithm first, because it is the simplest of all the sorting algorithms. However, it is one of the worst-case sorting algorithms with respect to runtime, and you will see why.

The bubble sort algorithm compares every two adjacent items and swaps them if the first one is bigger than the second one. It has this name because the items tend to move up into the correct order, like bubbles rising to the surface.

Let's implement the bubble sort algorithm as follows:

```
this.bubbleSort = function(){
  var length = array.length;              //{1}
  for (var i=0; i<length; i++){           //{2}
    for (var j=0; j<length-1; j++ ){ //{3}
      if (array[j] > array[j+1]){  //{4}
        swap(array, j, j+1);       //{5}
      }
    }
  }
};
```

First, let's declare a variable called `length`, which will store the size of the `array` (line {1}). This step will help us to get the size of the `array` on lines {2} and {3}, and this step is optional. Then, we will have an outer loop (line {2}) that will iterate the array from its first position to the last one, controlling how many passes are done in the array (which should be one pass per item of the array as the number of passes is equal to the size of the array). Then, we have an inner loop (line {3}) that will iterate the array starting from its first position to the penultimate item that will actually do the comparison between the current item and the next one (line {4}). If the items are out of order (that is, the current one is bigger than the next one), then we will swap them (line {5}), meaning that the value of the `j+1` position will be transferred to the `j` position and vice versa.

Now, we need to declare the `swap` function (a private function that is available only to the code inside the `ArrayList` class):

```
var swap = function(array, index1, index2){
  var aux = array[index1];
  array[index1] = array[index2];
  array[index2] = aux;
};
```

To make the swap, we need a temporary variable to store the value of one of the items in. We will use this method for other sorting methods as well, and this is the reason we will declare this swap code into a function so that we can reuse it.

If we use **ES6** (**ECMAScript 2015**), we can replace the preceding function with the following code (which uses the enhanced object properties that you learned in Chapter 1, *JavaScript—A Quick Overview*):

```
[array[index1], array[index2]] = [array[index2], array[index1]];
```

The following diagram illustrates the bubble sort in action:

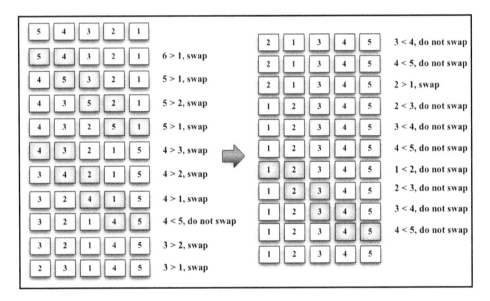

Each different section in the preceding diagram represents a pass made by the outer loop (line {2}), and each comparison between two adjacent items is made by the inner loop (line {3}).

To test the bubble sort algorithm and get the same results shown by the diagram, we will use the following code:

```
function createNonSortedArray(size){ //{6}
  var array = new ArrayList();
  for (var i = size; i> 0; i--){
    array.insert(i);
  }
  return array;
}

var array = createNonSortedArray(5); //{7}
console.log(array.toString());       //{8}
```

```
array.bubbleSort();                    //{9}
console.log(array.toString());         //{10}
```

To help us test the sorting algorithms that you will learn in this chapter, we will create a function that will automatically create a nonsorted array with the size that is passed by the parameter (line {6}). If we pass 5 as the parameter, the function will create the following array for us: [5, 4, 3, 2, 1]. Then, all we have to do is call this function and store its return value in a variable that contains the instance of the ArrayList class initialized with some numbers (line {7}). Just to make sure we have an unsorted array, we will output the array's content on console (line {8}), call the bubble sort method (line {9}), and output the array's content on console again so that we can verify that the array was sorted (line {10}).

 You can find the complete source code of the ArrayList class and the testing code (with additional comments) on the source code that you downloaded from the support page (or from the GitHub repository).

Note that when the algorithm executes the second pass of the outer loop (the second section of the previous diagram), the numbers 4 and 5 are already sorted. Nevertheless, on subsequent comparisons, we will keep comparing them even if the comparison is not needed. For this reason, we will make a small improvement on the bubble sort algorithm.

The improved bubble sort

If we subtract the number of passes from the inner loop, we will avoid all the unnecessary comparisons made by the inner loop (line {1}):

```
this.modifiedBubbleSort = function(){
  var length = array.length;
  for (var i=0; i<length; i++){
    for (var j=0; j<length-1-i; j++ ){ //{1}
      if (array[j] > array[j+1]){
        swap(j, j+1);
      }
    }
  }
};
```

The following diagram exemplifies how the improved bubble sort works:

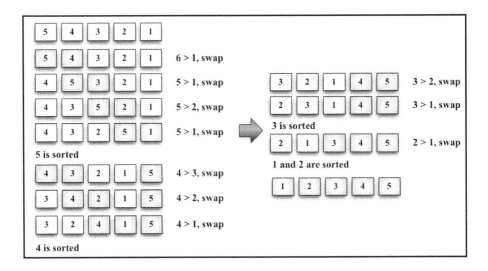

 Note that we did not compare the numbers that are already in place. Even though we made this small change to improve the bubble sort algorithm a little bit, it is not a recommended algorithm. It has a complexity of $O(n^2)$.

We will talk more about the big O notation in `Chapter 12`, *Algorithm complexity*, to learn more about algorithms.

The selection sort

The selection sort algorithm is an in-place comparison sort algorithm. The general idea of the selection sort is to find the minimum value in the data structure, place it in the first position, then find the second minimum value, place it in the second position, and so on.

The following is the source code for the selection sort algorithm:

```
this.selectionSort = function(){
   var length = array.length,         //{1}
   indexMin;
   for (var i=0; i<length-1; i++){    //{2}
      indexMin = i;                   //{3}
      for (var j=i; j<length; j++){   //{4}
        if(array[indexMin]>array[j]){ //{5}
           indexMin = j;              //{6}
        }
      }
      if (i !== indexMin){            //{7}
        swap(i, indexMin);
      }
   }
};
```

First, we will declare some of the variables that we will use in the algorithm (line {1}). Then, we have an outer loop (line {2}) that will iterate the array and control the passes (that is, which n^{th} value of the array we need to find next or the next `min` value). We will assume that the first value of the current pass is the minimum value of the array (line {3}). Then, starting from the current i value to the end of the array (line {4}), we will compare whether the value in the j position is less than the current minimum value (line {5}); if this is true, we will change the value of the minimum to the new minimum value (line {6}). When we get out of the inner loop (line {4}), we will have the nth minimum value of the array. Then, if the minimum value is different from the original minimum value (line {7}), we will swap them.

To test the selection sort algorithm, we can use the following code:

```
array = createNonSortedArray(5);
console.log(array.toString());
array.selectionSort();
console.log(array.toString());
```

The following diagram exemplifies the selection sort algorithm in action based on our array, which is used in the preceding code [5, 4, 3, 2, 1]:

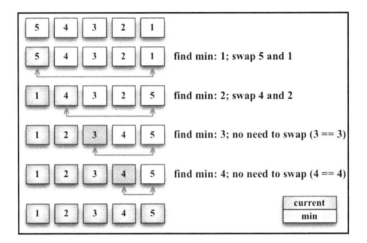

The arrows at the bottom of the array indicate the positions currently in consideration to find the minimum value (inner loop: line {4}), and each step of the preceding diagram represents the outer loop (line {2}).

The selection sort is also an algorithm of complexity $O(n^2)$. Similar to the bubble sort, it contains two nested loops that are responsible for the quadratic complexity. However, the selection sort performs worse than the insertion sort algorithm that you will learn next.

The insertion sort

The insertion sort algorithm builds the final sorted array one item at a time. It assumes that the first element is already sorted. Then, a comparison with the second item is performed: should the second item stay in its place or be inserted before the first item? So, the first two items will get sorted, he comparison will take place with the third item (that is, should it be inserted in the first, second, or third position?), and so on.

The following code represents the insertion sort algorithm:

```
this.insertionSort = function(){
    var length = array.length,        //{1}
    j, temp;
    for (var i=1; i<length; i++){      //{2}
        j = i;                         //{3}
        temp = array[i];               //{4}
```

```
    while (j>0 && array[j-1] > temp){ //{5}
      array[j] = array[j-1];          //{6}
      j--;
    }
    array[j] = temp;                  //{7}
  }
};
```

As usual, the first line of the algorithm is used to declare the variables we will use in the source code (line {1}). Then, we will iterate the array to find the correct place for the ith item (line {2}). Note that we started from the second position (index 1), instead of position 0 (as we considered the first item already sorted). Then, we initiated an auxiliary variable with the value of i (line {3}), and we also stored the value in a temporary value (line {4}) so that we can insert it in the correct position later. The next step is finding the correct place to insert the item. As long as the j variable is bigger than (because the first index of the array is and there is no negative index) and the previous value in the array is bigger than the value we are comparing (line {5}), we will shift the previous value to the current position (line {6}) and decrease the value of j. At the end, we will insert the value in its correct position.

The following diagram exemplifies the insertion sort in action:

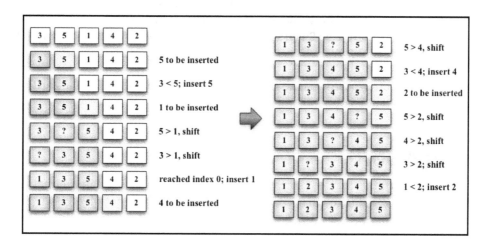

For example, suppose the array we are trying to sort is **[3, 5, 1, 4, 2]**. These values will be carried out in the steps performed by the insertion sort algorithm, as described in the following steps:

1. The value 3 is already sorted, so we will start sorting the second value of the array, which is the value **5**. The value **3** is less than the value **5**, so **5** stays in the same place (meaning the second position of the array). The values **3** and **5** are already sorted.
2. The next value to be sorted and inserted in the correct place is **1** (which is currently in the third position of the array). The value **5** is greater than **1**, so **5** is shifted to the third position. We need to analyze whether **1** should be inserted in the second position—is **1** greater than **3**? It's not, so the value **3** gets shifted to the second position. Next, we need to verify that **1** is inserted in the first position of the array. As 0 is the first position and there isn't a negative position, **1** needs to be inserted on the first position. The values **1**, **3**, and **5** are sorted.
3. We move to the next value: **4**. Should the value **4** stay in the current position (index 3), or does it need to be moved to a lower position? The value **4** is less than **5**, so **5** will get shifted to index 3. Should we insert **4** in the index 2? The value **4** is greater than **3**, so **4** is inserted in position 3 of the array.
4. The next value to be inserted is **2** (position 4 of array). The value **5** is greater than **2**, so **5** gets shifted to the index 4. The value **4** is greater than **2**, so **4** will also get shifted (position 3). The value **3** is also greater than **2**, and **3** also gets shifted. The value **1** is less than **2**, so **2** is inserted at the second position of the array. Thus, the array is sorted.

This algorithm has a better performance than the selection and bubble sort algorithms when sorting small arrays.

The merge sort

The merge sort algorithm is the first sorting algorithm that can be used in the real world. The three first sorting algorithms that you learned in this book do not give good performance, but the merge sort gives a good performance with a complexity of *O(n log n)*.

The JavaScript `Array` class defines a `sort` function (`Array.prototype.sort`) that can be used to sort arrays using JavaScript (with no need to implement the algorithm ourselves). ECMAScript does not define which sorting algorithm needs to be used, so each browser can implement its own algorithm. For example, Mozilla Firefox uses the merge sort as the `Array.prototype.sort` implementation, while Chrome uses a variation of the quick sort (which you will learn next).

The merge sort is a divide-and-conquer algorithm. The idea behind it is to divide the original array into smaller arrays until each small array has only one position and then merge these smaller arrays into bigger ones until we have a single big array at the end that is sorted.

Because of the divide-and-conquer approach, the merge sort algorithm is also recursive, as follows:

```
this.mergeSort = function(){
  array = mergeSortRec(array);
};
```

As in the previous chapters, whenever we implement a recursive function, we always implement a `helper` function that will be executed. For the merge sort, we will do the same. We will declare the `mergeSort` method that will be available for use, and the `mergeSort` method will call `mergeSortRec`, which is a recursive function:

```
var mergeSortRec = function(array){
  var length = array.length;
  if(length === 1) {        //{1}
    return array;          //{2}
  }
  var mid = Math.floor(length / 2),      //{3}
  left = array.slice(0, mid),          //{4}
  right = array.slice(mid, length); //{5}

  return merge(mergeSortRec(left), mergeSortRec(right)); //{6}
};
```

The merge sort will transform a bigger array into smaller arrays until they have only one item in them. As the algorithm is recursive, we need a stop condition—that is, if the array has a size equal to 1 (line {1}). If positive, we will return the array with size 1 (line {2}) because it is already sorted.

If the array is bigger than 1, then we will split it into smaller arrays. To do so, first we need to find the middle of the array (line {3}), and once we find the middle, we will split the array into two smaller arrays, which we will call left (line {4}) and right (line {5}). The left array comprises of elements from index 0 to the middle index, and the right array consists of elements from the middle index to the end of the original array.

The next steps will be to call the merge function (line {6}), which will be responsible for merging and sorting the smaller arrays into bigger ones until we have the original array sorted and back together. To keep breaking the original array into smaller pieces, we will recursively call mergeSortRec again, passing the smaller array to the left as a parameter and another call for the array to the right. Execute the following code:

```
var merge = function(left, right){
  var result = [], // {7}
  il = 0,
  ir = 0;
  while(il < left.length && ir < right.length) { // {8}
    if(left[il] < right[ir]) {
      result.push(left[il++]);   // {9}
    } else{
      result.push(right[ir++]); // {10}
    }
  }

  while (il < left.length){    // {11}
    result.push(left[il++]);
  }

  while (ir < right.length){   // {12}
    result.push(right[ir++]);
  }

  return result; // {13}
};
```

The merge function receives two arrays and merges them into a bigger array. During the merge is when the sorting happens. First, we need to declare a new array that will be created for the merge and also declare two variables (line {7}) that will be used to iterate the two arrays (the left and right arrays). While we can iterate through the two arrays (line {8}), we will compare whether the item from the left array is less than the item from the right array. If positive, we will add the item from the left array to the merged result array and also increment the variable that is used to iterate the array (line {9}); otherwise, we will add the item from the right array and increment the variable that is used to iterate the array (line {10}).

Next, we will add every remaining item from the `left` array (line {11}) to the merged result array and do the same for the remaining items from the `right` array (line {12}). At the end, we will return a merged array as the result (line {13}).

If we execute the `mergeSort` function, this is how it will be executed:

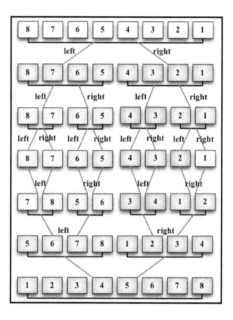

Note that first the algorithm splits the original array until it has smaller arrays with a single element, and then it starts merging. While merging, it does the sorting as well until we have the original array completely back together and sorted.

The quick sort

The quick sort is probably the most used sorting algorithm. It has a complexity of *O(n log n)*, and it usually performs better than other *O(n log n)* sorting algorithms. Similarly to the merge sort, it also uses the divide-and-conquer approach, dividing the original array into smaller ones (but without splitting them as the merge sort does) to do the sorting.

The quick sort algorithm is a little bit more complex than the other ones you have learned so far. Let's learn it step by step, as follows:

1. First, we need to select an item from the array called `pivot`, which is the middle item in the array.

2. We will create two pointers—the left-hand side one will point to the first item of the array, and the right-hand side one will point to the last item of the array. We will move the left pointer until we find an item that is bigger than the pivot, and we will also move the right pointer until we find an item that is less than the pivot and swap them. We will repeat this process until the left-hand side pointer passes the right-hand side pointer. This process helps to have values lower than the pivot before the pivot and values greater than the pivot after the pivot. This is called the partition operation.

3. Next, the algorithm repeats the previous two steps for smaller arrays (subarrays with smaller values and then subarrays with greater values) until the arrays are completely sorted.

Let's start the implementation of the quick sort via the following code:

```
this.quickSort = function(){
  quick(array,  0, array.length - 1);
};
```

Similarly to the merge sort, we will start declaring the main method that will call the recursive function, passing the array that we want to sort along with index 0 and its last position (because we want to have the whole array sorted, not only a subset of it), as follows:

```
var quick = function(array, left, right){

  var index; //{1}

  if (array.length > 1) { //{2}

    index = partition(array, left, right); //{3}

    if (left < index - 1) {              //{4}
      quick(array, left, index - 1);     //{5}
    }

    if (index < right) {                 //{6}
      quick(array, index, right);        //{7}
    }
  }
};
```

First, we will have the `index` variable (line {1}), which will help us separate the subarray with smaller and greater values so that we can recursively call the `quick` function again. We will obtain the `index` value as the return value of the `partition` function (line {3}).

If the size of the array is larger than 1 (because an array with a single element is already sorted at line {2}), we will execute the partition operation on the given subarray (the first call will pass the complete array) to obtain index (line {3}). If a subarray with smaller elements exists (line {4}), we will repeat the process for the subarray (line {5}). We will do the same thing for the subarray with greater values. If there is any subarray with a greater value (line {6}), we will repeat the quick sort process (line {7}) as well.

The partition process

The first thing we need to do is choose the pivot element. There are a few ways in which we can do this. The simplest one is selecting the first item of the array (the leftmost item). However, studies show that this is not a good selection if the array is almost sorted, causing the worst behavior of the algorithm. Another approach is selecting a random item of the array or the middle item.

Now, let's take a look at the partition process:

```
var partition = function(array, left, right) {

  var pivot = array[Math.floor((right + left) / 2)], //{8}
  i = left,                                          //{9}
  j = right;                                         //{10}

  while (i <= j) {                    //{11}
    while (array[i] < pivot) {  //{12}
      i++;
    }
    while (array[j] > pivot) {  //{13}
      j--;
    }
    if (i <= j) { //{14}
      swap(array, i, j); //{15}
      i++;
      j--;
    }
  }
  return i; //{16}
};
```

For this implementation, we will select the middle item as `pivot` (line {8}). We will also initiate the two pointers: `left` (low at line {9}) with the first element of the array and `right` (high at line {10}) with the last element of the array.

While the `left` and `right` pointers do not cross each other (line {11}), we will execute the partition operation. First, until we find an element that is greater than `pivot` (line {12}), we will shift the `left` pointer. We will do the same with the `right` pointer until we find an element that is less than `pivot`, and we will shift the `right` pointer as well (line {13}).

When the `left` pointer is greater than `pivot` and the `right` pointer is lower than `pivot`, we will compare whether the `left` pointer index is bigger than the `right` pointer index (line {14}), meaning whether the left item is greater than the right item (in value). We will swap these (line {15}), shift both the pointers, and repeat the process (starting again at line {11}).

At the end of the partition operation, we will return the index of the left pointer that will be used to create the subarrays in line {3}.

The `swap` function is the same we created for the bubble sort algorithm at the beginning of this chapter. We can also replace this function with the following ES6 code:

```
[array[index1], array[index2]] = [array[index2], array[index1]];
```

The quick sort in action

Let's take a look at the quick sort algorithm in action step by step:

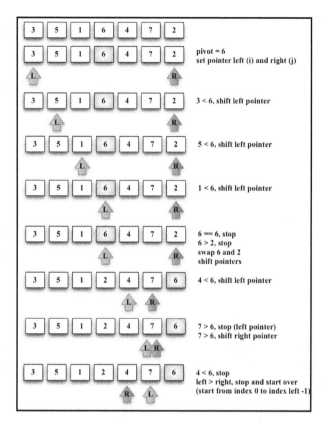

Given the **[3, 5, 1, 6, 4, 7, 2]** array, the preceding diagram represents the first execution of the partition operation.

The following diagram exemplifies the execution of the partition operation for the first subarray of lower values (note that **7** and **6** are not part of the subarray):

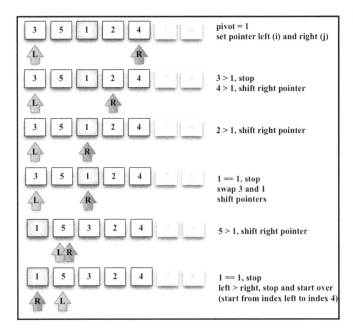

Next, we will continue creating subarrays, as seen in the following diagram but now with greater values than the subarray of the preceding diagram (the lower subarray with value **1** does not need to be partitioned because it only contains one item):

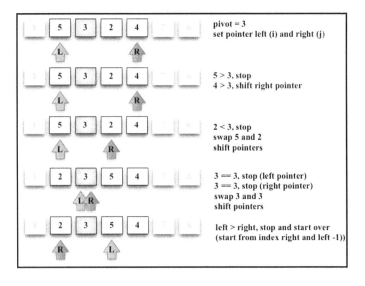

The lower subarray **[2, 3]** from the (**[2, 3, 5, 4]**) subarray continues to be partitioned (line {5} from the algorithm):

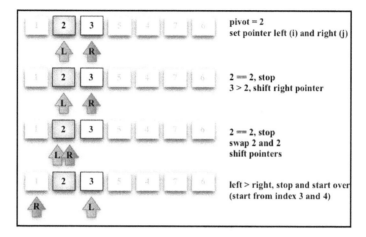

Then, the greater subarray **[5, 4]** from the **[2, 3, 5, 4]** subarray also continues to be partitioned (line {7} from the algorithm), as shown in the following diagram:

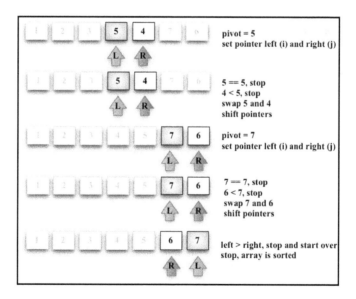

At the end, the greater subarray **[6, 7]** will also suffer the `partition` operation, completing the execution of the quick sort algorithm.

The heap sort

The heap sort is another efficient algorithm. The algorithm has this name because it sorts the array as if it were a binary tree. To do so, we need to manage the array as a binary tree considering the following information:

- Index 0 is the root of the tree
- The parent of any node N is *N/2* (with the exception of the root node)
- The left-hand side child of a node L is *2*L*
- The right-hand child of a node R is *2*R+1*

So for example, we can consider the **[3,5,1,6,4,7,2]** array as the following tree:

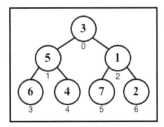

The heap sort algorithm is given as follows:

```
this.heapSort = function(){
  var heapSize = array.length;
  buildHeap(array);  //{1}

  while (heapSize > 1) {
    heapSize--;
    swap(array, 0, heapSize);     //{2}
    heapify(array, heapSize, 0); //{3}
  }
};
```

The first step is to build the heap structure (line {1}) in a way that array[parent(i)] ≥ array[i].

Then, as the second step, we will swap the first position (the bigger value in the array) with the last position of the current heap (line {2}). This way, the biggest value will be placed at its sorted position.

Step {2} might cancel the heap property. For this reason, we need to run a function called `heapify` that will transform the array into a heap again, meaning it will get the root of the current heap (the smaller value) and push it into the bottom of the tree again.

The `buildHeap` function is given as follows:

```
var buildHeap = function(array){
  var heapSize = array.length;
  for (var i = Math.floor(array.length / 2); i >= 0; i--) {
    heapify(array, heapSize, i);
  }
};
```

If we apply the preceding function to the **[3,5,1,6,4,7,2]** array, we will have the following steps until the heap is built:

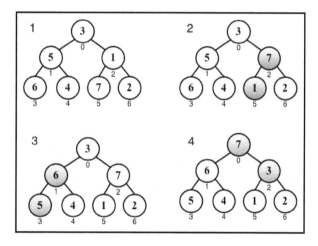

Finally, we will have the `heapify` function similar to the following:

```
var heapify = function(array, heapSize, i){
  var left = i * 2 + 1,
  right = i * 2 + 2,
  largest = i;

  if (left < heapSize && array[left] > array[largest]) {
    largest = left;
  }

  if (right < heapSize && array[right] > array[largest]) {
    largest = right;
  }
```

```
    if (largest !== i) {
      swap(array, i, largest);
      heapify(array, heapSize, largest);
    }
};
```

After the heap is ready, we can start the heap sort algorithm. These will be the steps {2} and {3} applied to the array.

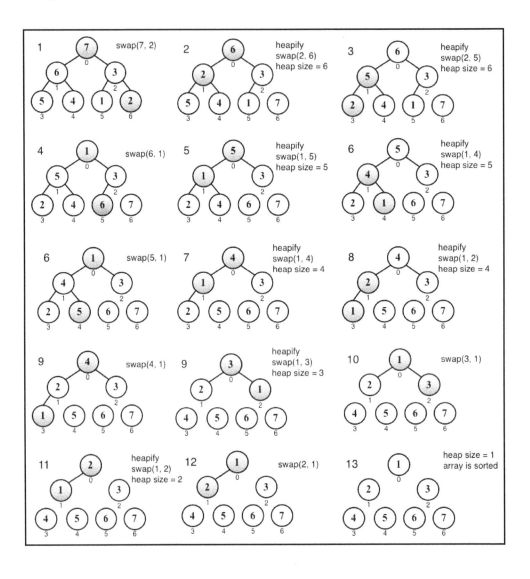

The counting, bucket, and radix sorts (the distribution sorts)

So far, you have learned how to sort an array without using any auxiliary data structure. There is also another type of sorting algorithm called the distribution sort in which the data is distributed from the original array in multiple intermediate structures (buckets), which are then gathered and placed on the original array.

The most famous distribution algorithms are the counting sort, bucket sort, and radix sort. These three algorithms are very similar.

 We will not cover these algorithms in this book. However, you can find the algorithms and examples within the source code bundle of this book or in the Github repository

at `https://github.com/loiane/javascript-datastructures-algo rithms`.

Searching algorithms

Now, let's talk about searching algorithms. If we take a look at the algorithms we implemented in previous chapters, such as the `search` method of the `BinarySearchTree` class (`Chapter 8`, *Trees*) or the `indexOf` method of the `LinkedList` class (`Chapter 5`, *Linked Lists*), these are all search algorithms, and of course, each one was implemented according to the behavior of its data structure. So we are already familiar with two-search algorithm; we just do not know their "official" names yet!

The sequential search

The sequential or linear search is the most basic search algorithm. It consists of comparing each element of the data structure with the one we are looking for. It is also the most inefficient one.

Let's take a look at its implementation:

```
this.sequentialSearch = function(item){
  for (var i=0; i<array.length; i++){ //{1}
    if (item === array[i]){           //{2}
      return i;                       //{3}
    }
  }
}
```

```
    return -1;   //{4}
};
```

The sequential search iterates through the array (line {1}) and compares each item with the value we are searching for (line {2}). If we find it, we can return something to indicate that we found it. We can return the item itself, the value `true`, or its index (line {3}). In the preceding implementation, we returned the index of the item. If we don't find the item, we can return -1 (line {4}), indicating that the index does not exist; the values `false` and `null` are among other options.

Suppose we have the **[5, 4, 3, 2, 1]** array and we are looking for the value **3**, then the following diagram shows the steps of the sequential search:

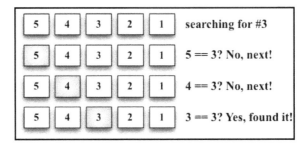

The binary search

The binary search algorithm works similar to the number guessing game, in which someone says "I'm thinking of a number between 1 and 100". We will begin by responding with a number, and the person will say "higher", "lower", or that we got it right.

To make the algorithm work, the data structure needs to be sorted first. These are the steps that the algorithm follows:

1. A value is selected in the middle of the array.
2. If the item is the one we are looking for, we are done (the value is right).
3. If the value we are looking for is less than the selected one, then we will go to the left and back to 1 (lower).
4. If the value we are looking for is larger than the selected one, then we will go to the right and back to 1 (higher).

Let's take a look at its implementation:

```
this.binarySearch = function(item){
  this.quickSort();  //{1}

  var low = 0,                    //{2}
  high = array.length - 1, //{3}
  mid, element;

  while (low <= high){ //{4}
    mid = Math.floor((low + high) / 2); //{5}
    element = array[mid];              //{6}
    if (element < item) {             //{7}
      low = mid + 1;                 //{8}
    } else if (element > item) {      //{9}
      high = mid - 1;                //{10}
    } else {
      return mid;                    //{11}
    }
  }
  return -1; //{12}
};
```

To get started, the first thing we need to do is sort the array. We can use any algorithm we implemented in the *Sorting algorithms* section. The quick sort was chosen for this implementation (line {1}). After the array is sorted, we will set the low (line {2}) and high (line {3}) pointer (which will work as boundaries).

While low is lower than high (line {4}), in this case, low is greater than high , which means that the value does not exist. So, we will return -1 (line {12}), find the middle index (line {5}), and hence have the value of the middle item (line {6}). Then, we will start comparing whether the selected value is less than the value we are looking for (line {7}), and we need to go lower (line {8}) and start over. If the selected value is greater than the value we are looking for (line {9}), we need to go higher (line {10}) and start over. Otherwise, it means that the value is equal to the value we are looking for, therefore we will return its index (line {11}).

Given the array in the following diagram, let's try to search for the value **2**. These are the steps that the algorithm will perform:

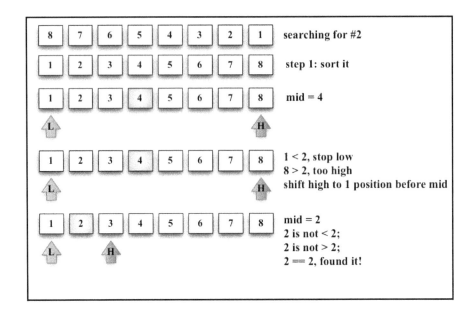

 The `BinarySearchTree` class we implemented in `Chapter 8`, *Trees*, has the `search` method, which is exactly the same as the binary search but applied to tree data structures.

Summary

In this chapter, you learned about sorting and searching algorithms. You learned the bubble, selection, insertion, merge, quick, and heap sort algorithms, which are used to sort data structures. You also learned the sequential search and binary search (which required the data structure to be sorted already).

You can apply any logic you learned in this chapter to any data structure or any type of data. You just need to make the necessary modifications to the source code.

In the next chapter, you will learn some advanced techniques used in algorithms.

11
Patterns of Algorithm

So far, we had fun discussing how to implement several different data structures, among them; the most-used are sorting and searching algorithms. Algorithm in the programming world is very interesting. In this chapter, you will learn more about this world, and we will also discuss the next steps in case you are interested in delving deeper into this world.

We will cover recursion, which was introduced in `Chapter 8`, *Trees*. We will also cover **dynamic programming** and **greedy algorithms**, and we will also cover some famous problems.

Recursion

Recursion is a method to solve problems that consists of solving smaller portions of the same problem until you solve the original larger problem. It usually involves calling the function itself.

A method or function is recursive if it can call itself directly, as follows:

```
function recursiveFunction(someParam){
  recursiveFunction(someParam);
};
```

A function is also called recursive if it can call itself indirectly, as follows:

```
function recursiveFunction1(someParam){
  recursiveFunction2(someParam);
};

function recursiveFunction2(someParam){
  recursiveFunction1(someParam);
};
```

Let's suppose we have to execute recursiveFunction. What would the result be? In this case, it would be executed indefinitely. For this reason, every recursive function must have a base case, which is a condition in which no recursive call is made (a stop point) to prevent infinite recursion.

JavaScript limitation on the call stack size

What happens when we forget to add a base case to stop the recursive calls of a function? It will not be executed indefinitely; the browser will throw an error, which is known as a stack overflow error.

Each browser has its own limitations, and we can use the following code to do some testing:

```
var i = 0;

function recursiveFn () {
  i++;
  recursiveFn();
}

try {
  recursiveFn();
} catch (ex) {
  alert('i = ' + i + ' error: ' + ex);
}
```

In **Chrome Version 37**, the function is executed 20,955 times, and the browser throws the error RangeError: Maximum call stack size exceeded. In **Firefox Version 27**, the function is executed 343,429 times, and the browser throws the error InternalError: too much recursion.

 Depending on your operating system and browser, the values might be different, but they will be close.

ECMAScript 6 has **tail call optimization**. If a function call is the last action inside a function (in our example, the highlighted line), it is handled via a "jump", not via a "subroutine call". This means that our code can be executed forever in ECMAScript 6. This is why it is very important to have a base case to stop recursion.

For more information about tail call optimization, visit `http://goo.gl/Z dTZzg`.

The Fibonacci sequence

Let's go back to the Fibonacci problem, which was covered in `Chapter 10`, *Sorting and Searching Algorithms*. The Fibonacci sequence can be defined as follows:

- The Fibonacci sequence of 1 or 2 is 1
- The Fibonacci sequence of n (for $n>2$) is the Fibonacci of ($n-1$) + Fibonacci of ($n-2$)

So, let's start implementing the Fibonacci function, as follows:

```
function fibonacci(num){
  if (num === 1 || num === 2){ //{1}
    return 1;
  }
}
```

We know the base case: the Fibonacci of 1 or 2 (line `{1}`) is 1. Now, let's finish its implementation:

```
function fibonacci(num){
  if (num === 1 || num === 2){
    return 1;
  }
  return fibonacci(num - 1) + fibonacci(num - 2);
}
```

We also know that if n is greater than 2, then Fibonacci (n) is Fibonacci ($n-1$) + Fibonacci ($n-2$).

Now, we have the Fibonacci function implemented. If we try to find the Fibonacci of 6, the following will be the result of the calls that are made:

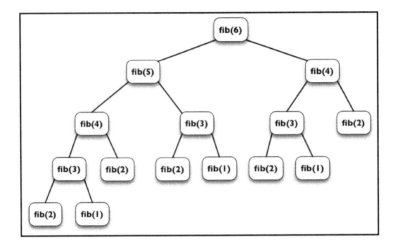

We could also implement the Fibonacci function in a nonrecursive way, as follows:

```
function fib(num){
  var n1 = 1,
  n2 = 1,
  n = 1;
  for (var i = 3; i<=num; i++){
    n = n1 + n2;
    n1 = n2;
    n2 = n;
  }
  return n;
}
```

Why use recursion? Is it faster? Recursion is not faster than the normal version; it is slower. However, note that recursion is clear to understand, and it requires less code as well.

 In ECMAScript 6, because of tail call optimization, recursion is not slower. However, in other languages, recursion code is usually slower.

So, we usually use recursion because it is easier to solve problems using it.

Dynamic programming

Dynamic programming (DP) is an optimization technique used to solve complex problems by breaking them in to smaller subproblems.

We covered some dynamic programming techniques earlier in this book. One problem we solved with dynamic programming was DFS in `Chapter 9`, *Graphs*.

 Note that the dynamic programming approach is different from the divide-and-conquer approach (as we used for the merge sort and quick sort algorithms). While the divide and conquer approach breaks the problem into independent subproblems and then combines the solutions, dynamic programming breaks the problem into dependent subproblems.

Another example is the Fibonacci problem we solved in the previous section. We broke the Fibonacci problem into smaller problems, as shown in the diagram of this section.

There are three important steps we need to follow when solving problems with DP:

1. Define the subproblems.
2. Implement the recurrence that solves the subproblems (in this step, we need to follow the steps for recursion that we discussed in the previous section).
3. Recognize and solve the base cases.

There are some famous problems that can be solved with dynamic programming:

- **The knapsack problem**: In this problem, given a set of items, each one with a value and volume, the goal is to determine the best collection of items out of the set in a way to maximize the total value. The constraint of the problem is that the total volume needs to be the volume supported by the "knapsack" or less.
- **The longest common subsequence**: This consists of finding the longest subsequence (a sequence that can be derived from another sequence by deleting some elements without changing the order of the remaining elements) common to all sequences in a set of sequences.
- **Matrix chain multiplication**: In this problem, given a sequence of matrices, the goal is to find the most efficient way to multiply these matrices (with as few operations as possible). The multiplication is not performed; the solution is finding the sequences in each of the matrices that need to be multiplied.
- **Coin change**: This consists of finding how many different ways we can make change in a particular amount of cents using a given amount of set denominations d1...dn.

- **All-pairs shortest paths in a graph**: This consists of finding the shortest path from vertex u to vertex v for all pairs of vertices (u,v). You learned about this problem in Chapter 9, *Graphs* using the **Floyd-Warshall** algorithm.

We will cover these problems in the next topics.

These problems and their solutions are very common in programming the interviews of big companies such as Google, Amazon, Microsoft, Oracle, and so on.

The minimum coin change problem

The minimum coin change problem is a variation of the coin change problem. The coin change problem consists of finding out in how many ways we can make change for a particular amount of cents using a given amount of set denominations **d1... dn**. The minimum coin change problem consists of finding the minimum number of coins needed to make a particular amount of cents using a given amount of set denominations d1... dn.

For example, the United States has the following denominations (coins): d1 = 1; d2 = 5; d3 = 10; and d4 = 25.

If we need to make change for 36 cents, we can use 1 quarter (25), 1 dime (10), and 1 penny (1).

How do we transform this solution into an algorithm?

The min-coin change solution consists of finding the minimum number of coins for *n*. But to do this, first we need to find the solution for every *x* < *n*. Then, we can build up the solution out of the solutions for smaller values.

Let's take a look at the algorithm:

```
function MinCoinChange(coins){
  var coins = coins;  //{1}
  var cache = {};     //{2}

  this.makeChange = function(amount) {
    var me = this;
    if (!amount) { //{3}
      return [];
    }
    if (cache[amount]) { //{4}
      return cache[amount];
```

```
      }
      var min = [], newMin, newAmount;
      for (var i=0; i<coins.length; i++){ //{5}
        var coin = coins[i];
        newAmount = amount - coin;   //{6}
        if (newAmount >= 0){
          newMin = me.makeChange(newAmount); //{7}
        }
        if (
          newAmount >= 0 && //{8}
          (newMin.length < min.length-1 || !min.length)//{9}
          && (newMin.length || !newAmount) //{10})
          {
            min = [coin].concat(newMin); //{11}
            console.log('new Min ' + min + ' for ' + amount);
          }
      }
      return (cache[amount] = min); //{12}
    };
  }
```

To be more organized, we created a class that will solve the min-coin change problem, given the denominations. Let's go through the algorithm step by step.

Our MinCoinChange class receives the coins parameter (line {1}), which represents the denominations of our problem. For the US coin system, it would be [1, 5, 10, 25]. We can pass any denominations that we like. Also, to be more efficient and not recalculate values, we will keep cache (line {2}).

Then, we have the makeChange method, which is also recursive and is the method that will solve the problem for us. First, if amount is not positive (< 0), then we will return an empty array (line {3}); at the end of the execution of this method, we will return an array with the amount of each coin that can be used to make change (the minimum amount of coins). Next, we will check cache. If the result is already cached (line {4}), then we will simply return its value; otherwise, we execute the algorithm.

To help us further, we will solve the problem based on the coins parameter (denominations). So, for each coin (line {5}), we will calculate newAmount (line {6}), which will decrease the value until we reach the minimum amount of change we can give (remember that this algorithm will calculate all makeChange results for x < amount). If newAmount is a valid value (positive value), then we will calculate the result for it as well (line {7}).

At the end, we will verify whether `newAmount` is valid, whether `minValue` (the minimum amount of coins) is the best result, and whether `minValue` and `newAmount` are valid values (line {10}). If all the verifications are positive, it means we have a better result than previously (line {11}. For example, for 5 cents, we can give 5 pennies or 1 nickel, 1 nickel being the best solution). At the end, we will return the final result (line {12}).

Let's test this algorithm via the following code:

```
var minCoinChange = new MinCoinChange([1, 5, 10, 25]);
console.log(minCoinChange.makeChange(36));
```

Note that if we inspect the `cache` variable, it will hold all the results for 1 to 36 cents. The result for the preceding code will be [1, 10, 25].

In the source code of this book, you will find some extra lines of code that will output the steps of this algorithm. For example, if we use the denominations 1, 3, and 4 and execute the algorithm for the amount 6, we will produce the following output:

```
new Min 1 for 1
new Min 1,1 for 2
new Min 1,1,1 for 3
new Min 3 for 3
new Min 1,3 for 4
new Min 4 for 4
new Min 1,4 for 5
new Min 1,1,4 for 6
new Min 3,3 for 6
[3, 3]
```

So, for the amount 6, the best solution is giving two coins of value 3.

The knapsack problem

The knapsack problem is a combinatorial optimization problem. It can be described as follows: given a fixed-size knapsack with a capacity to carry W amount of weight and a set of items that have a value and weight, find the best solution in a way to fill the knapsack with the most valuable items so that the total weight is less than or equal to W.

Here, we have an example:

Item #	Weight	Value
1	2	3
2	3	4
3	4	5

Consider that the knapsack can only carry a weight of 5. For this example, we can say that the best solution would be filling the knapsack with items 1 and 2, which together have a weight of 5 and a total value of 7.

 There are two versions of this problem. The *0-1* version, in which we can only fill the knapsack with the whole item, and the **fractional knapsack problem**, in which we can take fractions of the items. For this example, we will work with the *0-1* version of the problem. The fractional version cannot be solved with dynamic programming, but it can be solved with a greedy algorithm, which you will learn later on in this chapter.

Let's take a look at the knapsack algorithm, as follows:

```
function knapSack(capacity, weights, values, n) {

  var i, w, a, b, kS = [];

  for (i = 0; i <= n; i++) { //{1}
    kS[i] = [];
  }

  for (i = 0; i <= n; i++){
    for (w = 0; w <= capacity; w++){
      if (i == 0 || w == 0){ //{2}
        kS[i][w] = 0;
      } else if (weights[i-1] <= w){ //{3}
        a = values[i-1] + kS[i-1][w-weights[i-1]];
        b = kS[i-1][w];
        kS[i][w] = (a > b) ? a : b; //{4} max(a,b)
      } else{
        kS[i][w] = kS[i-1][w]; //{5}
      }
    }
  }
  return kS[n][capacity]; //{6}
}
```

Let's take a look at how this algorithm works:

- Line {1}: First, we will initialize the matrix that will be used to find the solution. This matrix is ks[n+1][capacity+1].
- Line {2}: We will ignore the first column and row of the matrix so that we can work only with indexes different from 0.
- Line {3}: Item i can only be part of the solution if its weight is less than the constraint (capacity); otherwise, the total weight will be bigger than the capacity, and this cannot happen. When this happens, we will simply ignore its value and use the previous one (line {5}).
- Line {4}: When we find that an item can be part of solution, we will choose the one with the maximum value.
- Line {6}: The solution can be found in the last cell of the two-dimensional table, which is found in the lower-right corner of the table.

We can test the following algorithm using our initial example:

```
var values = [3,4,5],
weights = [2,3,4],
capacity = 5,
n = values.length;
console.log(knapSack(capacity, weights, values, n)); //outputs 7
```

The following diagram exemplifies the construction of the kS matrix for our example:

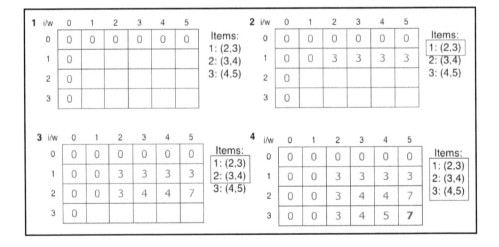

Note that this algorithm only outputs the maximum value that can be carried by the knapsack but not the actual items. We can add the following additional function to find the items that are part of the solution:

```
function findValues(n, capacity, kS, weights, values){
  var i=n, k=capacity;
  console.log('Items that are part of the solution:');

  while (i>0 && k>0){
    if (kS[i][k] !== kS[i-1][k]){
      console.log('item '+i+' can be part of solution w,v: ' +
      weights[i-1] + ',' + values[i-1]);
      i--;
      k = k - kS[i][k];
    } else {
      i--;
    }
  }
}
```

We can call this function right before line {7} of the knapsack function. If we execute the complete algorithm, we will have the following output:

```
Items that are part of the solution:
item 2 can be part of solution w,v: 4,3
item 1 can be part of solution w,v: 3,2
Total value that can be carried: 7
```

The knapsack problem can also be written recursively. You can find the recursive version within the source code bundle of this book.

The longest common subsequence

Another DP problem that is very often used in programming challenge problems is the **longest common subsequence** (**LCS**). This problems consists of finding the length of the longest subsequence in two string sequences. The longest subsequence is a sequence that appears in the same relative order but not necessarily contiguous (not substring) in both strings.

Consider the following example:

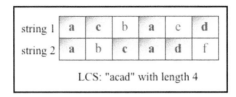

Now, let's take a look at the following algorithm:

```
function lcs(wordX, wordY) {

  var m = wordX.length,
  n = wordY.length,
  l = [],
  i, j, a, b;

  for (i = 0; i <= m; ++i) {
    l[i] = [];
    //{1}
    for (j = 0; j <= n; ++j) {
      l[i][j] = 0;
      //{2}
    }
  }

  for (i=0; i<=m; i++) {
    for (j=0; j<=n; j++) {
      if (i == 0 || j == 0){
        l[i][j] = 0;
      } else if (wordX[i-1] == wordY[j-1]) {
        l[i][j] = l[i-1][j-1] + 1;
        //{3}
      } else {
        a = l[i-1][j];
        b = l[i][j-1];
        l[i][j] = (a > b) ? a : b; //max(a,b)
        //{4}
      }
    }
  }
  //{5}
  return l[m][n];
}
```

If we compare the knapsack problem with the LCS algorithm, we will notice that both are very similar. This technique is called **memoization**, which consists of building the solution from a top manner, and the solution is given in the lower-right corner of the table/matrix.

Like, the knapsack problem algorithm, this approach only outputs the length of the LCS, but not the actual LCS algorithm. To be able to extract this information, we need to modify our algorithm a little bit by declaring a new matrix called `solution`. Note that in our code, there are some comments, and we need to replace the comments with the following code:

- Line {1}: `solution[i] = [];`
- Line {2}: `solution[i][j] = '0';`
- Line {3}: `solution[i][j] = 'diagonal';`
- Line {4}: `solution[i][j]=(l[i][j] == l[i-1][j]) ? 'top' : 'left';`
- Line {5}: `printSolution(solution, l, wordX, wordY, m, n);`

The `printSolution` function is given as follows:

```
function printSolution(solution, l, wordX, wordY, m, n){

  var a = m, b = n, i, j,
  x = solution[a][b],
  answer = '';

  while (x !== '0') {
    if (solution[a][b] === 'diagonal') {
      answer = wordX[a - 1] + answer;
      a--;
      b--;
    } else if (solution[a][b] === 'left') {
      b--;
    } else if (solution[a][b] === 'top') {
      a--;
    }
    x = solution[a][b];
  }
  console.log('lcs: '+ answer);
}
```

We can add the char to the answer whenever the direction of the solution matrix is diagonal.

If we execute the preceding algorithm using the `'acbaed'` and `'abcadf'` strings, we will get the output 4. The matrix l that was used to build the result will look similar to the following. We can use the additional algorithm to back track the LCS value, as well (this is highlighted in the following figure):

		a	b	c	a	d	f
	0	0	0	0	0	0	0
a	0	(1)	**1**	1	1	1	1
c	0	1	1	(2)	2	2	2
b	0	1	2	**2**	2	2	2
a	0	1	2	2	(3)	3	3
e	0	1	2	2	**3**	3	3
d	0	1	2	2	3	(4)	**4**

From the preceding matrix, we know that the LCS algorithm is **acad** with length **4**.

> The LCS problem can also be written recursively. You can find the recursive version within the source code bundle of this book.

Matrix chain multiplication

Matrix chain multiplication is another famous problem that can be solved with dynamic programming. The problem consists of finding the best way (order) of multiplying a set of matrices.

Let's try to understand the problem a little better. To multiply two matrices, A being a matrix m by n and B a matrix m by p. The result is matrix C, n by p.

Now, consider that we want to multiply A*B*C*D. As multiplication is associative, we can multiple these matrices in any order. So, let's consider the following:

- A is a 10 by 100 matrix
- B is a 100 by 5 matrix
- C is a 5 by 50 matrix

- D is a 50 by 1 matrix
- The result is a A*B*C*D 10 by 1 matrix

Within this example, there are five ways of doing this multiplication:

1. **(A(B(CD)))**: The total of the multiplications is 1,750.
2. **((AB)(CD))**: The total of the multiplications is 5,300.
3. **(((AB)C)D)**: The total of the multiplications is 8,000.
4. **((A(BC))D)**: The total of the multiplications is 75,500.
5. **(A((BC)D))**: The total of the multiplications is 31,000.

The order of the multiplication can make a difference in the total number of multiplications performed. So, how can we create an algorithm to find the minimum number of operations? The matrix chain multiplication algorithm is given as follows:

```
function matrixChainOrder(p, n) {
  var i, j, k, l, q, m = [];

  for (i = 1; i <= n; i++){
    m[i] = [];
    m[i][i] = 0;
  }

  for (l=2; l<n; l++) {
    for (i=1; i<=n-l+1; i++) {
      j = i+l-1;
      m[i][j] = Number.MAX_SAFE_INTEGER;
      for (k=i; k<=j-1; k++) {
        q = m[i][k] + m[k+1][j] + p[i-1]*p[k]*p[j]; //{1}
        if (q < m[i][j]){
          m[i][j] = q;
          //{2}
        }
      }
    }
  }
  //{3}
  return m[1][n-1];
}
```

The most important line of this code is line {1} because this is the one doing all the magic, meaning it calculates the number of multiplications of a given parenthesis order and stores the value in the auxiliary matrix m.

If we execute the preceding algorithm to our initial example, we will have the output 7500, as we mentioned before being the minimum number of operations. Take a look at this:

```
var p = [10, 100, 5, 50, 1],
n = p.length;
console.log(matrixChainOrder(p, n));
```

However, this algorithm does not provide us with the order of the parenthesis of the optimal solution either. We can make some changes to our code to be able to get this information.

First, we need to declare and initialize an auxiliary matrix s via the following code:

```
var s=[];
for (i = 0; i <= n; i++){
  s[i] = [];
  for (j=0; j<=n; j++){
    s[i][j] = 0;
  }
}
```

Then, on line {2} of the matrixChainOrder function, we will add the following code:

```
s[i][j]=k;
```

On line {3}, we will call the function that will print the parenthesis for us, as follows:

```
printOptimalParenthesis(s, 1, n-1);
```

Finally, we will have the printOptimalParenthesis function, which would be as follows:

```
function printOptimalParenthesis(s, i, j){
  if(i == j) {
    console.log("A[" + i + "]");
  } else {
    console.log("(");
    printOptimalParenthesis(s, i, s[i][j]);
    printOptimalParenthesis(s, s[i][j] + 1, j);
    console.log(")");
  }
}
```

If we execute the modified algorithm, we will also get the optimal order of the parenthesis, (A[1](A[2](A[3]A[4]))), which can be translated to (A(B(CD))).

Greedy algorithms

A greedy algorithm follows the problem-solving heuristic of making the locally optimal choice (the best solution at the time) at each stage with the hope of finding a global optimum (global best solution). It does not evaluate the bigger picture like a dynamic programming algorithm does.

Let's take a look at how we can solve the min-coin change and knapsack problems we covered in the dynamic programming topic using the greedy approach.

 We covered some other greedy algorithms in this book in Chapter 9, *Graphs*, such as **Dijkstra's algorithm**, **Prim's algorithm**, and **Kruskal's algorithm**.

The min-coin change problem

The min-coin change problem can also be resolved with a greedy algorithm. Most of the time, the result is also optimal, but for some denominations, the result will not be optimal.

Let's take a look at the algorithm:

```
function MinCoinChange(coins){
  var coins = coins; //{1}

  this.makeChange = function(amount) {
    var change = [],
    total = 0;
    for (var i=coins.length; i>=0; i--){ //{2}
      var coin = coins[i];
      while (total + coin <= amount) { //{3}
        change.push(coin);            //{4}
        total += coin;                //{5}
      }
    }
    return change;
  };
}
```

Note that the greedy version of MinCoinChange is much simpler than the DP one. Similar to the dynamic programming approach, we will instantiate MinCoinChange by passing the denominations as a parameter (line {1}).

For each coin (line {2}, starting from the biggest one to the smallest one), we will add the coin value to `total`, and `total` needs to be less than `amount` (line {3}). We will add `coin` to the result (line {4}) and also to `total` (line {5}).

As you can see, the solution is very simple. We will start with the coin with the greatest value and give the change that is possible with this coin. When we cannot give more coins for the current coin value, we will start giving change with the coin that has the second greatest value and so on.

To test the code, we will use the same code we used in the DP approach, as follows:

```
var minCoinChange = new MinCoinChange([1, 5, 10, 25]);
console.log(minCoinChange.makeChange(36));
```

The result will also be [25, 10, 1], the same result that we got using DP. The following diagram exemplifies how the algorithm is executed:

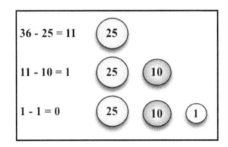

However, if we use the [1, 3, 4] denomination and execute the preceding greedy algorithm, we will get [4, 1, 1] as the result. If we use the dynamic programming solution, we will get [3, 3] as the result, which is the optimal result.

Greedy algorithms are simpler and also faster than dynamic programming algorithms. However, as we can note, it does not give the optimal answer all the time. However, on average, it would output an acceptable solution for the time it takes to execute.

The fractional knapsack problem

The algorithm to solve the fractional knapsack problem is a little different from the dynamic programming version. While in the *0-1 knapsack problem* we can only use the whole item to fill the knapsack, in the fractional knapsack problem, we can use fractions of the items. Let's use the same example we used before to compare the differences, as follows:

Item #	Weight	Value
1	2	3
2	3	4
3	4	5

In the dynamic programming example, we considered that the knapsack could only carry a weight of 5. For this example, we can say that the best solution would be filling the knapsack with items 1 and 2, which together have a weight of 5 and a total value of 7.

If we consider the same capacity for the fractional knapsack problem, we will have the same output. So, let's consider the capacity as 6 instead of 5.

In this case, the solution would be to use items 1 and 2 and only 25% of item 3. This would give a maximum value of 8.25 with a total weight of 6.

Let's take a look at the following algorithm:

```
function knapSack(capacity, values, weights) {
  var n = values.length,
  load = 0, i = 0, val = 0;

  for (i=0; i<n && load < capacity; i++) { //{1}

    if (weights[i] <= (capacity-load)) { //{2}
      val += values[i];
      load += weights[i];
    } else {
      var r = (capacity-load)/weights[i]; //{3}
      val += r * values[i];
      load += weights[i];
    }
  }
  return w;
}
```

The following is the explanation:

- Line {1}: While the total load is less than the capacity, we will iterate the items
- Line {2}: If we can use the total weight of the item, then we will add it to the total value (val) and update the current load of the knapsack
- Line {3}: If we cannot use the total weight of the item, we will calculate what is the ratio (r) that we can use

If we apply the same capacity 6 to the *0-1* knapsack problem, we will see that items 1 and 3 will be selected as part of the solution. In this case, we have two different outputs for the same problem but using different approaches to solve the problem.

Introduction to functional programming

So far in this book, we have used a paradigm called imperative programming. In imperative programming, we code each step of the program, describing in detail what needs to be done and in which order it needs to be done.

In this topic, we will introduce a new paradigm called functional programming. Functional programming was a paradigm used especially by academics, and thanks to modern languages such as Python and Ruby, it started becoming popular among industry developers as well. And thankfully, we can use JavaScript to program functionally, leveraging its ES6 capabilities as well.

Functional versus imperative programming

Developing in the functional paradigm is not difficult; it is just a matter of getting used to how the paradigm works. Let's code an example to note the differences.

Consider that we need to print all the elements of an array. We can use imperative programming and declare the following function:

```
var printArray = function(array){
  for (var i=0; i<array.length; i++){
    console.log(array[i]);
  }
};
printArray([1, 2, 3, 4, 5]);
```

In the preceding code, we iterated the array and logged each of the items.

Now, let's try converting the example to functional programming. In functional programming, the functions are the rockstars. We need to focus on what needs to be described, not how. Let's go back to the phrase "we iterated the array and logged each of the items." So, the first thing we will focus on is iterating the data, and then we will take action on it, which is logging the items. The following function will be responsible for iterating the array:

```
var forEach = function(array, action){
  for (var i=0; i<array.length; i++){
```

```
    action(array[i]);
  }
};
```

Then, we will create another function that will be responsible for logging the array elements to the console (we can consider it a **callback function**), as follows:

```
var logItem = function (item) {
  console.log(item);
};
```

Finally, we can use the functions we declared, a follows:

```
forEach([1, 2, 3, 4, 5], logItem);
```

Looking closely only at the preceding code, we can describe that we will log each item of the array to the console. And we have our first functional programming example!

A few things to keep in mind:

- The main goal is to describe the data and the transformation we need to apply on this data
- The order of the execution of the program has low importance, while the steps and their order are very important in imperative programming
- Functions and data collections are the rockstars in functional programming
- We can use and abuse functions and recursion in functional programming, while the loops, assignments, conditionals, and also functions are used in imperative programming

ES2015 and functional programming

With the new ES2015 functionalities, developing functional programs in JavaScript is even easier. Let's consider an example.

Consider we want to find the minimum value of an array. In imperative programming, to perform this task, we simply need to iterate throughout the array and verify that the current minimum value is bigger than the value of the array; if so, we will assign the new minimum value, as follows:

```
var findMinArray = function(array){
  var minValue = array[0];
  for (var i=1; i<array.length; i++){
    if (minValue > array[i]){
      minValue = array[i];
```

```
    }
  }
    return minValue;
};
console.log(findMinArray([8,6,4,5,9])); //outputs 4
```

To perform the same task in functional programming, we can use the `Math.min` function, passing all the elements of the array to be compared. To transform the array into single elements, we can use the ES2015 destructing operator (. . .), as in the following example:

```
const min_ = function(array){
  return Math.min(...array)
};
console.log(min_([8,6,4,5,9])); //outputs 4
```

Using ES2015 **arrow functions**, we can simplify the preceding code a little bit more:

```
const min = arr => Math.min(...arr);
console.log(min([8,6,4,5,9]));
```

The JavaScript functional toolbox – map, filter, and reduce

The `map`, `filter`, and `reduce` functions (which you learned about in Chapter 2, Arrays) are the base of functional programming.

Using the `map` function, we can transform or map a collection of data into another collection of data. Let's take a look at an example using imperative programming:

```
var daysOfWeek = [
  {name: 'Monday', value: 1},
  {name: 'Tuesday', value: 2},
  {name: 'Wednesday', value: 7}
];

var daysOfWeekValues_ = [];
for (var i = 0; i < daysOfWeek.length; i++) {
  daysOfWeekValues_.push(daysOfWeek[i].value);
}
```

Now let's consider the same example using functional programming, as follows:

```
var daysOfWeekValues = daysOfWeek.map(function(day) {
  return day.value;
});
```

```
console.log(daysOfWeekValues);
```

Using the `filter` function, we can filter values out of a collection. Let's consider an example:

```
var positiveNumbers_ = function(array){
  var positive = [];
  for (var i = 0; i < array.length; i++) {
    if (array[i] >= 0){
      positive.push(array[i]);
    }
  }
  return positive;
}
console.log(positiveNumbers_([-1,1,2,-2]));
```

We can write the same code using the functional paradigm, as follows:

```
var positiveNumbers = function(array){
  return array.filter(function(num){
  return num >= 0;
  })
};
console.log(positiveNumbers([-1,1,2,-2]));
```

Also, using the `reduce` function, we can reduce a collection to a specific value. For example, let's take a look at how to sum the values of an array:

```
var sumValues = function(array){
  var total = array[0];
  for (var i=1; i<array.length; i++){
    total += array[i];
  }
  return total;
};
console.log(sumValues([1, 2, 3, 4, 5]));
```

We can also write the preceding code as follows:

```
var sum_ = function(array){
  return array.reduce(function(a, b){
  return a + b;
  })
};
console.log(sum_([1, 2, 3, 4, 5]));
```

We can also mix these functions with the ES2015 functionalities, such as the destructuring operator and arrow functions, via the following code:

```
const sum = arr => arr.reduce((a, b) => a + b);
console.log(sum([1, 2, 3, 4, 5]));
```

Let's take a look at another example. Consider that we need to write a function to concatenate several arrays. To do so, we can create another array that will contain all the elements from the other arrays. We can execute the following code using the imperative paradigm:

```
var mergeArrays_ = function(arrays){
  var count = arrays.length,
  newArray = [],
  k =0;
  for (var i=0; i<count; i++){
    for (var j=0; j<arrays[i].length; j++){
      newArray[k++] = arrays[i][j];
    }
  }
  return newArray;
};
console.log(mergeArrays_([[1, 2, 3], [4, 5], [6]]));
```

Note that in this example, we are declaring variables and using loops. Now, let's execute the code written before using functional JavaScript programming, as follows:

```
var mergeArraysConcat = function(arrays){
  return arrays.reduce( function(p,n){
  return p.concat(n);
  });
};
console.log(mergeArraysConcat([[1, 2, 3], [4, 5], [6]]));
```

The preceding code does exactly the same task, but it is function-oriented. We can also simplify the code even more with ES2015, as shown by the following code:

```
const mergeArrays = (...arrays) => [].concat(...arrays);
console.log(mergeArrays([1, 2, 3], [4, 5], [6]));
```

From 11 lines of code to only one!

 If you want to practice JavaScript functional programming a little bit more, you can try these exercises (which are very fun to do!): http://rea ctivex.io/learnrx/

JavaScript functional libraries and data structures

There are some great JavaScript libraries that support the functional paradigm with utility functions and also functional data structures. In the following list, you can find some of the most famous functional JavaScript libraries:

- **Underscode.js**: `http://underscorejs.org/`
- **Bilby.js**: `http://bilby.brianmckenna.org/`
- **Lazy.js**: `http://danieltao.com/lazy.js/`
- **Bacon.js**: `https://baconjs.github.io/`
- **Fn.js**: `http://eliperelman.com/fn.js/`
- **Functional.js**: `http://functionaljs.com/`
- **Ramda.js**: `http://ramdajs.com/0.20.1/index.html`
- **Mori**: `http://swannodette.github.io/mori/`

 If you are interested in learning more about JavaScript functional programming, take a look at this book, also by Packt: `https://www.pack tpub.com/web-development/functional-programming-javascrip t`

Summary

In this chapter, you learned more about recursion and how it can help us solve some problems using dynamic programming. We covered the most famous dynamic programming problems, such as a variation of the min-coin change problem, the knapsack problem, the longest common subsequence, and matrix chain multiplication.

You learned about greedy algorithms and how to develop a greedy solution for the min-coin change problem and the fractional knapsack problem.

You also learned about functional programming, and we covered some examples of how to use JavaScript functionalities in this paradigm.

In the next chapter, we will cover the *big-O* notation and discuss how we can calculate the complexity of an algorithm. You will also learn more concepts that exist in the algorithm world.

12
Algorithm Complexity

In this chapter, we will to cover the famous **big-O notation** (introduced in Chapter 10, *Sorting and Searching Algorithms*) and the NP-Completeness theory and also take a look at how we can have some fun with algorithms and boost our knowledge to improve our programming and problem-solving skills.

Big-O notation

In Chapter 10, *Sorting and Searching Algorithms*, we introduced the concept of big-O notation. What does this mean exactly? It is used to describe the performance or complexity of an algorithm.

When analyzing algorithms, the following classes of functions are the most commonly encountered:

Notation	Name
$O(1)$	Constant
$O(log(n))$	Logarithmic
$O((log(n))c)$	Poly-logarithmic
$O(n)$	Linear
$O(n^2)$	Quadratic

$O(n^c)$	Polynomial
$O(c^n)$	Exponential

Understanding big-O notation

How do we measure the efficiency of an algorithm? We usually use resources such as CPU (time) usage, memory usage, disk usage, and network usage. When talking about big-O notation, we usually consider CPU (time) usage.

Let's try to understand how big-O notation works using some examples.

O(1)

Consider the following function:

```
function increment(num){
    return ++num;
}
```

If we try to execute the `increment(1)` function, we will have an execution time equal to x. If we try to execute the increment function again with a different parameter (let's say `num` is 2), the execution time will also be x. The parameter does not matter; the performance of the function increment will be the same. For this reason, we can say the preceding function has a complexity of *O(1)* (which is constant).

O(n)

Now, let's use the sequential search algorithm we implemented in `Chapter 10`, *Sorting and Searching Algorithms*, as an example:

```
function sequentialSearch(array, item){
    for (var i=0; i<array.length; i++){
        if (item === array[i]){ //{1}
            return i;
        }
    }
    return -1;
}
```

If we pass an array with 10 elements ([1, …, 10]) to this function and look for element 1, in the first attempt, we will find the element we are looking for. Let's suppose the cost is 1 for each time we execute line {1}.

Now, let's suppose we are looking for element 11. Line {1} will be executed 10 times (it will iterate through all the values of the array and it will not find the value we are looking for; therefore, it will return −1). If line {1} has a cost of 1, executing it 10 times has a cost of 10, which is 10 times more than the first example we used.

Now, suppose the array has 1000 elements ([1, …, 1000]). Searching for element 1001 will result in line {1} being executed 1000 times (and then returning −1).

Note that the total cost of execution of the sequentialSearch function depends on the number of elements of the array (size) and also on the value we are looking for. If the item we are looking for exists in the array, then how many times will line {1} be executed? If the item we are looking for does not exist, then the line {1} will be executed the size-of-the-array times, which we call the worst-case scenario.

Considering the worst-case scenario of the sequentialSearch function, if we have an array with size 10, the cost will be 10. If we have an array with size 1000, the cost will be 1000. We can conclude that the sequentialSearch function has a complexity of $O(n)$—n being the size of the array (input).

To see the preceding explanation in practice, let's modify the algorithm to calculate the cost (the worst-case scenario), as follows:

```
function sequentialSearch(array, item){
  var cost = 0;
  for (var i=0; i<array.length; i++){
    cost++;
    if (item === array[i]){ //{1}
      return i;
    }
  }
  console.log('cost for sequentialSearch with input size ' +
  array.length + ' is ' + cost);
  return -1;
}
```

Try executing the preceding algorithm using different input sizes so that you can see the different outputs.

O(n²)

For the $O(n^2)$ example, let's use the *bubble sort* algorithm:

```
function swap(array, index1, index2){
  var aux = array[index1];
  array[index1] = array[index2];
  array[index2] = aux;
}

function bubbleSort(array){
  var length = array.length;
  for (var i=0; i<length; i++){          //{1}
    for (var j=0; j<length-1; j++ ){ //{2}
      if (array[j] > array[j+1]){
        swap(array, j, j+1);
      }
    }
  }
}
```

Consider that lines {1} and {2} have a cost of 1 each. Let's modify the algorithm to calculate the cost as follows:

```
function bubbleSort(array){
  var length = array.length;
  var cost = 0;
  for (var i=0; i<length; i++){ //{1}
    cost++;
    for (var j=0; j<length-1; j++ ){ //{2}
      cost++;
      if (array[j] > array[j+1]){
        swap(array, j, j+1);
      }
    }
  }
  console.log('cost for bubbleSort with input size ' + length + '
is ' + cost);
}
```

If we execute `bubbleSort` for an array with size 10, the cost will be 100 (10^2). If we execute `bubbleSort` for an array with size 100, the cost will be 10,000 (100^2). Note that the execution will take even longer every time we increase the input size.

Note that the code from the *O(n)* complexity has only one for loop, whereas $O(n^2)$ has two nested for loops. If the algorithm has three for loops iterating through the array, it will probably be $O(n^3)$.

Comparing complexities

We can compare the different big-O notation complexities mentioned previously using a chart as follows:

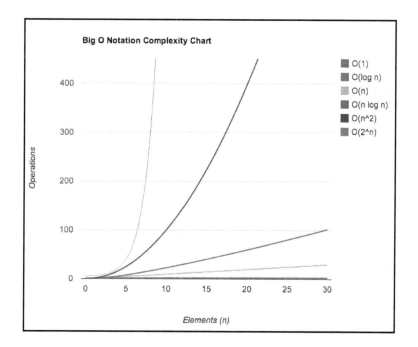

This chart was also plotted using JavaScript! You can find the source code used to plot this chart inside the `bigOChart` folder under `chapter12` of the sample code files included with this book.

In the following section, you will find a cheat sheet that shows the complexities of the algorithms we implemented in this book:

Data Structures

The following table show the complexities for Data Structures:

Data Structure	Average Cases			Worst Cases		
	Insert	Delete	Search	Insert	Delete	Search
Array/ Stack/ Queue	*O(1)*	*O(1)*	*O(n)*	*O(1)*	*O(1)*	*O(n)*
Linked List	*O(1)*	*O(1)*	*O(n)*	*O(1)*	*O(1)*	*O(n)*
Doubly Linked List	*O(1)*	*O(1)*	*O(n)*	*O(1)*	*O(1)*	*O(n)*
Hash Table	*O(1)*	*O(1)*	*O(1)*	*O(n)*	*O(n)*	*O(n)*
Binary Search Tree	*O(log(n))*	*O(log(n))*	*O(log(n))*	*O(n)*	*O(n)*	*O(n)*
AVL Tree	*O(log(n))*	*O(log(n))*	*O(log(n))*	*O(log(n))*	*O(log(n))*	*O(log(n))*

Graphs

The following table show the complexities for Graphs:

Node/ Edge Management	Storage Size	Add Vertex	Add Edge	Remove Vertex	Remove Edge	Query
Adjacency List	$O(|V| + |E|)$	*O(1)*	*O(1)*	$O(|V| + |E|)$	$O(|E|)$	$O(|V|)$
Adjacency Matrix	$O(|V|^2)$	$O(|V|^2)$	*O(1)*	$O(|V|^2)$	*O(1)*	*O(1)*

Sorting Algorithms

The following table show the complexities for Sorting Algorithms:

Algorithm (applied to Array)	Time Complexity		
	Best Cases	Average Cases	Worst Cases
Bubble Sort	*O(n)*	$O(n^2)$	$O(n^2)$
Selection Sort	$O(n^2)$	$O(n^2)$	$O(n^2)$

Insertion Sort	$O(n)$	$O(n^2)$	$O(n^2)$
Merge Sort	$O(n\ log(n))$	$O(n\ log(n))$	$O(n\ log(n))$
Quick Sort	$O(n\ log(n))$	$O(n\ log(n))$	$O(n^2)$
Heap Sort	$O(n\ log(n))$	$O(n\ log(n))$	$O(n\ log(n))$
Bucket Sort	$O(n+k)$	$O(n+k)$	$O(n^2)$
Radix Sort	$O(nk)$	$O(nk)$	$O(nk)$

Searching Algorithms

The following table show the complexities for Searching Algorithms:

Algorithm	Data Structure	Worst Case
Sequential Search	Array	$O(n)$
Binary Search	Sorted Array	$O(log(n))$
Depth First Search (DFS)	Graph of $|V|$ vertices and $|E|$ edges	$O(|V| + |E|)$
Breadth First Search (BFS)	Graph of $|V|$ vertices and $|E|$ edges	$O(|V| + |E|)$

Introduction to the NP-Completeness theory

In general, we say an algorithm is efficient if it is $O(n^k)$ for some constant k, and this is called a polynomial algorithm.

Given a problem in which there is a polynomial algorithm even for the worst case, the algorithm is denoted by P (polynomial).

There is another set of algorithms called **NP (nondeterministic polynomial)**. An NP problem is a problem for which the solution can be verified in a polynomial time.

If a problem P has an algorithm that runs in polynomial, we can also verify its solution in polynomial time. Then, we can conclude that P is subset of, or equal to NP. However, it is unknown whether $P = NP$.

NP-Complete problems are the hardest problems in an NP set. A decision problem L is NP-Complete if:

1. L is in NP (that is, any given solution for NP-complete problems can be verified quickly, but there is no known efficient solution).
2. Every problem in NP is reducible to L in polynomial time.

To understand what the reduction of a problem is, consider L and M as two decision problems. Suppose algorithm A solves L. That is, if y is an input for M, then algorithm B will answer *Yes* or *No* depending upon whether y belongs to M or not. The idea is to find a transformation from L to M so that the algorithm B can be part of an algorithm A to solve A.

We also have another set of problems called NP-Hard. A problem is NP-Hard if it follows property 2 (of NP-Complete), and it does not need to follow property 1. Therefore, NP-Complete set is also a subset of the NP-Hard set.

 Whether $P = NP$ or not is one of the biggest questions in computer science. If someone finds the answer to this question, it would have a major impact in cryptography, algorithm research, artificial intelligence, and many other fields.

The following diagram represents the Euler diagram for the **P**, **NP**, **NP-Complete**, and **NP-Hard** problems, considering that $P <> NP$:

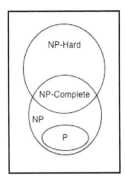

As examples of NP-Hard problems that are not NP-Complete problems, we can mention the **halting problem** and **Boolean Satisfiability problem** (**SAT**).

As examples of NP-Complete problems, we can also mention the subset sum problem, traveling salesman problem, and vertex cover problem.

For more information about these problems, refer to `https://en.wikipe dia.org/wiki/NP-completeness`.

Impossible problems and heuristic algorithms

Some of these problems we mentioned are impossible to solve. However, there are techniques that can be used to achieve an approximate solution in a satisfactory time. A technique would be using heuristic algorithms. A solution produced by heuristics might not be the best of all solutions, but it is good enough to solve the problem at the time.

Some examples of heuristics are local search, genetic algorithms, heuristics routing, and machine learning. For more information, take a look at `http://goo.gl/gxIu9w`.

Heuristics are a great and fun way of trying to solve a problem. You can try to pick a problem and develop a heuristic for your college or master's degree thesis.

Having fun with algorithms

We do not learn algorithms only because we need to study them in college or want to become developers. You can become a better professional by boosting your problem-solving skills using the algorithms you learned in this book as a way of solving problems.

The best way of boosting our knowledge in problem solving is practicing, and practicing does not need to be boring. In this section, we will present some websites that you can go to and start having fun with algorithms (and even earn some cash while doing so!).

Here is a list of some useful websites (some of them do not support sending the problem's solution in JavaScript, but we can apply the logic we discussed in this book to other programming languages as well):

- **UVa Online Judge** (`http://uva.onlinejudge.org/`): This site contains a set of problems used in several programming contests around the world, including the ACM **International Collegiate Programming Contest** (**ICPC**), which is sponsored by IBM. (If you are still in college, try to participate in this contest and, if your team wins, you can travel around the world with all expenses paid!) This site contains hundreds of problems in which we can use the algorithms learned in this book.

- **Sphere Online Judge** (`http://www.spoj.com/`): This site is similar to UVa Online Judge but supports more languages (including JavaScript submissions).
- **Coder Byte** (`http://coderbyte.com/`): This site contains 74 problems (easy, medium, and hard difficulty) that can also be solved with JavaScript.
- **Project Euler** (`https://projecteuler.net/`): This site contains a series of mathematical/computer programming problems. All you have to do is input the answer to the problem, but we can use algorithms to find the answer for us.
- **Hacker Rank** (`https://www.hackerrank.com`): This site contains 263 challenges divided into 16 categories (you can use the algorithms that you learned in this book and much more). It also supports JavaScript, among other languages.
- **Code Chef** (`http://www.codechef.com/`): This site also contains several problems and hosts competitions online.
- **Top Coder** (`http://www.topcoder.com/`): This site organizes programming tournaments, usually sponsored by companies such as NASA, Google, Yahoo!, Amazon, and Facebook. Some contests give you the opportunity to work with the sponsoring company, and some contests can give you cash prizes. The website also offers great tutorials for problem solving and algorithms.

Another nice thing about the previous websites is that they usually present a real-world problem, and we need to identify which algorithm we can use to solve this problem. It is a way of knowing that the algorithms we learned in this book are not only educational but can also be applied to solve real-world problems.

If you are starting a career in technology, it is highly recommended to create an account on GitHub (`https://github.com`) for free, and you can commit the source code you write to solve the problems from the previous websites. If you do not have any professional experience, GitHub can help you build a portfolio, and it can also help you get your first job!

Summary

In this chapter we covered big-O notation and also discussed how we can calculate the complexity of an algorithm by applying this concept. We introduced the NP-Completeness theory, a concept that you can dive into if you are more interested in learning more about solving impossible problems and using heuristics for an approximately satisfactory solution.

We also presented some websites on which you can register to for free, apply all the knowledge you acquired while reading this book, and even be offered your first job in IT!

Happy coding!

Index

www.ingramcontent.com/pod-product-compliance
Lightning Source LLC
Chambersburg PA
CBHW062107050326

40690CB00016B/3243